Praise
"Why Simple Things Are Difficult

"A frank, witty and informed look at the
society in which we think we live."

"I laughed out loud."

"Very enjoyable and thought-provoking to read."

"This will resonate with a huge amount of people."

"Essential reading for anyone wanting to know
why things are the way they are."

"Every chapter gives you something to think about."

"People need to read this."

"A guide to things we take for granted without understanding them."

"Explains the things you didn't even realise need explaining."

"Only someone like you could write this."

WHY SIMPLE THINGS ARE DIFFICULT

An Alternative Look at Society

RAYMOND G PLUM

Cover image by: Yesna99, 99Designs
Book design by: SWATT Books Ltd

Printed in the United Kingdom
First Printing, 2024

ISBN: 978-1-0686685-0-0 (Paperback)
ISBN: 978-1-0686685-1-7 (eBook)

Raymond G Plum
Bedfordshire, UK

raymondgplum@gmail.com

Dedicated to:

All those who provide charitable social care and those who need or rely on this essential help.

Contents

PREFACE

"True wisdom comes to each of us when we realise how little we know about life, ourselves and the world around us."
(Socrates, 469–399BC, Greek philosopher)

We are constantly being told how good things are, how things are continually improving, how everything is quicker and easier and how much help and support there is available to us. If this is so, then why does it not feel that way to me and why do even the simplest things seem so difficult? Why is it a struggle to get things done? Why is it such a problem to find someone who is willing and able to help me? And why does it seem like I always have to do it myself or find my own answers, when there is supposedly so much help and support around to help us?

This book attempts to explain why so much of our modern, affluent, caring, efficient way of life can be so frustrating and difficult. It explores some common misconceptions and explains why many accepted theories don't work in practice. It goes on to look at our human behaviours, choices and decisions and how these are influenced and steered by different aspects of society, such as finance, businesses, machines and government. The final part then provides an alternative look at our society as a whole, the direction it is heading in and even goes as far as exploring a more optimistic version of society that contrasts starkly with our society today.

Each chapter raises thought-provoking questions and unconventional ideas, providing a rare opportunity to see our society from a very different perspective. It is openly candid and opinionated and is peppered with anecdotes, humour, real examples and outbursts of ranting throughout. However, it does not expect or need your acceptance or agreement, but instead raises questions that you are invited to ponder and judge for yourself.

I have a curious and analytical mind and, for the last 30 years, an enjoyable technical engineering career. Most of this has been spent constantly questioning, sorting, learning, trying to understand, making links between cause and effect, comparing, contrasting, analysing and spotting things that are inconsistent or contradictory. Consequently, I perhaps think about and see the world a bit differently from many people. However, the more I realised that my unconventional opinions and personal frustrations were more widespread, shared, replicated and reinforced by colleagues, friends and associates, the more I started to wonder if they were more symptomatic of our society and the way we live. Therefore, the first question for you to ponder is whether you think this collection of views, ideas and rants exposes some underlying problems within our society or whether they are just the opinionated frustrated moans and groans of yet another grumpy old man with something to say.

In my early fifties I received a birthday card that simply read:

> The 3 stages of man.
> Know it all.
> Say it all.
> Sod it all.

This inspirational spark made me realise that I did have something to say, and the result is this book. It is my opportunity to "say it all" before it is too late. Without that spark, the affirmation of others and the vital contribution of those who helped to convert my initial, incoherent ramblings into this legible form you have before you, this book would not have been possible. It has been very time-consuming, often arduous, mostly enjoyable and even therapeutic in parts, but it was always driven on by my hope that it would raise money for charity and so I sincerely thank those who made this possible, specifically the publisher SWATT Books. Finally thank you for your purchase, which will contribute towards the care charities that provide some benefit to those who need it.

I hope you enjoy the book and get something useful from it.

PART 1:

THE THEORIES

01

DON'T BELIEVE A WORD

"The single biggest problem with communication
is the illusion that it has taken place."
(George Bernard Shaw, 1856–1950, winner of Nobel Prize for Literature)

Humans and possibly a few other animal species have developed language to communicate. The development of language is so fundamental to the evolution of human society and the way we live that it is very difficult to envisage a world in which language does not exist in one form or another. It is undoubtedly one of the strongest and most beneficial skills humans have; we are so reliant on words that they are one of the very first things we start to teach our children. Words allow us to exchange information and ideas, which leads to shared goals and co-operation, which ultimately leads to working collaboratively and the advancement of technology. It is probably true that without some method of communication comparable to that of words, we would still be living in the Stone Age era even now, millions of years after it started. Words are really that fundamental to how we operate and co-operate. Beyond this purely practical role, they can be a powerful inspirational tool and a form of artistic expression, with poems, songs and literature all painting wonderful images of worlds that we can never visit physically. Some people claim that body language accounts for most of human communication, with subtleties of posture, eye contact, gestures, tone and facial expression subconsciously informing us whether someone is authentic, lying or confident. While this is true to some extent, both body language and tone of voice are absent from all forms of written communication. Furthermore, regardless of whether communication is written, spoken, signed or in Braille, all the raw informational content of language is concentrated in words. Without words, body language and tone alone can't communicate simple things such as "I've lost something blue" or "The cat is stuck in the shed again." Therefore, this chapter looks at our use of language, words and their informational content.

However, regardless of how important they are or how much we rely on them, they are not perfect, and they are often very ambiguous. When my son asked, "Can I eat the chocolate cake in the fridge?" my wife replied "No, you can eat it at the table with everyone else". In my profession of engineering and many others like teaching, medicine and law, the clarity and precision of language is important, as any misinterpretation or inaccuracy can have serious effects. Perhaps spending so long in engineering has made me more attentive to this natural ambiguity of words and the problems it can cause. Therefore, this first chapter looks at how the natural ambiguity of words is magnified and extended by our own conscious, subconscious, lazy or intentional misuse of words and language. It explains why it is often difficult to receive a clear explanation or to get a simple answer to a simple question. We start with perhaps our oldest misuse of words, dishonesty.

Dishonest words

The main characteristic of 'dishonest words' is that they are already known to be false at the point of being spoken. The good old-fashioned lie has been around for just about as long as speech itself and is something we are all guilty of from a very young age, if only to get another biscuit. Dishonest words are intended to mislead or misguide others, to make people believe something false or do something they otherwise wouldn't do. Often they are driven by selfish reasoning, like getting an extra biscuit, politicians gaining votes, people receiving financial compensation or just claiming a day off work sick. However, words don't have to be this dishonest to be misleading: consider the popular phrase "I'll get back to you."

Misleading words

If you are honest, how many times does someone actually "get back to you" after saying this? In my case, it is probably about 30%, which means around two out of three have misled me. This doesn't have to be malicious or dishonest – they just say the words because they form a commonly accepted phrase. Whilst many sincerely intended to help or respond, others may innocently forget, whilst the more dishonest use the phrase to mean "I'm going to leave now and totally forget what we have talked about". Here are a few more examples of words I find misleading rather than explicitly dishonest (along with my cynical interpretation when I hear them added in brackets below).

"Your call is important to us."
(But not important enough to answer it or spend a
bit more money to employ more people.)

"We've improved our customer service."
(That means I'm going to have to do more of it myself.)

"Let's have a meeting to discuss it."
(Let's talk about it for 30 minutes, so no one can
complain that nothing has been done.)

Alternatively, the misinterpretation may be caused by those receiving the words and not the fault of the person saying them. Some may recognise the example of reporting up through a management chain, starting from the person doing the work through to director level, where each step has a small misinterpretation or extrapolation, just like a game of Chinese Whispers.

- I've not started it yet.
- It's about to start.
- It's just started.
- It's started.
- It's progressing.
- It's part way through.
- It's part complete.

- There's some left to do.
- It's almost done.

Emotive words

Another way to mislead someone is by using emotive language. Some specific words such as 'racist', 'vile', 'unpatriotic' and 'disloyal' can trigger our emotions, which tend to be far stronger than our more conscious analytical thoughts. These emotive words can immediately swamp or dominate our reaction and understanding, without even considering the content in the rest of the statement. For example, "The paedophile wanted to make a large charitable donation to the school". Here the emotive word "paedophile" makes you emotionally think "no this is wrong", but replace the word with "person" and it seems like the right thing to do. In this way using emotive language can disguise or dominate the rest of the sentence and so mislead or misguide us away from the real content of the words.

Standard words

'Standard words' are not misleading, but they are not very useful or informative either. Their main characteristic is having only the minimum amount of information. A good example is post-match interviews with professional footballers, who just repeat the same standard phrases regardless of the game or the result, such as "work as a team", "continue to improve", "concentrate on the next game" etc. I recently tested this theory, by correctly predicting about 70% of the footballer's responses, knowing nothing more than the final score, which was displayed at the bottom of the screen. Perhaps I just got lucky or perhaps they have all been professionally trained to regurgitate this bland, standardised tripe in every post-match interview. Other perpetrators of this type of standard language are contestants on talent shows who "gave it everything", sportspeople who "need to continue improving", businesses that "must remain competitive in the market" or politicians who claim they "need to act in the best interests of all those involved". This use of standardised, bland language even appears in children's school reports, as below.

"This term your child's achievements are in line with expectations and their predicted level of attainment. However, with further work at school and home they could improve further."

Parents may read this and be pleased, but it actually says very little. It could equally apply to either the laziest troublemaker or the most hard-working, academically gifted child in the school. Although standard words are relevant to the subject, they are bland, generic, uninteresting and quickly become repetitive and boring. Standard words are most easily spotted by the reactions they prompt – "heard it before", "not again", "not worth listening to", "blah blah blah" – but at least they are not a total waste of time like 'empty words'.

Empty words

'Empty words' are like standard words, just worse. Empty words either say nothing at all or only the blindingly obvious. Empty words are so bland that they don't even relate to one subject and can be applied to almost anything. This type of word misuse involves taking the simplest of statements, like "let's do our work", and converting it into something like "we should all communicate and collaborate as a team to achieve our goals and succeed". This phrase could be used at work (you may have used it yourself or heard your boss say it?), but it is just as applicable to a football team, a committee, a mountain rescue attempt, children playing on an obstacle course, friends doing a jigsaw or a couple decorating a bedroom in their new home.

Another common set of empty words is "in a timely manner", such as "It will be processed in a timely manner". It is true, everything happens "in a timely manner". The nucleus of an atom splits in a timely manner, new galaxies form in a timely manner, food cooks, plants grow and paint dries in a timely manner. It is impossible for anything to happen that isn't "in a timely manner" and so the words are utterly useless and contain no information at all about how long something should take. So don't tell me (or anyone else) that something will be done "in a timely manner" – I know that already!

The words "I don't know" carry more useful information, because at least then you know this person is either unable or unwilling to help. In my opinion, there are only two reasons for someone to use empty words: one is to waste other people's time and the second is to draw attention to themselves and neither is of any use whatsoever. What triggers people to say stuff like this? Why? What does this type of language achieve? I cannot begin to comprehend the benefit of using the maximum number of words to say absolutely nothing at all. It defeats the object of using words in the first place. (That was the first rant of the book, but there'll be plenty more.)

This type of empty language is common and often involves phrases like "appropriate", "progressing" or "in due course". These should be a warning sign that all useful content is being replaced by bland words. Finally, what is the point of using the phrase "moving forward"? Are these people trying to imply that after some serious consideration of all the alternatives, that on this occasion they have consciously decided not to break the laws of physics and travel back in time, but instead have chosen to "move forward" in time at the same pace as the rest of us? We are all moving forward, every single moment of our lives, so it is just a ridiculous and useless thing to say. These types of empty phrases are heard far too often, they are embarrassingly common in the world of business and politics, they are completely worthless and they are certainly not worth wasting any more space on this page.

Contradictory words

'Contradictory words' involve saying two contradictory things in the same sentence. It would be easy to say this is invalid and that words should not be used in this way, but it is common to hear things like "we have significant financial constraints, but we will continue to improve" or "we need to increase production by 30%, with more efficient use of the reduced resources available". Intuitively these are not possible. More recently there is a noticeable trend to answer questions with "Yes, no" or "No, yes" and you can't get more contradictory than this. To me this is a warning sign that the response is probably going to contain contradictions.

Dual meaning words

This is a much more subtle and clever use of words which often goes unnoticed, primarily because this is part of the intention. As the name suggests, 'dual meaning words' can say two different things at the same time. This means that two people with two opposing views can happily agree to the same sentence as supporting their own views and being acceptable. I overheard a good example of this whilst working in an office, where someone was being told to read a large, dull document. The response given was "I'll waste no time at all in reading it". When the coast was clear I asked if they realised what they had said. The phrase can be interpreted either as "I'll do it immediately" or as "I won't bother doing it at all". They smiled, confirmed that they knew exactly what they had said and intended, but the person who left happy had absolutely no idea. Similarly, the word "quite" can mean "a bit" or "very", when saying "I'm quite interested" and the phrase "for all we know" can mean either "everything we know" or "we haven't got a clue". My son has his own version of this when asked "How much cake would you like?" he responds, "A healthy slice", which can mean either a great big portion (because he is a growing lad) or a small low-calorie slice (because we shouldn't feed children too much sugar and fat). As we naturally look for agreement from others, most people will assume that the words are agreeing with their own personal view. If you listen carefully, you can often hear this from politicians who want both sides to agree with what they are saying, such as "Action will be taken after full consideration". This could be interpreted as "they are going to take action" by those that want action or as "they are going to consider it fully before doing anything" by those who are opposing the action. Both sides can be equally happy with the sentence and interpret it as support for their own viewpoint.

Incomprehensible words

This Satz describes the problem when using fremd Sprache to explain an einfach Begriff to other Leute. If you were confused, frustrated or annoyed by the inclusion of a few German words in the previous sentence, then this is precisely how it is for other people whenever jargon, acronyms, terminology or overly complex descriptions are used. Any of these can be just as incomprehensible as using words from a foreign language. The main premise of language is to communicate and explain things, so that other people can understand what you mean or want. Therefore, using any type of incomprehensible language simply undermines the premise of using language in the first place. In just the same way that it is pointless to use empty words to say nothing, it is equally pointless to say words that are incomprehensible to your audience, and this includes all those ridiculous job titles like "Health and Leisure Initiative Operative".

Presumptuous words

This type of word misuse assumes that people have mastered the art of mind reading or telepathic communication. Speaking for myself, I don't yet have any mind reading capability, I've not even got the lowest level of qualification in extra-sensory perception (ESP), and I don't know anyone who has, so why do people assume it is OK to use phrases like those below (again followed with my reaction in brackets).

- "Are you available?" (when, what for and for how long?)
- "Can you give me their number?" (whose?)
- "Will you be at the meeting?" (which one, we have three?)

This is just a result of trying to be quick or efficient, using the fewest number of words possible, but in doing so it omits the most important content. It can be caused by haste or laziness, which we all suffer from occasionally, but some people are prone to doing it much more regularly or habitually. Perhaps they are just trying to be really efficient, and no actual harm is done other than being really inefficient and breeding confusion, delay and extra effort.

Simple mistakes

There is one more type of word misuse to which thankfully no one is immune. In my view the 'simple mistake' is the best type of word misuse, as it is both unintentional and provides a real benefit, as it can provide humour instead of frustration. Just saying the wrong thing is sometimes comical, such as "I know it like the top of my head", an incorrect combination of the two common phrases "I know it like the back of my hand" and "I don't know it off the top off my head". A similar one is "I've got a brain the size of a sieve". Other types of mistakes include spoonerisms, unintended innuendos, mispronunciation and simply not being able to get the right words out, which all form the basis of those humorous outtake shows, which invite us to laugh at people struggling with their words.

Despite all these different types of misuse being of very little help or assistance to anyone, how much of what you hear or say each day falls into one of these categories? Who is generating these frustrating, time-wasting 'words of no use' and, more importantly, why?

Ambiguity of words

The psychologist Bertram Forer did an experiment in the late 1940s to show how people interpret words in a way that is best suited to their own personal preference.[1] In this experiment, a range of people judged a description of their own individual personality to be accurate, even though every person had unknowingly been given exactly the same text from a newspaper astrology article. The vagueness of these empty, standard words allowed each person to interpret the bland content differently, to accurately match their own personality. This ability to interpret bland words differently means that people are much more likely to agree and ultimately accept them. This perhaps explains why the use of ambiguous empty or standard words is becoming more common. Just take all the content away and people can't disagree with you.

Even in the simplest cases, when the writer genuinely thinks they have provided all the information needed, the words can still be unclear and ambiguous. Consider the following.

"I sat on the chair at my desk, but it was broken."

Is it the chair or the desk that was broken? Similar confusion can occur whenever pronouns like "it", "that" or "they" are used, as often it is not clear which noun (chair or desk) is being referred to. Even in these simplest of cases, it is still difficult to make words clear and unambiguous. This is important because the connections between the words, our interpretation and our understanding are so strong that even our perception and reasoning can be manipulated by the subtlest changes in the words used.

Words and our perception

There have been many studies on words and the human mind that clearly show how people's perceptions can be influenced by words alone. The Loftus and Palmer car crash experiment in 1974 investigated how changing a single word within a question can alter people's perception of what they saw.[2] It is possible to imagine a very similar effect if you are asked to taste something that has been modified from the original. Here the question might be:

"What is your feedback on the modified taste?"

Would your answer be different if the word "modified" was replaced by any of these words: distorted, adjusted, altered, changed, enhanced, improved or optimised? Studies show that it would, even though you were tasting exactly the same thing. This shows how human perception and reasoning can be manipulated by the words used, and you would be both naive and wrong if you thought that this type of manipulative wording is not used to influence people all the time, in politics, adverts, negotiations and probably even this book.

The urge to talk

From the day we are born we are all encouraged to make sounds and talk, so for the vast majority of people it is a very easy and enjoyable thing to do. This ease, combined with the power and influence of words and language, means that many people are happy to talk at any opportunity. Talking is so accepted and encouraged, that the propensity for talking seems to be the one female trait that can be openly commented on without attracting some kind of critical response. Perhaps this is because it is commonly accepted that too much talking is far better than the alternative of not talking enough.

Informally people can choose to talk about whatever they want, and this social use of language is of no relevance here. However, in more formal settings such as work, schools, businesses, committees and other organisations, and in the vast majority of meetings, talking has a very important role. There is a need for people to use clear language to explain, understand, contribute, clarify, agree and decide what actions to take. Nonetheless, how much of this formal language you read, write, say or hear consists of bland standard, empty or contradicting words like the following (again, with my disparaging interpretations in brackets)?

- The committee discussed it last week. (So, what did they decide, was anything done?)
- We need to have a conversation. (Just that, or do you intend to agree and decide to do something afterwards?)
- It is progressing. (That only says it is somewhere between not started and not finished.)
- We are working on it. (They don't know, or they don't want to say.)
- It is something that is subject to priorities. (Aren't most things, is it high or low priority?)
- We should be more efficient and more productive. (Easy to say on its own, now give some options or suggestions of how you intend to actually do it.)
- We need to review and agree. (You want to talk more, before anything actually gets done.)
- I'll talk to someone. (Just talk to them or ask them to do something specific, by a certain time and let everyone know?)
- We have listened and learned. (We messed up big time and we hope by saying this you will quickly forgive and forget our mistake, so we can just carry on doing more of the same stuff in future.)

And don't forget the classic "it will be done in a timely manner". All this frustratingly bland talk is of very little use, so why do some people choose to talk like this and equally why is it considered acceptable or even professional? This is explored a little further using meetings as an illustration.

Meetings

Many people who attend meetings feel the need to justify their attendance by providing some kind of contribution, but with an audience they don't want to embarrass themselves or generate unnecessary disagreement. One solution is to contribute in the least controversial way, using only words that the other people can interpret differently to match their own preferences and easily accept (just like Forer's astrology text and all those empty, standard, contradicting or dual meaning words). Not by coincidence, these useless contributions tend to come from those with the least real contribution to make, which is best summarised by this Plato quote:

> "Wise men speak because they have something to say,
> fools because they have to say something."

Meetings used to be promoted under slogans of "solving problems", "forming an agreement" or "deciding what action to take". More recently meetings tend to be focused on "having a conversation", "open discussions" or "maintaining a dialogue". The emphasis and expectation have moved away from agreement, decision or action, towards inferring that nothing more than a good old chinwag or a bit of a natter is all that is needed. No wonder meetings have a reputation for being little more than a "talking shop".

Unfortunately, acceptance and tolerance of this type of bland, generic, empty language just exacerbates the whole problem. The more it is tolerated, the more it is deemed acceptable and the more people will follow suit and use similarly bland language. It is a self-feeding loop where apathetic tolerance promotes further use and acceptance. Eventually talking this bland nonsense becomes normal or correct; it may even be respected or considered professional. Ultimately it leads to professional help and support being provided in the form of words like these:

> "Your query has been acknowledged and will
> be dealt with in a timely manner.
> We will let you know when and how we intend to deal with it.
> Thank you for contacting us and your custom is important to us."

All too frequently this type of nice polite, professional (bland) words and phrases translate into something like this in the real world:

> "We have already relegated your problem down to a query because
> it is not as important to us as it is to you. It is likely to sit in our
> computer database for a while without anyone looking at it, so be
> prepared to wait a while and you may end up having to remind us of

it several times before anything happens. When we do offer some assistance, it will only be one of our few standard basic fixes, that you may have already tried yourself several times whilst waiting for us to respond. We will then consider this belated brief verbal advice as a full resolution and instantly close your query (because that's good for our statistics). In the highly likely event that your problem persists, you will need to go online and raise another different query, so you can then go through the whole identical process again. We are both polite and nice so don't get frustrated with us (even if that is the most natural and likely outcome), as any sign of frustration or anger will be treated as a sign of verbal abuse. Thank you and please give us some more of your money in the future."

More and more people are falling into the trap of believing that a few bland words are a form of help or will solve the problem. Other people assume that constantly filling their time with endless, supposedly productive, discussions and conversations means that things are getting done and things are going well. They all confuse "talking" with "doing". Using this bland, standard, uninformative language to replace decisions, actions and helpful practical advice only adds delays, misunderstanding and frustration. It also makes resolving the real issue or problem more difficult.

Actions speak louder than words

Whenever we need assistance, the first thing we tend to do is ask someone for help or support. Perhaps that person cannot help directly, but they know Sam can help and so promise to talk to them. Later you discover that Sam spoke to one of their team, so now you can relax thinking help is being provided. However, apart from some talking nothing has happened yet, nothing has changed and nothing will change until somebody does something that isn't just words.

To reinforce the same point further, we can extrapolate this simple example to a hypothetical situation on a much grander scale. Now imagine that someone has an idea that could solve the world's problems. Thinking the idea was so good, they told the Prime Minister, who also thought it was a brilliant idea and decided to explain the idea to every other world leader. They also all agreed it would solve all the world's problems and collectively agreed to tell the whole population of each country about the idea, until every single person on the planet agreed it would solve the world's problems. After all this has happened, the question now is "Is the world a better place?" The answer of course is NO, the world is exactly the same as it was, with all the same problems. Not a single person has taken any action yet, nothing has happened or changed, and absolutely nothing will change until physical actions are taken (and in this particular hypothetical situation, it would need plenty of them).

As obvious as it may seem here, this distinction between words and actions is very important if people are not to confuse "discussing something" with actually "doing something". Unfortunately, there seems to be a growing number of people who perceive that generating yet another set of empty, standard words is going to be useful or that repeatedly having good conversations is progress. I'm also fed up with people using the throw away remark "We had a good discussion" as sufficient justification of their time and contribution, because unless something was agreed, decided or done, then the discussion was in fact completely useless. Rather ironically, although words alone do absolutely nothing, they are a brilliant tool for providing excuses when things are not done.

Whilst the importance and role of words cannot be underestimated, they all suffer the same problem. The sound of every spoken word dissipates and dies as it travels through air, some of the sound enters our ears and by some amazing interaction between the physical vibrations of the air and the biological and chemical reactions in the ear, it gets converted into minute electric signals that become thoughts within our brain, sitting there as memories. When we read written words from paper or screen there is a different, but equally amazing, interaction between the electromagnetic light waves with chemical and biological reactions in the eye and again the written words become thoughts and memories in our brain, which may ultimately turn into better understanding or new ideas. But without action, all those words remain nothing more than silent, dormant, fanciful ideas, false hopes, fictitious claims and ignored intentions, which quickly become distant fading memories, decaying away to nothing in the deep dark recesses of our minds. It is only action that converts words into something real, as summarised in the chain below.

WORDS – INTERPRETATION – KNOWLEDGE –
DECISION – ACTION – PHYSICAL WORLD

This chain reinforces the fact that if words are to be of any practical use, then they must be both acted on and consistent with the real world (I once heard someone say that "if reality contradicts the words, then the words will be incorrect"). Words are easy to generate and are not constrained by reality, they can say absolutely anything ("I'll just use these two bananas to pick up this full-sized tractor and fit it inside this small teapot"). In stark contrast, actions are very real and constrained by time, people, cost, performance, complexity and any other number of real-world effects, including the laws of physics. Everything is easy to say, the difficulties only start when you try to do it, such as the health spokesperson who told the public not to touch our face during a COVID-19 announcement, just before licking their finger to turn the page of their notes.[3] Perhaps this is the reason why some people prefer to remain in the relative comfort of just "talking" and are much less interested in the more difficult reality of actual "doing".

For all those artistic, creative, supportive, encouraging, explaining, consoling and supportive words, which are so important to everyone at various times of our lives, action and doing are not necessary to make the words worthwhile, because the benefit is in the mind only. However, for all the practical day-to-day things in life, like putting the kettle on, repairing a bike or going to work, both written and spoken words are absolutely useless at actually doing things. The conclusion is something already very well known – "ACTIONS SPEAK LOUDER THAN WORDS" – but it is perhaps much more accurate and correct to say, "ALL WORDS ARE SILENT, UNTIL ACTION IS TAKEN". This is the reason for the title of this chapter and why you should not believe a word.

"All words are silent, until action is taken."

02

SOME FEEDBACK ABOUT FEEDBACK

"We are of different opinions at different hours."
(Ralph Waldo Emerson, 1803–1882, philosopher)

Today you cannot have a meal, visit a location, buy something or even use a website without being told "Your feedback is important to help us improve". It seems that feedback has become fashionable to the point of obsession. I've even been asked to provide feedback within the first few seconds of opening a website. I've not even had time to read the title yet – what possible opinions could I have formed? The only possible opinion is that this feedback request has just interrupted me, is a waste of time and made the website worse. However, most people, including many influential and very successful people, promote feedback as the way to improve. You may have guessed already that my view of feedback does not entirely agree with this, so this chapter looks at what feedback is, how it works and what it can realistically achieve.

I'm a strong supporter of teaching, instruction, giving opinions, recommendations, reviews, criticism and any other type of advice. They are essential and humanity depends on them to educate and protect future generations and to provide the support that we all need from time to time. Neither am I particularly concerned if people want to group all these together under the label of 'feedback'. However, I do object to the assumption that this collective relabelling as 'feedback' automatically implies that they are now going to create improvement. Simply relabelling something does not mean that it magically inherits all the properties and characteristics of the new label. Relabelling 'chocolate cake' as a 'healthy snack' does not help people dieting, it simply means the new label is more misleading. To quickly introduce this idea, take the example of someone giving a speech and two audience members offering their opinions. One says they should speak more slowly, whilst the other recommends speaking more quickly. Many would accept these opinions as a form of feedback, so surely the speaker should now be able to improve, but how? The feedback is contradictory. Simply changing the label of these contradicting 'opinions' to 'feedback' does not make them any more capable of generating an improvement, just as relabelling my 'car' to 'train' doesn't make it any more capable of avoiding traffic jams. Relabelling opinions as feedback might change people's perceptions or expectations of what is possible, but it does not and cannot change what they can actually achieve.

Therefore, what follows is a brief explanation of the origins of feedback, what true feedback is, how it works and why it can reliably produce improvements in the fields of science and engineering. This is then compared with the more fashionable opinionated version of feedback we are asked to provide almost every hour of every day, highlighting the differences and limitations of it.

How feedback works

One of the first uses of feedback was probably an early version of the mechanical float valve used during Roman times, in which a float follows the water level, and a solid arm provides mechanical feedback of the water level to restrict further water flow. This is so reliable it is still used today, and you can see it in action by removing the lid of your toilet cistern and flushing the toilet. One of the first scientific uses of feedback was in steam engines, where waste heat was simply piped or 'fed back' to help pre-heat the cold water, making it easier to boil and improving the efficiency of steam engines. Once the practical and financial benefits of using an output to aid future operation instead of just losing or forgetting it were established and matured, the approach soon spread. Relatively quickly the use of feedback in other engineering applications coalesced and evolved into the basic principles of all feedback control systems, based on the three steps in the diagram below.

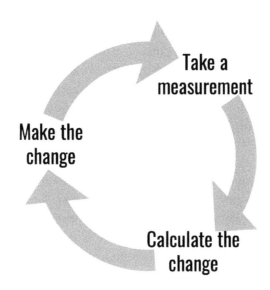

For a simple temperature control system for a room this becomes:

- Measure current room temperature (19°C).
- Calculate the difference between desired temperature setting (20°C) and measured room temperature (19°C).
- Apply some change or correction in the form of heating (or cooling if the room was too hot).

This application of heat will raise the room temperature, but if left uncontrolled it will make the room too hot. It is therefore necessary to measure the room temperature again a bit later and repeat the whole loop again, creating a 'feedback control loop'. It is this type of feedback loop that reliably improves the performance and stability of almost every electrical appliance from temperature controls, washing machines and car engines to autopilots.

How well these feedback control loops operate depends on several things, specifically the accuracy of the measurement, how good the calculation is and how accurately the change is applied. If a room at 19°C is measured inaccurately as 21°C, then the calculation will say the room must be cooled further instead of raising the temperature closer to 20°C. Equally, if the heater was too powerful, the application of heat could easily send the room above the desired 20°C setting, so forcing the control loop to switch to cooling next time. This introduces a very important point about using feedback, which is stability. For a feedback control system to be stable and operate well, the 'measurement', the 'calculation' and the 'application' must work together, be tuned and be in balance. Without this balance, any change applied will be slightly worse than expected, but this is only the start of the problem. The 'slightly worse' behaviour is then fed back again to make it 'even worse', and this is precisely what happens when you hear the horrible 'feedback' screech from a sound system. Some skilled musicians, normally the lead guitarist in a rock band, can use their skill to re-introduce this finely tuned balance by providing some additional precise measurement and response to what is essentially an unstable feedback loop. Without this balance or tuning, feedback is very prone to creating unstable behaviour, so most poor feedback control systems do become unstable. An awful lot of skilful tuning, in the form of engineering design and testing, is needed to ensure we do not experience this instability very often.

Feedback in engineering

In engineering, feedback control loops are designed and extensively tested to achieve a specific aim, such as keeping the room temperature close to 20°C or using cruise control to keep your speed at 50 mph. Engineering feedback control loops rely on both 'accuracy of measurement' and 'precision of application', which can be provided by the type of equipment listed below.

- GPS to measure your position.
- Gyroscopes to measure rotation rates (used in games that rely on tilting your phone).
- Tachometer to measure shaft rotation speed (like the rev counter in your car).
- Electric motors to apply rotation.
- Hydraulics to apply pushing forces.
- Brakes to provide resistance forces.

Within some cost versus performance constraints, each of these reliably provides an accurate measurement or applies a specific change. Combining these with carefully designed calculations and huge amounts of testing produces stability, reliability, performance improvements or better efficiency in most of the tools, toys and machines we use. Ultimately this is all for our benefit.

Naturally, the accuracy and precision needed depends on the product. A Formula One car would be uncontrollable if the precision used to measure and apply the changes was similar to that used in a remote-control toy car. The complexity of the calculations also varies greatly. There are relatively simple temperature controls, more complicated control of spin speeds, vibration levels and weight distribution in your washing machine and complex engine management systems that need to measure and control fuel flow, engine speed, automatic gear selection, temperature and efficiency, to name a few. The role of autopilots is to change the inherently unstable situation of large lumps of metal up in the air into controlled and stable flight, so that they don't crash to the ground or wobble around too much. Although in science and engineering accurate feedback is used to reliably control instability and make improvements, it is not that simple or easy. One of the first things that engineering students learn about 'feedback control theory' is that inaccurate or poor use of feedback can quickly make things worse; it can even make natural and very stable situations become unstable. For completeness, the timing, delay or response of the application of change is also important in ensuring stability, but this engineering detail does not need to be considered any further.

Human feedback

In many ways, human feedback in the form of opinions, reviews, surveys etc. mimics that of engineering feedback; it is very similar in concept and application. Initially a measurement or assessment is made, secondly there is a calculation of what needs to change and finally some change is implemented. In both cases this loop repeats, but that is where the similarity ends. The success of feedback control in engineering relies on accurate measurements, unambiguous instructions, precise application and prolonged testing or tuning. Human feedback cannot rely on these same contributions, so it shouldn't be too surprising that the results and consequences are different. Unfortunately, giving our opinions the confusing label of 'feedback' is what allows people to assume that a few quick ticks and couple of scores on a survey is all that's needed to reliably provide improvements.

Human feedback is different from engineering feedback in many ways. Firstly, our measurements and assessments are less accurate. Does ticking the 'satisfied' box mean "Perfectly happy, please don't change anything" or "It's acceptable but could be better"? Secondly, our calculation of what to change (or not) gets entangled with our opinions, viewpoints, biases, emotions and many other more practical influences, such as the time available or cost. Thirdly, our instructions on what to change are more ambiguous and easier to misinterpret. Furthermore, people are not as reliable as machines at applying the changes accurately or as instructed, so the correct application of the change is far from guaranteed. People are quite good at not doing the things they are supposed to, but also good at doing other things they are not supposed to. Consequently, human feedback includes the notions of both positive feedback (do more of this) and negative feedback (do less of that). This means that, although human feedback can work in theory, it struggles to deliver in practice. The sections below illustrate how this drift from the optimistic theory to practical reality occurs.

Feedback from a skilled person

Feedback from skilled people such as doctors, teachers, coaches, therapists etc. is similar to engineering feedback. It is based on a lot of knowledge and understanding, which is equivalent to the knowledge built up in engineering design and testing. Also, like engineering, skilled feedback is targeted towards specific needs, to solve a particular problem, and the instructions are often clear and precise (take these tablets three times a day, keep your back straight, use more adjectives etc.). However, the application of change is up to the recipient; it is limited and variable according to their interpretation, capability and effort. Unfortunately, not all skilled feedback is clear – just remember some of your bad teachers. Similarly, two doctors may provide different diagnoses or treatments, and different sports coaches may recommend different training techniques. This type of contradictory feedback can lead to mixed messages and an erratic or unstable response, such as when two parents with different rules and standards leads to erratic behaviour and arguments, involving phrases like "Well dad said I could".

Feedback from individuals

Feedback is not limited to skilled people, and many genuine and competent people such as family, friends and colleagues also provide feedback on a much wider, less targeted range of topics such as these:

- Performance review of your work by your boss.
- Advice to a friend.
- A review or assessment of someone else's work.
- A parent checking a child's homework.

In this type of situation, a friend might simply recommend what they would do in your situation, and your boss might provide feedback to speed up and spend less time checking everything. Alternatively, a parent might assess their child's homework and say it is not very clear and tell them to rewrite it or structure it differently. In all these cases the first step of measurement has become less accurate, more subjective and more opinionated. Similarly, instead of being accurate and precise, the feedback instructions become vaguer: "Do more of that" or "Do that differently". There are countless ways to do it differently, but little indication on which to choose. Equally "do more of that" gives no indication of how much more – just a fraction or quadruple it? The important characteristics that make feedback work reliably are starting to disappear.

Whilst most of this 'individual feedback' is well meant and probably useful, it is also more likely to be wrong, inaccurate or easily contradicted by equivalent feedback from other individuals. The parent's advice to restructure the child's homework might be judged as incorrect by the teacher or school friends. Similarly, the person told to speed up by their boss might then be told by someone else the following day that they should be more careful and do more checks. How can someone speed up and do more checks? It makes the feedback inconsistent, just like the example at the start of this chapter, where the speaker was told to speak more slowly and more quickly. Worse still, a few days later individuals can contradict their own initial feedback with a different set of instructions.

This starts to highlight how inconsistent individual feedback makes it much more difficult or even impossible to make the correct change and how it can cause unstable flips from one thing to another.

Feedback from a varied group

Just as feedback from a couple of individuals can differ, feedback from larger groups like those listed below is even more likely to contain a spread of opinion and contradiction.

- Collective feedback from a wide selection of work colleagues.
- School collecting feedback from the parents, students or both.
- Collecting market research on the high street.
- Feedback questionnaires and surveys.

Now the range of topics is huge, such as a restaurant menu, the layout of a website or the transport system. Although people are interested or have strong opinions on these topics, they are also less skilled in assessing or measuring them. A couple of late trains will result in terrible feedback, even if 99.99% are on time. This type of 'collective human feedback' gathered via questionnaires and surveys will contain a wide spread of opinions and so the measurement now becomes statistical in nature. It is well known that statistical measurements can produce accurate results, even from a varied unskilled group. This is what happens at school fetes, where people pay £1 to guess the number of sweets in a jar or the weight of the cake. Individually the estimates (measurements) are wildly inaccurate, but collectively the average across all entries is often a reasonably close match to the real answer.

This type of statistical approach is used in many feedback questionnaires and surveys, but without any numerical estimation or quantitative scale. They don't ask us to estimate the room temperature, number of rooms or the weight of the dessert. Instead, they offer a choice of several ranked options (or buckets) to choose from, without any indication of the size of each option (or bucket) or the distance between them. The most common and recognisable of these are a 'five-point ordinal scale' like the ones below.

Score on a scale of 1–5, where 1 is bad and 5 is good.

Strongly agree, Agree, Neither agree or
disagree, Disagree, Strongly disagree.

Far too much, Too much, About right, Too little, Far too little.

The feedback from this type of ordinal scale could be used to control the temperature of a room, using the scale 1 is much too cold, 2 is cold, 3 is just right, 4 is warm and 5 is too hot. The average can only indicate whether people want the room warmer or colder, but not by how much. This approach may be acceptable and work well in this extremely simple example, but things are seldom this simple. The next section looks at the example of how a hotel may use all our important ordinal feedback to make the hotel better for us.

Hotel improvements

Perhaps the first question would be how satisfied the customer was overall, with scores of 5 or 4 being content and scores of 1, 2 or 3 being displeased in some way. Now further questions are needed to find out what is displeasing them, by individually scoring the restaurant, the room, the hotel staff, the service etc. Assuming it is the restaurant that scored poorly, what needs to change? The food quality, portion size, service, cleanliness, range of drinks? Even more questions are needed. If it is the portion size that is not right, then is the main dish too small or is the dessert too big? If the service was poor, was it waiting to be seated, waiting for the food or waiting for the bill? As each has a different solution. If the food quality was bad, was it too salty or spicy, not enough vegetables or meat, not enough choice? Without more and more questions and a feedback survey that looks more like a 12-page multiple-choice exam paper, it is not possible to know precisely what is wrong and needs changing.

This type of statistical collective feedback only tells you that something is not good enough in a general area (the restaurant), but not what needs to change or by how much. This is where I think the theory of using collective feedback falters. These questionnaires and surveys only provide indications that something needs to change, but don't provide any detail about what to change or by how much. It would be like telling the room temperature controller "Change something, might be the heater, might be the cooler or humidity, might be the fan speed, no idea how much to change it by, no more clues, just do it and make sure it is better for everyone". How can the right change or improvement be made: sheer guess work, toss a coin, crystal ball? Collective human feedback can have large statistical validity and numerical accuracy, but it provides very little specific instruction on what actually needs to change. Without this there is no way of knowing if the changes are the right ones or not; you might change something and actually make things worse. You become trapped in a loop like this:

- See what people think.
- Try changing this.
- See what people think again.
- Now try changing something else.
- See what people think.
- Now try changing that.

Some may see this as precisely how our feedback is used and should be used, to provide continual improvements. In fact, it is much closer to the inaccurate, poorly designed feedback control systems that engineering students are warned about, the ones that create the instability. I view this as a continual loop of unstable change, which is explained further a bit later. For now, the problem is knowing specifically what changes and improvements to make, assuming of course that the true intention of all our important feedback is to make the improvements that people want.

An alternative to a 12-page exam-style survey would be to simply ask for a clear explanation via questions like, "If any part of the restaurant was unsatisfactory, please explain why." Those who choose to scribble a short hint like those below just recreate the same problem of not being specific enough (as indicated by the contents of the brackets).

- "The chips were a joke." (Not enough, too cold, overcooked, soggy?)
- "The wine was off." (Which bottle of wine? There may be one bad batch of wine, but the restaurant won't scrap all the wine it has in stock and won't open all the bottles to check.)
- "We waited too long." (Too be served, for the food or for the bill? Each has a different solution.)

- "Not enough choice." (For main course, dessert, seating, wine or all of these?)

Today we are very much acclimatised to these types of surveys. My reaction is mostly "Oh no, not another one". They are so common and frequent that many people complete them quickly, leaving plenty of time to fill in several more later that day. In general, we don't have that much time for them and perhaps we don't give them the full consideration and attention that those collecting the feedback think we should. We are so acclimatised, accepting, tolerant and blind to being asked for more feedback that many people pay little attention to what they are being asked, they are not consciously aware of the questions they are answering. This problem is perfectly demonstrated in the Dave Gorman TV show *Life Is Goodish*, Series 3 Episode 8: "A German Tradition",[1] where a street survey was conducted using only questions about that particular survey itself.

Conversely, clearer, more detailed explanations like "The fish dish was served cold and there were not enough vegetables" provide useful targeted feedback. Now the chef can be instructed more precisely (or ticked off) and hopefully it won't happen again. These clear targeted explanations are very similar to the useful review comments that people leave and are another form of feedback.

Reviews

These personal reviews are extremely useful, so we should appreciate the time and effort spent by the people who choose to write them. But why should these 'reviews' (which are a collection of contradicting, inconsistent, human views and opinions) be more useful or more valuable than collective human feedback (which is a collection of contradicting, inconsistent, human views and opinions)? The answer is simple.

REVIEWS ARE NOT TRYING TO BE SOMETHING THEY ARE NOT.

Personal reviews are a collection of opinions that can be read, ignored, believed, dismissed, questioned, interpreted and most importantly used differently by each individual, for their own personal and specific purpose. In this respect they are extremely useful in making your own personal choices that affect only you or very few other people. If you think about it, these personal reviews often contain much more useful information and specific details about how to improve, than the popular five-point ordinal surveys.

- The hotel food was good, but the rooms were dirty.
- This product is poorly built and breaks easily.
- The performance is fantastic, but the instructions don't explain how to...

This is probably because these people have chosen to write these reviews with the genuine intention to provide useful information to others and not just to indicate some generalised level of satisfaction. What these useful, important, individual reviews don't do is pretend that they can change and improve things for the benefit of everyone.

Regardless of the format, be it a few tick boxes, a long five-point ordinal survey, a scribbled hint or a clear and detailed review, all forms of collective human feedback suffer yet another fundamental problem when trying to improve things for everyone. Even if the feedback is clear and the change correctly implemented, not everyone is going to get what they wanted. Some or hopefully most may be happy, but some will now see it as worse than before and their next feedback will say change it again, probably back to how it was. To summarise, this all means that consistent feedback from a few likeminded people is good way to steer and direct change in the direction they want it to go. However, collective human feedback from a wide spread of people is poor at making changes that benefit the majority and is much more prone to just making continual unstable change, as demonstrated below.

Unstable change

In this crude example, assume one third of the population prefer red, one third prefer blue and one third prefer yellow. A business produces a product and chooses to make it blue and then asks for feedback using the question "Do you like the colour? YES/NO". One third of the feedback will say YES (those who like blue), but two thirds will say NO (those who like red or yellow). As the feedback now says that people don't like the colour, they change the colour to red and the next set of feedback again says one third YES (the people who like red are now happy) but two thirds again say NO (those who prefer blue or yellow). Again, the feedback says the colour must be changed, so this time it is changed to yellow. You can now guess what is going to happen. Now the one third who like yellow say YES and the other two thirds say NO, so it is changed back to blue again. This is an unstable feedback control system in operation. Inconsistent (but genuinely human) feedback is being used to change the product in line with feedback and it results in an unstable, ever-changing oscillation going blue, red, yellow, blue, red, yellow, blue. In this crude example nothing is getting better, the product is not improving, it is just continually changing in an unstable manner, in response to genuine collective human feedback.

The colours could be any characteristic that people have differing opinions about, such as temperature, weight, shape, taste, lighting, location, service, capability, options, complexity, quantity, sound, layout or any other type of characteristic. In a restaurant this could result in the portion size constantly changing between small, medium and large. The preferences of the people do not need to be exactly equal for this unstable effect to materialise and take hold. Any fairly even spread across a range of different preferences, as occurs naturally in any population, would produce the same unstable result.

Another human trait exaggerates this effect further. There is a natural perception that if you want change than you need to say so and, equally, if you don't say anything then things will stay the same. This means many contented people choose not to provide feedback, because they don't want to spend their entire lives constantly reaffirming all the things that they want to remain the same, such as "don't change the portion size", "don't change the location of the pedestrian crossing", "don't change the school entrance" and definitely "don't change the layout of your website again, because I've only just got used to this one". This means that any collective human feedback is biased towards those who want change. In the blue, red, yellow example, there would be less feedback from those who like the colour and more from those who don't, so exaggerating the proportion of people that don't like the colour. The same unstable cycle exists, but now the need for change is emphasised further. In feedback control theory this is called an amplification or gain factor. It is therefore important to not treat the feedback in isolation, but to look at what is really happening.

To demonstrate this in a more realistic example, assume that 100,000 people have purchased the same product and are asked to provide feedback. Let's assume 1000 people respond (that is only 1% of customers), with 700 saying it is difficult to use and 300 saying it is easy to use. This feedback indicates that 70% of users are finding it difficult to use. Surely this means there is a need to change it and ensure it is easier to use (even though there is still no indication of which part is difficult). However, if we now assume that most of the 99,000 people who chose not to provide feedback found everything acceptable and didn't want to waste their time confirming everything was OK, then now only 700 people out of 100,000 (only 0.7%) are finding it difficult to use, strongly implying that no change is needed, and that the vast majority of customers are happy. I sincerely hope that all those people who use collective feedback already know all this (and most true statisticians will), but those that don't are simply using feedback to feed an unstable, uncontrolled loop of constant change.

Therefore, in contradiction to all those persistent, pestering claims that "Your feedback is important to help us improve", I've attempted to demonstrate why it is actually very difficult for these feedback surveys to make the specific improvements you want, and instead how they are very prone to making continual unstable changes. The wider problem can now be seen: there are lots of requests, from lots of places, for lots of feedback, from anyone and everyone, to produce the type of collective feedback most likely to cause continual unstable change. Fortunately (not) for all of us, this worst possible type of feedback is only being used to change, modify and dare I say 'improve' every product, meal, service, visitor experience, website and public amenity we use. Instead of improvement, what we actually experience is the frustration of continual, unstable change. Despite all this, our unreliable opinionated feedback might be the best information there is, so instead of concentrating on what it can't do, the next section looks at what it can do.

What can it do?

A huge amount of time and effort is spent requesting, collecting and analysing all this feedback, using mathematical principles ranging from simple percentages, rates of change, distributions and variances, all the way through to modern, multi-layered (dimensional), complex analysis techniques and presumably the use of artificial intelligence algorithms in the near future. So, it must be useful for something.

As already indicated, it is capable of highlighting areas that the majority consider unacceptable and need to be fixed, such as cleanliness. Some analysis techniques show how data changes over time. A statistic which declines over time from 70%, 60% to 50% could highlight either a decline in standards or a change in public opinion. A falling statistic for "enough vegetarian choice" could indicate a growing preference for vegetarian food, allowing the restaurant to react to this new trend and keep customers happy by changing the menu. Strictly speaking this is not so much feedback as a type of 'feed forward', where measurements are used to predict the future and then make changes in anticipation of that prediction.

Beyond this, these feedback statistics also provide a very good measure of business performance. "How did you hear of...?" questions highlight which advertising works best. "Would you recommend...?" questions provide great statistics for advertising like "Over 90% would..." and ratings for level of service and satisfaction might be used to calculate the targets for next year or bonus payments. Is it a step too far to suggest they are also very useful measure of whether savings or cutbacks are starting to affect customer satisfaction? These valid uses all have a common thread. All this important feedback is predominantly for the benefit of those requesting it and not to make improvements for us. I can't imagine a single person giving feedback who says they would prefer to hang around waiting on a customer service helpline for an extra 15 minutes, repeatedly listening to how important their call is. Most would say that they want their call answered immediately by a real knowledgeable person who is able to provide practical help straight away. How come that feedback never gets implemented into an improvement? The people that collect feedback are not stupid either; if their true intention was to make the specific changes that the majority wanted, they would ask for plenty of the specific review-style comments. However, if they want nothing more than a collection of very useful and statistically valid performance indicators, then these simple feedback surveys do a grand job of it.

What this means is that all our time and effort providing all that 'important feedback' is predominantly not for our benefit at all, but for those collecting it. This was the sentiment that got customer surveys relegated to Room 101 in the TV show of the same name.[2] Perhaps the last two questions on every feedback survey should be something like this:

- Did this survey allow you specify the changes you would specifically like?
- Do you think the improvements you want are being implemented by us?

The statistics from these two feedback questions would be very interesting.

Incestuous feedback loop

This brief analysis shows how the different types of feedback vary and how they produce different results. Feedback is good when it categorically highlights that something is wrong, but it is not so effective when it becomes opinionated and variable. As stated at the start of this chapter, I am a strong supporter of teaching, instruction, reviews, giving opinions, recommendations, criticism and any other type of advice and people have been doing this long before the advent of engineering. However, it is only recently since the advent and success of feedback control theory in science and engineering that the generic label of 'feedback' has spread to cover and include many of these different types of human opinions and judgements. This change of label has blurred the divisions between the different types of feedback and confused what 'feedback' can or can't do. In this confusion people are becoming acclimatised (or brainwashed) into the idea that all feedback produces improvements. People are becoming trapped in this invalid and incestuous loop.

Feedback produces improvement.
This change is based on feedback; therefore,
it must be an improvement.
More feedback is required to improve further.

It is wrong to assume, expect, imply or believe that those same human opinions are any better at generating improvements than they were half a century ago. Our collective feedback is far more likely to generate continual unstable change than improvements, so the next chapter looks at what all these changes and improvements are.

———————————————————————

"How can people's collective feedback produce improvement, when people's collective opinions can't even agree on what the improvement should be."

03

WHAT IMPROVEMENT? (OR WHAT IMPROVE MEANT)

*"The best and easiest thing to improve
is yourself, so start there."*
(Anonymous)

Over the last 5, 10, 50, 100 years there have been huge improvements that have provided massive benefits to all aspects of modern life, including medicine, engine efficiency, flight safety, digital communications, satellites, new materials like carbon fibre and solar power to name but a few. These are all technological advancements, but similar improvements occur across other fields such as sports and arts, which then go on to inspire others. Improvement has become an essential and expected part of our lives. After all, who wants to watch a sports team that isn't trying to get better? What would happen if parents or taxpayers learnt that a school or hospital wasn't trying to improve? Businesses want to improve all the time, and who would employ someone who wasn't trying to better themselves? This obsession with improvement spans all aspects of modern life and rarely does a day or an hour go by without hearing the word 'improvement', often accompanied by its inseparable friend 'feedback'. Under their combined banner of 'continual improvement', the pace of change is increasing and has coincided with a growth of exasperated, frustrated outbursts like "Oh no, they've changed it again" or "Why have they done that, it worked before?" This chapter looks at what all these improvements really are.

Things must change

All improvements must come from something changing; if nothing changes then nothing can get any better or worse. It is a reasonable starting point to assume that not every change is an improvement, although in my experience a few ignorant people seem reluctant to accept even this simple premise, by blindly defending every change as being part of continual improvement. Just to prove this point, consider the extreme example of demolishing a junior school during a half-term break! This would change the children's education, and would certainly change the plans of most parents, as well as changing the shape of the bricks, amongst many other things, but hopefully no one reading this would claim that this rather dramatic change was actually an improvement. To continue in the same vein (not demolishing schools, but the idea that not all changes are improvements), a football fan who watches the score change from a 2-0 lead to a 2-3 loss would not view this as an improvement, whilst an opposing fan would judge the same change as a huge improvement. The same singular change can simultaneously be seen as improvement to some and a detriment to others. This rather simple fact is equally valid for a change in the smell of soap, the taste of food, the colour of something or the packaging of a product, in fact just about everything that people can have differing opinions about. Whether something is changed for better or worse is therefore often a subjective judgement, based on our own personal perspective and it is a little presumptuous of those making changes to claim or tell us it is an improvement. Perhaps they are only trying to convince us that we should see it as an improvement before we have had a chance to make up our own mind?

Real improvement

Therefore, rather than using the dictionary definition of improvement, 'become better', where 'better' is very subjective, a more reasonable attempt at a clearer definition for a 'true improvement' or a 'real improvement' could be:

REAL IMPROVEMENT:
A change which provides some tangible benefit to people or activities, without generating a larger tangible detriment to other people or other activities.

Every change made is likely to produce an improvement to something, like demolishing schools improves the amount of hard-core rubble available for local builders to use. Changing the shape of wheels from circle to square would improve storage. It is therefore the adverse effects of a change that prevent it becoming a real improvement, as in these everyday claims.

- "We have improved the layout of your monthly statement." (I used to know where to look, now I need to find where the information is and check it is the same.)
- "We have improved our customer service." (So instead of being able to ask a knowledgeable person for help, I must now do it all myself, by spending hours searching websites for information and answers or have a Chatbot tell me it doesn't understand my question, despite me typing it out in six different ways.)

Are these cases of improvement or just change? Here the implication is that improvement is for the public or customers' benefit, so it is justifiable that people bemoan yet another improvement that doesn't benefit them. However, many changes and improvements are not made for the benefit of people at all, but for the reasons below.

- Legislation or laws
- Financial
- Environmental
- Health
- Politics
- Selfish personal gain

Using the environmental example, rinsing, cleaning and sorting our rubbish into different bins is more difficult and time-consuming than just throwing everything into the same bin, but many people see this as acceptable and do it because there is a much wider, more important benefit for the environment and future generations. The overall benefit or 'gain' is greater than the overall 'pain' and it is this balance that makes a change a real improvement or not. An improvement which saves 1 hour for 4 people (4 hours of gain) but results in 15 minutes of extra effort for 20 people (5 hours of pain) produces an overall detriment, visualised in the simple balance diagram below.

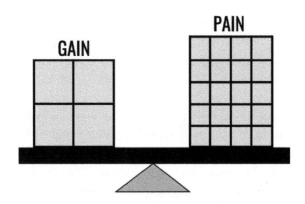

As difficult as it is to accept, there is no fundamental difference between this simple attempt at time saving and demolishing a school. They both improve something locally, but both have bigger detriments elsewhere. Furthermore, just like the football supporters, those who experience the detrimental pain are often a different group from those that experience the beneficial gain. In the real world it is rare to get something for nothing, so it is only by considering both the gain and the pain of changes that real improvements can be made. Real improvements are not as easy as just sticking the label 'improvement' on every change made or hiding frequent changes under a banner of 'continual improvement'.

Find the real improvement

Below is a game in which you can consider which changes constitute real improvements (but to make it a little harder, expect some level of sarcasm and ranting).

Vending machines

Living in one location has allowed me to observe six changes to the vending machines used in a single location over a 10-year period. Starting with a cash-only payment, they improved to chargeable tags, then to rechargeable tags, to charge cards, to a new supplier of charge cards, to a combination of charge cards and cash and finally back to cash-only payment. The result of all this continual improvement over 10 years was the same as the starting point. How can six consecutive improvements result in no change at all? It was this example that first started my analytical thoughts of what is really happening when people use the term 'improvement' to describe changes. Incidentally, if these changes were driven from user feedback, then this becomes a real case of the 'blue, red, yellow, blue' example from the previous chapter.

Taps

There was a time when I was able to use all the taps I encountered with ease, without instruction or problem. After a lot of improvements over a decade or more, I'm now lucky if I can use a quarter of them first time. The first improvements involve making taps look sleek, stylish and minimalistic, which includes removing those ugly red and blue spots, along with all other clues on how to change the temperature. The second improvement is for some taps to decide how much water you need to wash your hands, which can be anything from a couple of egg cups up to 60 seconds of full force that makes every attempt to wash your trousers as well. However, by far the best improvement is the invention of every possible new and different way to switch a tap on. Is it a push or a lift, is it a twist or a turn, a press, a wave, a hold, a movement, a double press, a voice command or stamping on a button on the floor? The number of movements now required to get water out of a modern tap redefines what a tap dance is.

To add insult to injury, they then spoil the sleek, modern, stylish design by sticking a bright yellow triangle next to it, taunting you that if you are clever enough to get water out of the tap, then it "may be very hot", because every clue on how to control the temperature has been removed! Finally, to make taps even easier and simpler to use, they are now placing motion-activated taps close to motion-activated driers and soap dispensers, then conveniently hiding them all from our view.

Frantically waving your hands, desperately trying to find and activate one of these hidden devices (of which only two out of three seem to work) in the right order would constitute a reasonable format for some low-quality, but hilarious, game show. Can all these really be improvements?

Traffic flow improvements
The mere mention of variable speed limits is likely to touch a nerve and raise the voice of many drivers. We are told that they improve traffic flow and prevent traffic jams, yet they always seem to end up with one anyway. What is the benefit of slowing down earlier, if you are only going to have to stop anyway? I can see how they might reduce accidents, which is a type of improvement on its own, but the claim is that they improve traffic flow. Here the additional pain is having to slow down, but often without the gain of not having to stop.

Smart fridge
One of the big trends for product improvement today is to make a 'smart' product, which is connected to the internet. In many cases this can be considered a real benefit, such as controlling your home heating while at work etc. Some more debatable examples can be seen as gimmicks: does your washing machine need to be smart or is a delay timer enough? A recent example that caught my eye was a smart fridge with a camera inside (yes this is real). Do you really need to see the inside of your fridge from anywhere? It is unlikely to be very exciting to watch and if you do want to get something out, you will have to stand up to get it anyway. Alternatively, it might be useful to see if you have run out of milk whilst at the shop, but I would suggest if you could afford a smart fridge, you could probably also afford an extra pint of milk or block of cheese and so shouldn't need to check anyway.

Improving the layout of your store
Occasionally a local supermarket will rearrange all the aisles and claim "we are improving the layout of your store". This means there will be some temporary disruption before the improved layout is finished and we all get the benefit. In my case the benefit is that my semi-automatic shop routine, which used to take about 45 minutes, is now extended

(sorry improved) by an extra 30 minutes spent walking up and down the aisles looking for things I can't find, whilst making myself an inconvenient obstruction to other shoppers, as they do the same to me. So, this improvement changes my reasonably slick routine into a kind of indoor treasure hunt, trying to find the new location of the last few items on my list. I like puzzles more than most, but I don't want someone to say "We've hidden the eggs somewhere in the store for you" 30 minutes before I pick my child up from afterschool club. This kind of improvement is not done for my personal benefit and, by inference, yours either. It is intended to disrupt our semi-automatic shopping routine, so we see more products and ultimately buy something extra. Presumably the sales figures show this disruptive approach works.

The answer

As surprising or disturbing as it may be, the real improvement from the selection above is for traffic flow. Variable speed limits are designed to keep all cars rolling at the highest average speed possible, even if this is a rolling crawl. This is because once a car is stationary it takes longer to start rolling again. All the cars behind must wait an extra second or two per car, whilst one or more of the following is done:

- Take the handbrake off and select gear.
- Put the phone down.
- Finish explaining something to the kids.
- Restart the engine.

If each car in a stationary line of 300 cars takes just one extra second to start moving again then the person at the back of the line must be stationary for an extra five minutes, which is plenty of time for many more cars to join the back of the stationary line and stop. It is therefore easier and quicker to get everyone through this 'sticky patch' if every car just keeps rolling, even very slowly. Whether you like them or not, variable speed limits are actually a real improvement. Whilst those at the front have some pain and wonder why they have to slow down, many cars behind gain and keep rolling, wondering why there is a speed restriction when everything seems to be rolling along fine.

Our judgement of change

Our judgement of change is individual. We look for things that are beneficial, help us, and make things simpler, quicker or easier, but we don't like anything that causes complications, disruption and delays, or makes something more difficult than it was before, like taps. It is this need to adjust, learn or adapt to change that we judge as detrimental pain. Changes which are almost invisible to us, like better battery life, a new feature on your phone that you never use or more cleaning power, don't generate any pain because they don't affect us. We can blissfully ignore them whilst getting some benefit. Therefore, something can definitely improve if the change does not disrupt or disturb us in any way. Our judgement of change is also influenced by how frequent or regular it is. A one-off reorganisation of a computer file system is tolerable, but if it keeps changing repeatedly, you never know where to find things and it keeps breaking all the hyperlinks. In the past, constantly reorganising a music CD or record collection would produce the same effect – it just doesn't help, at least in the short term. Below is a general indication of some different types of changes and the different levels of gain, pain and regularity they have.

Changes in technology

The introduction of a brand-new technology is relatively rare, as it tends to follow years of scientific research and development. Examples include the steam engine, light bulb, radar, new medicines, internet, MRI (magnetic resonance imaging) scans and atomic clocks (used for GPS), to name just a few. Although there can be some short-term pain as people acclimatise to a new technology (like GPS), this tends to be greatly outweighed by significant long-term benefits (or gain) for the vast majority of people. These relatively rare technology leaps then allow more frequent changes that provide us with new capabilities, change how we do things or provide better performance.

Change of capability

This type of change involves adding or removing some capability, including adding GPS to cars, adding autofocus to cameras or providing vegan options in bakeries. This type of change tends to be quite common, as it inspires new interest and entices new customers. Adding capability (providing something new) is often considered beneficial, unless it adversely affects some existing capability or feature. Introducing vegan options won't be judged as beneficial if it is achieved by replacing all the most popular meat options. The disappointed meat-eaters will outweigh the pleased vegans. Introducing cameras to fridges is also capability change which does not cause any detriment, other than to someone's bank balance, but it could also be judged as a bit gimmicky with little real benefit either.

Functional changes

A functional change does not change what something does, only how it is done. Staying with the bakery theme, you are normally handed your food in a paper bag or box on top of a clean counter, but equally it could be dropped on the floor and kicked to you under the counter, so you must bend down to pick it up. You are still getting your pastries in the same packaging, but it is just done a different way. Other functional changes include replacing mechanical devices with electric motors, powering cars with batteries instead of fossil fuel or replacing switches with touch screen menu options. You get the same capabilities, but via a different method. Just like changes in capability, functional changes also entice new customers, so they are common. However, by changing how something works, people must also adapt, they are affected in some way and so some detriment is involved. Just as I struggle to adapt to different taps that all just provide water, some functional changes can be viewed as change for change's sake: "It just does the same thing, and it was OK before".

Performance and reliability change

Performance changes do not provide a new capability or do something differently, they only change a characteristic of something that already exists, such as longer battery life, better fuel economy, faster travel, quieter operation, smoother surface etc. Again, performance changes entice customers and are relatively common, but they generally provide a performance gain without affecting or disrupting us. Increasing performance does not produce any detrimental pain. The same is not true of reducing performance, where an old, tired vacuum cleaner makes housework harder. This is where repair and maintenance changes are needed.

Repair and maintenance change

Repair and maintenance aim to return something back to its normal condition. Other than a bit of time, effort and inconvenience during the maintenance, the change does not affect us in any other way, but equally does not provide any new benefits. There is little pain or gain, and things just go back to normal, so on balance repair and maintenance changes tend to be fairly neutral.

Process and procedural change

Processes or procedures are a method for doing something and they range from operating procedures at work and application forms through to regulatory processes, amongst many more. They aim to instruct, guide or control people's activities, so inevitably any changes will require people to adapt or change, to do something in a new or different way. There is always some detrimental pain, even if the intended gain is greater. Written processes are also relatively easy to change and so they can change very often.

Cosmetic change

Judging whether a cosmetic change in colour, shape, size, layout etc. is more personal and subjective, as it doesn't add or remove anything. Most cosmetic changes are relatively easy to make, so they can be frequent. Fortunately, most cosmetic changes do not affect us much, so there is not much pain generated either. However, changing the layout of a website can make it harder to use initially, so some pain can be generated while we adapt.

The table below attempts to summarise these oversimplified points to provide a very rough indication how people judge the different types of change, via a descending scale from best to worst. It also suggests that those things which are easiest to change are changed more frequently. Certainly the cosmetic layout of websites change more frequently than the screen technology used to display them.

TYPE OF CHANGE	HOW OFTEN DOES IT CHANGE	HOW OFTEN DOES IT DISRUPT PEOPLE (pain)	HOW OFTEN DOES IT BENEFIT PEOPLE (gain)	PEOPLE'S RESPONSE (judgement)
Technology	Rare	Often	Mostly	Very good
Performance	Often	Rare	Often	Very good
Capability	**Often**	**Often**	Often	Good
Functional	**Often**	**Often**	Sometimes	Mixed
Repair	Occasional	None	None	Neutral
Cosmetic	Very often	Occasional	None	Subjective
Process	**Very often**	**Always**	Occasional	Poor

Those changes that make us adjust or adapt frequently (see bold font in table) affect us the most and generate the most pain. Whilst capability and functional changes often provide gain in return, process changes which only tell us to do something differently (store it here in this format, now use this tool not that one) tend not to provide us with the same level of benefit or gain in return. If these very broad assumptions are fair (and that doesn't mean finding a single example that don't fit the general mould) then the worst type of changes are those which regularly disrupt people (high pain) whilst providing least benefit (low gain), which seems entirely reasonable. People don't like being constantly affected by change if they are not getting much in return. Therefore, the dubious award of "Worst kind of change" goes to process changes and the prize is to have a chapter dedicated to this subject at the end of Part 1.

Post-change inefficiency

Adapting to the changes that affect us does not come for free. Readjustment takes some time and effort (or pain). Just as this is true for the bigger changes explained above, it is also true for all those little day-to-day changes that happen all the time, whenever someone thinks "wouldn't it be good if we just..." or "it would be better if we..." Whenever keys and tools are moved, computer files and folders are renamed, or names, labels, terminology or page layouts are changed, a bit of confusion and delay follows. A 5-minute job now becomes a 30-minute job, and all those little natural subconscious actions are replaced slower conscious ones. For a short while at least, things are more difficult; we get the pain without the gain. This is 'post-change inefficiency'.

There is surprisingly little on the internet about change causing temporary inefficiency (these days, change is always about improvement). It's like it doesn't exist and I've just made it all up (which I might have done – that is for you to decide). Is it just a figment of my imagination, that it takes me longer to find the eggs after the supermarket aisles have has been reorganised, or that every time they change a computer tool at work it takes me some time to learn how to use it? Am I going slightly mad or does the consensus view of the internet want to ignore this post-change inefficiency? Incidentally, one article I did find is called "The inefficiency of change",[1] but it has a different emphasis to the point being made here and is much more in keeping with the business chapter in Part 3.

Whether the changes are planned, unplanned, large or small, any changes which affect people will create some level of short-term post-change inefficiency. This temporary readjustment may be slightly frustrating at the time and may be quite trivial for some infrequent or one-off changes, but just one occasional change is not part of the philosophy of continual improvement. If things stop changing then things stop improving, so they must be changed again and again and again. Constant change continually affects people, creating continual post-change inefficiency. It doesn't matter whether you recognise post-change inefficiency as real or whether it is just an affectation inside the mind of a frustrated grumpy old man who can no longer use taps, because the theory of continual improvement has much stronger opposition. These much more ominous opponents are the imposing, unflinching, uncaring laws of physics, laws of nature and their close relative the 'law of diminishing returns'.

Continual improvement versus diminishing returns

The law of diminishing returns is often explained using the analogy of emptying a bath of water (without using the drainage plug hole). At first it is easy to make a few big improvements by using a large bucket to remove large amounts of water, but it soon becomes hard to remove a lot of water and you need a smaller vessel, like a cup. Now the amount of water removed on each attempt is much less, the improvements (or gains) become smaller, and more attempts and effort (scoops of water) are needed. Eventually, after more water has been removed with the cup, an even smaller vessel, like a spoon, is needed and now a lot of effort (or pain) is needed for very little progress (or gain). The law of diminishing returns demonstrates that initially a few big improvements can made, but as more improvement attempts are made, the gains become smaller while the effort or pain increases. Therefore, attempting to improve something that has already been improved a few times, like the layout of a supermarket, the fuel economy of a car, the organisational structure of a business or a government cabinet reshuffle, is likely to produce only small gains or benefits, which struggle to outweigh the effort or pains of making the change. This is something which is well known by scientists, engineers, sportspeople, musicians or anyone who has had to empty a bath with a bucket.

Science and engineering

Engineers can't just make batteries last 10% longer, cranes lift 20% more or make buildings 30% higher, because it is difficult and takes a lot of time and effort to design, develop and test how to do it. Scientists can't just cure 10% of cancers this year or make a material that's twice as strong because the law of diminishing returns gets in the way every time. The laws of physics and nature dictate what can be done, when something will break, overheat or reach capacity, or how hard something is to do, not that fashionable pair of words: continual improvement. The best we can do is continue the long, hard, slow battle of scientific research to understand the laws of physics and slowly but surely push the limit of what is achievable. Occasionally, someone will make a new technology discovery, like the invention (or discovery) of carbon fibre, which will initially allow a couple of bucket-sized improvements to be made, before returning to the slow effort of using cup and then spoon to make small incremental changes until it is good enough and practical enough for people to use.

Individuals

People are a little different and it is natural and instinctive for people to improve, expanding the scope and range of what they are capable of, like learning to play a musical instrument, getting a better job, trying a new sport or even writing a book when you've only ever worked with numbers. These attempts to improve are accompanied by lots of failed attempts, wasted effort, uncertainty, changing preferences and internal personal battles, which are all an acceptable part of improving ourselves. Importantly, however, all this time and effort is personal. Except for the wailing violin that can be heard down the street or a lack of housework getting done, all this extra effort tends not to affect many other people, so there is very little pain for others. After some initial improvements you become competent or reasonably good. Then the law of diminishing returns is waiting there again, and it becomes increasingly difficult to get better. Runners can't just say "I will run 5 minutes faster than my best time today", they must train for months shaving a few seconds off their best time. A guitarist or piano player can't just learn a new piece of music and any reasonably good golfer can't just lower their golf handicap by four shots overnight. In all cases the accuracy, strength, timing, skill and endurance needed to get better are all limited by the physical world and the law of diminishing returns. It takes more and more effort to make smaller and smaller improvements.

In some cases, this search for more improvement, just one more teaspoon of gain, can have a large disruptive effect on something which is already close to optimal or working very well. This is something which a few unfortunate professional golfers have experienced, when trying to improve their already near-perfect swing. The same has happened to snooker players trying to improve their cueing action. This unfortunate occurrence introduces yet another strong opponent to the idea of continual improvement: if you improve (or change) something enough times, you will eventually break the parts that work well.

Business organisations

Despite this, continual improvement has become the mantra of many businesses and organisations, who continually set targets like 5–10% efficiency improvements year on year. Where does this improvement come from? They all exist and operate in the same real world, with the same physical laws, with the same limits on time, accuracy, power, efficiency etc. Whilst sport, music, science, engineering and people all have to battle against reality and the law of diminishing returns, it seems strange that these large complex organisations believe they can miraculously make continual improvements year after year, with yet another improvement plan or initiative. Any reasonably competent business or organisation that has existed for a few years or more will already be operating in a reasonably efficient, optimised state. Those more obvious, early bucket-sized improvements will have already been made, making further smaller gains harder, whilst the likelihood of disrupting those things that already work well increases. Even with all the best and genuine intentions, when a business is operating well, there will be a tipping point where the relatively small cup and spoon improvement gains will be outweighed by the combined pains of post-change inefficiency and disrupting or breaking things that already worked well.

It is of course possible to acknowledge the existence of this tipping point. You can accept things are sufficiently good or efficient enough and choose not to make any more changes. You can accept reality and simply stop trying to improve, and in doing so you have just put the concept of continual improvement in the bin, exactly where it belongs. The theory of continual improvement only works when the continual changes do not adversely affect or disrupt others, like when musicians practise and scientists do experiments. However, in the real, complex world we inhabit, in businesses and large organisation, this rarely happens. A change that provides some localised gain to one group often goes on to disrupt or affect the activities of another group, who then experience the pain of yet another bloody so-called improvement. All that is happening here is a ridiculous never-ending game of 'pass the burden' (the full name is 'pass the burden, call it an improvement and hope no one will notice').

Here lies a subtle contradiction and a good dose of irony. By spending time and effort seeking small continual improvements to something that already works reasonably well, you are just as likely to continually create disruption, post-change inefficiency and frustration. This is the reason why all those amazing, endless, continual improvements just seem to make things more difficult, inefficient and frustrating. Every time tools, information, hierarchy structures, controls, organisations, systems and processes get changed, a year or two later someone realises that improvement didn't work as expected and makes another change. The law of diminishing returns and post-change inefficiency join forces and make it difficult to produce a real improvement.

Real improvement is difficult

In this game of pass the burden, any changes intended to provide localised benefits then need to be dressed up or disguised as improvements, so that others will be more willing to accept them. In this way a reduction in customer service staff might be dressed up with a phrase like:

"Our customer service improvements put you
in control with a few simple clicks."
(Meaning... we've now passed the burden on
to you, so you can do it all yourself.)

Other similar examples of passing the burden include:

- Making something more complicated, then expecting others to understand it.
- Introducing a new procedure, then expecting others to do it.
- Passing part of your job on to others to do for you.

For many changes, the people who get the gain are different from those who get the pain. Those who experience the pain of an improvement without the gain can and will justifiably view it as yet another unnecessary, irritating, frustrating change. Using a localised benefit as a justification for using the label 'improvement' is the start of a very steep and very slippery slope, at the bottom of which is the claim that demolishing schools improves the amount of rubble available to local builders to use. For those wanting to play this game, it is possible to claim that absolutely any change is an improvement.

Making a real improvement is difficult and requires some conscious effort and time to consider who the change could affect and how. It is easy to put the blinkers on and focus only on the local gains, but much harder to consider, assess or even care about the consequences of change, the pain experienced by others. To some extent, this game of pass the burden can be avoided by asking questions like:

- If I make this change, do I know who it will affect?
- Do I need to check how it will affect them, before making the change?

- Is this change going to cause a big problem for anyone (even if it is minor and acceptable to most people)?
- If I make this change, what could it disrupt or break?
- Could this change affect things I'm not even aware of, and how do I check?

These extra considerations and checks would be cumbersome to do formally and, in most cases, would be entirely unnecessary and impractical. However, without any conscious thought, understanding or check whether any of these may be relevant, there is absolutely no way of being aware of the possible disruption or pain. It is these types of checks that prevent demolishing a school from being a real improvement and help to ensure the overall gain is greater than the overall pain, by trying to do the following:

- Minimise the post-change inefficiency for others (make it easy for people to adjust).
- Do not affect people unnecessarily (don't make the effects of the change widespread if the benefits are only localised to a few people).
- Ensure that those it affects get the benefit (don't benefit a few, to the detriment of many).

In reality, it is extremely rare that you get something for nothing, but not enough people realise this. If people do not recognise that their changes can adversely affect others, they cannot understand that changes and improvements have limits, boundaries and consequences. Under this illusion that every change will make things better, these inconsiderate disruptive changes will continue to flourish. Ignorance doesn't make a change an improvement. Neither do the assumptions like these.

"If this part is better, it will be better overall."

"If I just change this, then..."

"The feedback said change this, so it must be an improvement".

In my experience, if you highlight this and demonstrate the disruption caused, those who are the most ignorant will go on to defend their change with glib remarks like "It is part of continual improvement" or "Thank you for your feedback, we will consider it in future". I've even been told directly that "Every change is an improvement". I'll let you imagine the tone and content of my response to ridiculous statements like that. Perhaps these claims are a little unfair. Perhaps most people do carefully consider the potential disruption of a change, but this does not prevent a lot of bad, so-called improvements from happening. Perhaps some decide to selfishly take the local benefit (like supermarkets changing layouts), or perhaps other stronger influences sway the choices and decisions. Both these aspects are explored further in Parts 2 and 3.

Continual ignorance and continual consequences

Over the last couple of decades, the idea of continual improvement has grown into a cyclic obsession. Everything must be improved; changes make improvements; everything must be changed. It has created a culture where change is good, leading to a mindset and a freedom to make lots of changes all the time. The focus is only on the gain with little regard for the consequences. The pain is always an acceptable by-product because an improvement is being made. When changes break things or don't provide improvement, the theory of continual improvement can only interpret this as "more changes are needed to improve it". It cannot be interpreted as evidence that something is already close to optimal, performing well or difficult to improve further. To put this more bluntly, the concept of continual improvement does not have any method or option for saying "You know what, this is pretty damn good, and it is good enough". It has no recognition of the tipping point, where the constant effort (pain) required to implement and adjust to continual changes is higher than small improvement gains. It can only suggest that you carry on changing things because that's what makes things better. It allows people to use the phrase "It is part of continual improvement" to justify every single change they make, regardless of how poor or disruptive it is. It means that any change, to anything, by anyone, at any time can be described as an improvement.

The word 'improvement' has become completely devalued by habitual overuse and misuse. It is so frustrating to hear the word 'improvement' applied to things that make something more difficult, more time-consuming, more inefficient, more unreasonable or more nonsensical.

In a moment of higher cynicism, I even predicted that the current dictionary definition of the word 'improvement', "get better", will be replaced with the definition "a change". I think my fundamental problem here is that I still hold on to the rather old-fashioned concept that making something less reliable, making something more difficult or changing something that works into something that doesn't work simply aren't improvements. Therefore, if this chapter does anything to subdue the belief in continual improvement or reduce the habitual overuse and misuse of the word 'improvement', then it has been very worthwhile. However, this does not mean we should stop trying to improve. It just means that real improvement is difficult and, in some cases, not even possible. It suggests that people should distinguish between the 'pass the burden' tinkering type of changes and those that truly try to resolve significant fundamental problems.

The next chapter looks at why the assumptions that collective human feedback and continual improvement work well are wrong. It is because they are built around a type of false logic.

"Anything that passes the burden on to others is just a change, not an improvement."

04

FALSE LOGIC

*"There is nothing worse than someone who
doesn't know that they don't know."*
(Advice from my boss at work, 1991)

hapter 1 demonstrated how sentences that initially seem reasonable can contain ambiguity, inconsistency and even contradiction. False logic is an extension of this, where several sentences, ideas or sets of information that initially seem perfectly acceptable are, after a little consideration, found to be fundamentally wrong or impossible. One well-known example of this is these two sentences.

THE SENTENCE BELOW IS TRUE
THE SENTENCE ABOVE IS FALSE

At first glance, nothing appears wrong (especially for those who have not seen this before) and when you realise that the bottom sentence refers back to the top sentence it still seems acceptable. It is not until you explicitly follow the logic for several steps, that you realise these two sentences form an infinite, contradicting loop that can never be true. These infinite loops are not the topic of this chapter, but for those interested they are explored in detail in the book *Godel, Escher, Bach* by Douglas Hofstadter.[1] The reason we accept them is because the human brain has evolved an important survival trait to decide quickly "should

I play dead, run away, hide or fight?" We immediately trust and act on our instincts, with more conscious thinking taking much longer and coming later. This evolutionary need and ability to make quick survival decisions also makes us susceptible to jumping to incorrect, invalid or even impossible conclusions. This is the subject of this chapter.

The first time I became aware of false logic was watching the BBC show *Yes, Prime Minister* in the late 1980s,[2] where it was used to comic effect and called 'politicians' logic'. This comical use of false logic is possible because initially the falsehood remains hidden, and you accept what you hear or see. It is only when the unexpected contradiction is revealed that you realise you also missed it, and this adds to the comic value. Whilst laughing at others, you can secretly laugh at yourself as well. Another of my favourite examples is the following phrase that I saw on a t-shirt.

"There is a time and place for spontaneity."

Again, the phrase initially seems to be entirely innocent and correct, until you start analysing it and find the inherent contradiction hidden inside these eight words. Before we move onto the more serious side, false logic is understandably a common cause of confusion and misunderstanding in young children, such as this example.

All fish live and swim in water.
Dolphins live and swim in water.
Dolphins must be fish.

A similar example and a fond personal memory of mine involved my daughter when she was very young. Whilst taking a long walk through a forest, we came across a map with the customary red dot to show us "You are here", which prompted her to ask, "How does it know we are here?" Inside my young daughter's mind, the logic was something like this.

The map knows all the routes through the wood.
But the map does not know where we have walked.
So how does the map know we are here?

False logic does not only affect young children. The examples below illustrate the various types of false logic that affect adults as well.

Types of false logic

The first type of false logic is where a logically true statement is reversed to produce an invalid statement, such as the dolphin example and another about getting to work below.

All fish live and swim in water.
...incorrectly reverses to...
Everything that lives and swims in water is a fish.

People drive to work.
...incorrectly reverses to...
People at work have driven there.

Furthermore, the belief that constant changes make 'continual improvements' is also based around a similar reversal of logic, as in this chain of logic.

> All improvements need something to change.
> Changes lead to improvements.
> My change will lead to an improvement.

Here the first line "All improvements need something to change" incorrectly reverses to "When something changes, there are improvements", which is equivalent to the middle statement. Although some people believe this to be true, and it can sometimes be true, it is certainly not always true, as you will quickly discover if you change your wheels from circles to squares. Had this reversal of logic been made more obvious, with the first line reading "All changes produce improvements" then our common sense would immediately interject and shout, "That's not right" and the falsehood would be spotted.

A second type of false logic occurs when a logical statement is negated instead of reversed. Although this can be true as in the next 'reproduction' example, it is certainly not true in the 'smoking' and 'unemployment' examples that follow it.

Living things reproduce.
...which correctly negates to...
Non-living things don't reproduce.

Smoking gives you cancer.
...incorrectly negates to...
If you don't smoke, you won't get cancer.

This political party will reduce unemployment.
...incorrectly negates to...
Other political parties won't reduce unemployment.

A third type of false logic occurs when the same word or item is interpreted differently within the same chain of logic. The optimistic belief that collective human opinions produce improvements suffers this problem with the word 'feedback'. Below it is interpreted as "scientific feedback" in the first line but as "opinions and reviews" in the third line.

- Scientific feedback reliably improves performance.
- Humans can offer opinions and reviews.
- Human opinions and reviews are feedback.
- Therefore, human opinions and reviews can be used to reliably improve performance.

Again, you can believe this to be true, and in some cases it may be true, but it is incorrect to think that it is always true.

Other types of false logic include the use of 'circular logic' like "It is a great painting because they are a great painter", which ignores the fact that a good painter can produce bad paintings or incorrectly assuming a cause and effect: "If I wash my car, then a bird poos on it".

Finally, our logic can be affected by the introduction of red herrings, which strictly speaking do not break the logic, but produces a diversion away from it. When a child complains "I'm tired" the emphasis should be on "Are you really tired and, if so, why?" The red herring response of "I work twice as hard as you" only diverts the question towards "Who works the hardest?" or "Who is most tired?" instead. The remainder of this chapter shows how these different types of false logic affect our decision making in everyday life. It looks at how our understanding of the real world and our common sense can sometimes jump in and save us and the situations when it can't.

Common sense and abstraction

We have all grown up in the real physical world and have a huge amount of experience and understanding of it. We rely heavily on this real-world common sense. It can prevent us from falling foul of false logic, as in this more subtle example.

- Intelligence requires learning.
- Learning takes time.
- Older people have had more time to learn.
- Older people are more intelligent than younger people.

Although there are likely to be many influences that we are unable to understand or explain properly, our ingrained day-to-day experience of the real world, our common sense, intuitively tells us that older people are not more intelligent than younger people and this helps us reject the conclusion. However, not everything is quite so simple as this. As the subject becomes more complex or more abstracted away from our real-world experience, it becomes increasingly difficult for our intuition and common sense to step in and help us understand or decide. The next few examples, which progressively abstract away from the reality we are familiar with, are only here to highlight this, so feel free to skip the examples if or when this happens.

Example 1

The first case is what we should do with information.

- Databases are good for storing and accessing information.
- I have some information.
- I should put it in a database.

Although this might be true much of the time, the chain above indicates that all information you have should be put in a database. Intuitively we know this is not correct, as it really depends on what the information is, how many people need to see it and how long it needs to be stored for.

Example 2

To increase the level of abstraction from our real-world experiences further, this next chain of statements is based on familiar shapes and the much less familiar awareness of how the length of sides is related to their area. The logic is initially provided in words, like other examples, but a diagram is also provided to help clarify these words.

- A square piece of paper has all sides of length A + B.
- The square can be divided into four sections (as shown by the dotted line below), one square with all sides of length A (top left), one square with all sides of length B (bottom right) and two rectangles, each with opposites sides of length A and the other opposite sides of length B.
- The large square (of sides A + B) can contain a smaller rotated square, so that one side of the rotated square forms a diagonal line, which divides one of the rectangles (top right), forming one of four identical triangles in the corners of the original large square.
- The total area of these four outer triangles is the same as the total area of the two rectangles.
- Therefore, the area of the rotated middle square is the same has the total area of the two smaller squares (the one with sides of length A and the one with sides of length B).

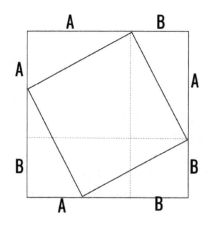

How does this more abstract chain of statements relate to your knowledge of the real world and how much did your common sense help? Is this chain of logic true or false? This is starting to demonstrate that the further we abstract away from our understanding and everyday experience of the real world, then the less we can rely on our common sense to 'kick in' and help. Some may recognise this example as a proof of the famous Pythagoras theorem learnt at school ($C^2 = A^2 + B^2$), where C is the length of the sides of the rotated square.

Example 3

The final step is a complete abstraction from reality, removing all links from our everyday experiences, in the form of a raw logical problem. This pure logical puzzle has four letters, each letter has a numerical value of 1 or higher (no letter has a value of zero) and all you need to do is to work out the correct order of the letters and determine whether the final statement is logically true or false.

- The two letters with a value of 1 are next to each other.
- The letter with the highest value is next to the letter T.
- The letter Q has a value equal to the sum of the values either side of it.
- The letter S is earlier in the sequence than D, but has a value greater than that of D.
- Therefore, the value of Q is equal to the sum of S and D.

Where was your common sense this time? When all connection to the familiar real world is removed, our common sense is completely disabled and silent. Or perhaps it just shouted, "Run away and ignore this horribly abstracted problem that I can't comprehend".

Collectively, this group of short examples demonstrate how our good old common sense helps in situations that relate closely to our real-world experiences, but becomes less useful as the level of abstraction from the real world increases. Once this abstraction has happened, we are left with a choice to ignore it, blindly accept it or a lot of hard work and logical rigour to understand it, as those of you who completed the final abstract logic puzzle will know. Incidentally the answer to the question is TRUE, the order of the letters is SQTD, where both T and D have value 1.

The value of S and Q are indeterminate (there is not enough information to know it), however because Q is S + T, then Q = S + D. I chose the letters such that if you increment each letter by one in the alphabet it spells TRUE (the answer).

Beyond these silly examples, any form of abstraction away from the real world that we intuitively know will disable our common sense. Combine this with our natural inclination to jump to conclusions and other real-world pressures such as time, money and complexity, and it produces a toxic combination in which false logic can flourish. False logic is not just limited to comedy, young children or the pages of this book. It is far more common and frustrating than you would think, as is demonstrated by the following real examples.

A few real examples

This first real case has affected millions of people in the UK. The following (grossly oversimplified) chain of false logic applies to house prices and the market forces of supply and demand.

- The theory of supply and demand works very well for items that are bought and sold.
- Houses are bought and sold.
- The theory of supply and demand will work very well for houses.

Those of an inquisitive nature may wish to puzzle over this to see if they can unearth the hidden break in the logic chain before reading on. This logic chain is invalid due to a very significant, but not so obvious, difference between houses and other everyday products like kettles, cars and sofas. Even if you can afford it, there is a natural limit to the number of kettles you will buy, because the value of everyday objects decreases until they become worthless and get thrown away. Conversely, the value of houses tends to increase over time. Therefore, providing you have enough money, it is financially beneficial to buy one or more, even if the extra ones are not used or rented. This means there is no natural limit to the demand and so house prices continue to increase with this demand. Adding further fuel to the fire, when other people recognise this is a profitable activity, they also start to do the same thing and they too can buy more and more. Therefore, the theory of supply and demand works in one situation, for everyday items like kettles that become worthless, but not when the products increase in value, like houses.

In complex environments, which include anything involving people, multiple influences, financial markets, uncertainty or beliefs, then it only takes a small subtle change to break the chain of logic. Here the incorrect assumption, "If it works well for this, then it will work for that" breaks the logic chain. There are parallels here with our use of feedback (if it works there, it will work here). In the complex world it is not true; this is just how the real world works.

The next example occurred when my children's school wanted to ensure that parents were acknowledging important information, by using the following approach.

- There is important information regarding the school.
- All parents/guardians need to know this information.
- We will email the information to all parent/guardians.

So far, so good, this seems very reasonable and something that most people would accept (including me). Astonishingly, the important information about the school was this: "It is unacceptable that far too many parents/guardians are not acknowledging or responding to information sent to them via email". Adding this to the top of the logic chain forms an inconsistency that even my children spotted as being a bit daft. It is like saying "Blind people are not paying attention to all these written notices we have stuck on the wall, so we need to put up more written notices". How can you tackle the problem by feeding it further? I know, let's put out this fire by drowning it with petrol.

The final real-life example is about tax avoidance and based on the sensible idea that we should not tax people's conscience, because being conscientious is generally considered to be a good thing and something to encourage. During the TV show *The Last Leg* shown on Channel 4, one of my favourite comedy actors David Mitchell made a brilliant logic chain, in his typical ranting style, to show how tax avoidance amounts to nothing more than a tax on your conscience.[3] Those interested will have to look it up, as there is too much to repeat here without infringing copyright.

False logic is everywhere. It disrupts or invalidates our decision making all the time, not maliciously or intentionally, it just isn't recognised at the time. Our fallible minds quickly jump to conclusions and try to fill in the gaps, particularly when things are complex, ambiguous or when we only see a small part of the logic chain. All this is a perfect recipe to allow another bit of false logic to slip through unnoticed and produce yet another of those annoying, frustrating decisions that just seem to contradict common sense. Anyone reading this and thinking "I'm too clever for this to happen to me" is probably just blissfully ignorant of all the times it has happened to them. As stated at the start of this chapter "There is nothing worse than someone who doesn't know that they don't know". That is not intended to be condescending or insulting, it is simply the nature of this particular beast. False logic is very good at remaining hidden and being difficult to spot.

Battle against false logic

The best defence against false logic and bad decisions is our understanding of how the real world operates and our common sense. Beyond these we must rely on a purer, more mathematical analysis which is not as easy, as all those who skipped the SQTD letters puzzle will testify. Some people have the ability to ask a few crucial questions, quickly pick up on the contradictions and prevent mistakes, which is a good but unfortunately rare skill to have. For the rest of us, the best we can do is attempt to keep track of the critical pieces of information that build up the logic chain, so the reasoning behind the decision can be understood. If these critical pieces start to conflict with each other, if they are not clear or well understood or whenever they are glossed over with empty words, then the FALSE LOGIC alarm bells should start to ring. You should proceed with more caution. To make a decision we only have to believe that we are correct, but our brains are quite easy to fool and that doesn't mean we are correct.

The more we weaken our natural defences in the ways listed below, the less chance we have of spotting the presence of false logic.

- Abstraction away from the real world that we intuitively understand.
- More complexity with lots of logical steps.

- Seeing or having only part of the logic chain.
- Misinterpretation or ambiguity, allowing invalid links and bridges to be built through the logic chain.
- Lack of understanding, making it harder to know if different statements agree or contradict, leading us to make links by assumption.

Being unaware of false logic makes it much more difficult to identify, just as being unaware of how a change will affect others makes it impossible know if it is an improvement or not. On the occasions when you do spot false logic being used to make a decision, it can be difficult to speak out without it sounding rude: "Don't be so stupid, can't you see the contradiction that makes your decision ridiculous". Alternatively, not saying anything means that the impossible contradiction will just get noticed much later, when someone else will have a bigger problem to deal with. Often the best approach is to simply question the logic used, using simple, clear statements: "In the meeting we said X, Y and Z, but I'm not sure X is compatible with Z".

Regardless of how the contradictions of false logic are spotted and announced, you can almost guarantee that someone will have a vested interest in the decision. Many decisions are not made on logic alone, but are based on some other bias or opinion, such as financial need, politics or selfishness (all of which are considered further in Parts 2 and 3). To sway the decision, the contradictions need to be ignored or glossed over, and the best tool for this job is yet another set of ambiguous words. This does not make those decisions right or wrong, it just means that the dormant false logic and contradiction within the decision can ruin the outcome later, when it encounters the real physical world and becomes apparent for what it is. The real physical world cannot accept contradiction; it cannot be persuaded by words, optimism, belief or hope. It has absolutely no awareness or concern for the bad decision, who made it, when or how. The physical world will simply obey the laws of physics and follow the laws of nature and show the contradiction for exactly what it is: impossible. There is a moral here: the real world will always win. You can convince yourself your decision is right, but if it is not, the real world will eventually show you that your decision is wrong. The real physical world will not allow ignorance, beliefs or desires that are inconsistent with reality to win.

This hidden beast of false logic has many victims and that's before you start counting the second tier of victims who suffer from the consequences of those bad decisions. Our common sense, intuition and understanding are our best defence against false logic and it is these essential human qualities that distinguish us from computers. The more we abstract our decision making away from our real-world experiences, the more we disable these important human traits. This is investigated further in the next chapter, which looks at our use of information.

———————————————————

"The real physical world is the only true judge of decisions and actions."

05

BINFORMATION

*"Everybody gets so much information all day
long that they lose their common sense."*
(Gertrude Stein, 1874–1946, novelist and poet)

Ever since the emergence of computers in the 1970s, the ability to record, store, access, use and ultimately benefit from information has grown exponentially. We now live in what is quite rightly called the Information Age, following on from its predecessors the Industrial, Middle, Iron, Bronze and Stone ages. It would be foolish to claim that this technological revolution is not massively beneficial to everyone and, as with many technology advancements, it is truly a real improvement. The access and use of maps, music, videos, user guides, reviews and other information is nothing short of a modern miracle, even if this miracle does require some mildly frustrating infrastructure, such as setting up accounts, remembering passwords and waiting for yet another update (or change) to download. However, none of this is the subject of this chapter, and neither is the type of information stored, as that is surely the choice of those using the information. Instead, this chapter looks at how this new ability to store huge amounts of information affects our use and interaction with that information.

Information and knowledge

Stored information shares many of the characteristics of words. Both are essential and beneficial, whilst both can be ambiguous, contradictory or incorrect, but principally both do absolutely nothing on their own. It is only our access and understanding of the information that makes it useful. Earlier our use of words was condensed down to the following chain.

WORDS – INTERPRETATION – KNOWLEDGE –
DECISION – ACTION - PHYSICAL WORLD

In the case of computer-stored information, the equivalent chain would be this.

INFORMATION – ACCESS – UNDERSTANDING –
KNOWLEDGE – DECISION – ACTION – PHYSICAL WORLD

This is the first main point of this chapter: there is a fundamental difference between information and knowledge. This is a simple fact, made explicitly clear by the statement "Information is not knowledge", the origin of which is unclear, but is attributed in various forms to Albert Einstein, James Gleick, Frank Zappa, Clifford Stoll and Arthur C. Clarke. My own version is "If someone gives you a physics book, then you have all the information, but it does not mean that you now understand physics". My computer contains a huge amount of information (about 0.6 terabytes), but I only have access to a fraction of that information, and I don't have a good understanding of most of that. I don't know who sang certain songs or the precise email address of a friend, for example. For most of our simple everyday needs, using this modern-day miracle is almost subconscious. There is very little effort accessing, understanding and deciding what action to take (play, delete, call etc.) for music, videos, maps, contacts etc.

However, a lot of the information we use is much more complex than just a song or map and it is used in much more complicated ways. The huge, complex sets of information held by schools, hospitals, businesses, governments etc. are too large and complicated for our brains to comprehend. Often, they need to be used in different ways, for different reasons, by different people, at different times or even simultaneously.

We therefore need computer tools to bridge the gap from the raw stored INFORMATION to our KNOWLEDGE and subsequent use of it. In our Information Age, this bridge is achieved by a collection of common computer tools such as spreadsheets and databases, which generally work very well if they are suitable for the job. Unfortunately, these tools also influence and change our relationship with information, and that is the subject of this chapter, starting with a real example.

Bloody bonkers

Recently my wife and I both booked appointments to give blood, on the same day, at the same donation centre. Mine was at midday and my wife's was late afternoon. Naturally our appointments were stored in a database tool along with all the other appointments. About a week before the appointment date, a change in work commitments meant I could no longer attend my midday donation, but this wasn't a problem as I could just swap appointments with my wife. Problem solved – or so it seemed. I rang up to swap the appointments, but I was informed by the very polite representative that this wasn't possible. Remarkably the database tool, which allowed these two appointments to be booked initially, would not allow the same two the appointments to be booked the other way round. More ridiculously, I was then told that I could in fact take my wife's slot, but that she could not take mine. It was bloody bonkers!

Any reasonable or sensible person could easily comprehend that swapping two appointments (that had already been booked and accepted) would not affect anything else. Unfortunately, it was not the polite, reasonable, sensible person that was now controlling the information. It was the computer database tool that was dictating how the appointment information was viewed, what could be changed and how the information could be used. Unknowingly the database tool was needlessly throwing away a blood donation that could save someone's life – WHY? Even in these critically important aspects of our lives, it is simply wrong to state, assume or believe that these computer tools do not influence or affect how we access, understand and ultimately use information.

What is binformation?

Any information that we cannot access or understand is not very useful, and neither is information that is incorrect or doesn't help us to learn, decide and act. It is rubbish information. Binformation is therefore a collective label for any information that doesn't flow through the chain above. Various types and examples are briefly described below.

Rubbish in, rubbish out

A lot of raw numerical and text data, such as ages, prices, names, addresses etc. is entered by hand. When it is entered incorrectly, the tools simply do not know and will regurgitate the same incorrect information to an unsuspecting person in the future. This is precisely what happened when I received a phone call, asking to speak to the parent or guardian of a 50-year-old man, presumably because the age had been entered as 5 instead of 50 by mistake. This is commonly known as "rubbish in, rubbish out" and it is not the computers' fault. These simple mistakes are easy for people to make. Most of the time the consequences are just mildly irritating or comical, but occasionally they can be much more serious, such as if they delay a passport application, calculate an incorrect salary or affect medical treatment.

Once this type of 'rubbish in' mistake has been made, the effect can spread. If that information is used in calculations or to create statistics and charts, these will also be incorrect to some extent. The error from one incorrect number in the average of a large set of data will be very small, whilst a similar error used in a calculation can have a bigger effect. Imagine using a tool to calculate the total cost of 180 items costing £67.74 each and being provided with the answer of £13,813.20. This very useful and practical use of tools is so common that we are all used to taking the answer and using it immediately; this is the real problem. We are so accustomed to believing the answers provided by computers that we rarely question their validity or correctness. If the computer says it is true, then it must be true, just like the example above. However, it isn't true and the answer isn't correct. The incorrect answer of £13,813.20 came from the calculation 180 x £76.74, not 180 x £67.74. The correct answer is actually £12,193.20. As the price was incorrectly entered, the 'rubbish in' produced 'rubbish out'. Although very common, human error is not the problem here. What is important is the realisation of how often people blindly trust the answers provided by computers, without question or understanding, just as many will have trusted the answer to the calculation above. The paragraphs below outline other ways in which computers can provide us with incorrect information that is likely to be used blindly, without question or understanding.

More rubbish in

Another way of putting 'rubbish in' is by making it unclear what is expected or needed. Using bland, generic labels and terminology for column headings or drop-down menu options will result in different people, with different interpretations, entering different information.

- "Name": is that the author, the person entering the data or the manager responsible?
- "Date": is that the date of input, result, review or the initial problem?
- "Item": is that the product, the document or the problem?
- "Cost": is that in pounds, dollars or euros?

Perhaps this is specific to engineering, but I've used many computer tools which use ambiguous labels like "type", "process", "category", "stream", "component", "item", "entry", "package" or "group". What do these mean? The person who designed the tool and chose the labels knows precisely what they mean and why they were chosen, but many users won't. Unless all users of the tool enter and interpret the information consistently (not easy in a world of constant change – sorry, improvement), most of the good information will be contaminated with some rubbish binformation.

Auto-corruption

Even when information is entered correctly, it is still possible to get 'rubbish out'. This is because many computer tools have auto-correct features like those on your phone, to make things more convenient for the user. These features can all be disabled (if you know how) so, again, no blame can be placed on the providers of this helpful and convenient selection of annoying, interfering, know-it-all, superior functions that irritatingly override your input with some pseudo random guess at what it thinks you might be trying to say. If not disabled, these auto-correct, or more specifically auto-format, functions within spreadsheets are very efficient at converting numbers like "23.10" to "23rd October" or "3/8" to "3rd August" without telling you it has done so. Similar things happen to some acronyms that get auto-corrected (or auto-corrupted would sometimes be a more accurate name) to become days of the week or months of the year WED, THUR, JAN, FEB, MAR etc. Once this auto-format damage has been done, the correctly typed number "23.10" will be corrupting both the information and any analysis using it. Again, the result is a different type of 'rubbish out' for us to believe and use in ignorance.

The widespread use of spreadsheets means there is a lot of potential for this type of data corruption, damage or oversight. There are known problems in areas of finance, genetics, health records and COVID-19 records, as reported in an article in *The Conversation*, an online source of news and views from a large collection of UK universities.[1] It indicates that between 5% and 30% of spreadsheets are likely to contain some form of error. Regardless of the true scope, this type of auto-corrupted binformation is again used in ignorance and trusted as good information.

Computer models

Computers are capable of far more than just storing and providing access to information. Their ability to do millions of calculations incredibly quickly makes them capable of calculating very complex behaviours in something called computer models or mathematical models (I was a mathematical modeller for about 7 years). This type of model has been used for decades across a wide range of industries, including weather prediction, studies of animal populations, the spread of viruses, engineering, finance, architecture, traffic flows, satellite trajectories and computer games amongst many more. Primarily this is because it is much quicker and cheaper to test initial ideas and concepts on a computer than build and test a physical (hardware) product. However, in some cases real testing is just not possible – you can't physically change the weather or animal populations just to see what happens – so mathematical modelling is the only option. These mathematical models are based around the laws of physics, chaos, nature and sometimes more nebulous behavioural models. Once you think you have all the maths correct and have checked and tested the model, it then becomes a very flexible, immensely powerful and relatively cheap technique for investigating things such as these.

- How effective a lockdown will be in restricting the spread of a virus.
- The maximum load a bridge or building can withstand before collapsing.
- How the performance and stability of a feedback control loop will change if the measurement accuracy is reduced, or the application of the change is delayed.
- What the weather will be like at the weekend.

However, even at this stage it is impossible to know how correct your model of a building, plane or washing machine is, until you have built it and tested it. What if the steel used is weaker than the strength assumed in the model? This problem is best summarised by a phrase used by the head of the mathematical modelling department I worked in.

"All computer models are wrong, but some are very useful."

This was not just a quip or sarcastic comment, it was a crucial, professional warning to never take model results for granted, never blindly believe they are true. The subject of my MSc dissertation was how and why mathematical models can be wrong, from the obvious errors through to many more subtle reasons. Mathematical models contain millions or billions (or perhaps even trillions) of calculations, so one error hidden deep in all that complexity could invalidate the answer. This can be demonstrated by two real examples.

- The finance models that are used to predict and control the financial markets indicated that a financial crash was massively unlikely. However, the models did not accurately represent reality. The models were simply wrong and that incorrect answer misled the financial world into a false sense of security that a financial crash just couldn't happen.

- On 15th October 1987, just before terrible gale force winds hit the south of the UK, a famous BBC weatherman told people that there would be no gale force storms in the UK that evening.[2] He didn't do this because he wanted to mislead people, he did it because all the computer models were wrong and predicted that the strong winds would be south of the English Channel.

Both these "very useful" mathematical models were "completely wrong" on those occasions. What all computer models do, along with databases and spreadsheets to a lesser extent, is condense something very complex into a small amount of information that is easier to comprehend. In doing so, they remove a lot of the context, understanding and knowledge around the answer. It becomes very difficult to know if the answer from a mathematical model is good information or rubbish binformation. People are put into the position of accepting and using the answer blindly, exactly as some of you did with the earlier calculation. The problem is not the use of these incredibly powerful and useful tools, the danger lies in blindly accepting and using the answers without understanding. It is therefore important to use these models with the mindset that they can be wrong and then convince yourself that the answers are good and correct, rather than blindly accepting that the answers are always valid.

Even right is wrong

The modern computing miracle means that children's schooling and homework can be done online via various educational tools. I have nothing against these tools, I think it is essential for their generation to use them, as this is the world that they will grow up in (even though it would drive me up the wall). My problem with these educational tools is their susceptibility to tell you that right answers are wrong, which is something I've experienced many times when helping my children with homework. Here are just two examples.

1. Factorise the following: 3y + 3

My son knew the correct answer to this and immediately typed 3(y+1), only to be told it was incorrect. Despite his frustration and confusion, I convinced him that his answer was perfectly correct and that he had learnt and understood how to factorise correctly. We did the question again, but this time entered the answer as 3(y + 1), noting an extra space either side of the "+" symbol, which the computer now marked as correct.

2. Which king married Anne Boleyn?

The correct answer could be entered as "Henry VIII", "Henry the eighth", "Henry 8th" or "Henry the 8th" and any teacher would hopefully accept any of these answers as correct, but the computer can mark some, most or all except one, as wrong.

These (inadequate) tools are not testing knowledge of maths or history. They are much closer to a weird pedantic guessing game, where you must guess the location of the hidden spaces, capital letters and the exact syntactical format of the answer stored inside the computer. It's like having a combination lock: "Let's try this combination of spaces and capital letters and see if that works". Telling a child that these correct answers are wrong will confuse the hell out of them. This is not the fault of the online approach to education. The fault lies with poor computer tools that are not properly checked or tested before they are let loose to disrupt and confuse the learning efforts of thousands of children who use them. The same problem also occurs in other computer tools, like when I was told my credit card number was wrong, because I failed to correctly guess whether the payment tool wanted spaces, hyphens or nothing between the blocks of four digits – ARRRGH. When computer tools operate (or are designed) inadequately like this, they are not educating children or helping people, they are accentuating the expectation that people are subservient to the machine, the machine is always right and people must change their answer to what the machine wants (there is more of this in Parts 2 and 3).

Littering

Similar to other types of litter and rubbish, another kind of binformation is all that rubbish information that is just left lying around. The useful information that we "Just copy there for now" will quickly become binformation when it is forgotten about, becomes out of date or whenever we can't remember precisely what it was. We are all capable of (and probably guilty of) this type of information littering, simply because it so quick and easy to do.

Old and outdated

Add to all this the information that used to be good and valid information, before some of those constant tinkering and continual improvement changes quickly made it out of date, invalid, useless or misleading.

Large databases

As mentioned at the start, for those who need to use huge amounts of complex information, database tools are essential for bridging the gap between the stored raw information and our understanding of it. These large sets of complex data are collected by entering data, which can be a rather tedious and repetitive job, especially if entering this information is a subsidiary task to a more interesting main role, like fixing cars. If the database tool is difficult to use or asks for too much information, this unappetising job becomes more difficult and frustrating. I was told about the following example from the automotive (car) industry, where a new database tool was used to record all the faults, parts components and time taken for each repair.

This computer tool had over 80 boxes to complete, many with very long drop-down menus to ensure that only valid values could be entered. After some time, when people had got used to using the tool and the level of information had built up, the database started to produce some strange statistics about certain faults on certain components. After some investigation the problematic components were all found to be near the top of the long drop-down menus. What was happening? Once the users became familiar with the time-consuming tool, many became lazy and instead of meticulously finding the right option, they just started clicking options near the top of the huge drop-down menus. The real fault on the car had already been fixed so why waste time completing all these 80 boxes, when you could be doing something much more enjoyable like fixing another real problem? Again, as rubbish went in, rubbish binformation came out. If these large, complex database tools are to be useful and not misused, then they really need to be easy to use.

These examples all demonstrate how we can be presented with binformation instead of good information. As we become less aware and more detached from how that information was generated, we become more trusting of the answers and information provided. Increasingly people blindly accept what the computer presents to them.

Access to the information maze

Returning to the information chain, we must first get access to the information. Looking through someone else's personal filing system is a little like trying to read their mind, as everyone prefers to file things differently. We follow a maze of directory paths, then retrace our steps to follow a different path until we gain access to what we want. On the scale of large organisations or the internet this would simply be impossible, so our modern information miracle provides hugely powerful search engines that do a remarkably impressive job of finding the relevant information (and some not so relevant), using nothing more than a vague description or a few words. Between these two extreme cases of small personal filing systems and the hugely powerful internet lie database tools, with their own smaller search features. In my experience, most are very good if you already know precisely what you are looking for beforehand, like a reference number or an exact title. However, beyond this, performance becomes unreliable. For those searches that list any file, containing any word or any number from your search, the results border on useless. They might as well finish by reporting "Hope you find your needle in this haystack". As a last resort, you may go to the extreme of asking a real knowledgeable person, in the hope they don't just give you one of these common, but rather empty and unhelpful, responses.

- "I've put it in the system." (Any clues as to where or what it is called?)
- "You'll find the information on our website." (Only if you know which menu options to look under.)
- "You'll find it in the database." (Only if you have a login account, access rights, know how to use the tool and know what to look for.)

If you spend long enough searching these mazes and learning the tools, eventually you start to learn and understand where things are stored. It is this knowledge and experience that provides a solution, not just more stored information and user instructions hidden somewhere else in the same information maze. Any information that can't be found or accessed can't be used, and so becomes yet another type of useless binformation.

Using database tools

Although some small database tools can be simple and quite intuitive to use, many are necessarily complicated, making them less intuitive to use. This is easily overcome by good practical, active hands-on training, a good dose of experience and help from people who can already use the tool properly. The alternative, faster, cheaper, less-effective option comprises a passive demonstration, accompanied by a very large instruction manual. Has this type of tick box, "Let them sort it out for themselves", pass the burden type of training ever happened to you? Once you finally find the few relevant pages you need within the huge instruction manual, it is disappointing to discover that the instructions approximate to the garbage below:

1) Choose the top-level menu option or tab that no longer exists because the names and labels change with almost every update of the tool.

2) From the list select the option which closely resembles two or three of the choices available but is not an exact match to any of those listed.

3) Enter your information in a very specific format that hasn't been described or defined, so you will have to guess at it several times before the tool accepts it.

4) Save your entries by ticking a box that doesn't exist, because it has been replaced by some other type of confirmation method.

This frustrating mismatch between the current updated tool and the outdated instructions is probably due to the endless, continual, cosmetic tinkering and updating (sorry 'formally controlled continual improvements') of the tool. Unfortunately nobody can be bothered with the laboriously dull task of keeping the manuals up to date with all those wonderful, helpful improvements that are being made to the tool.

The next section moves away from entering, calculating and accessing information, onto the next step in the chain, UNDERSTANDING, and this requires context.

Importance of context

Once we have access to information, the context of that information is vital in forming our understanding. What is your understanding of information that says "98% thought that fire fighters should be paid more"? It depends on the context. If the information was collected from a large nationwide survey with a high participation rate, then you would understand that the general population thinks that fire fighters are underpaid. Conversely, if the information was taken from a survey of fire fighters only after a three year pay freeze, you would rightly understand the same information in a very different way and think this was inevitable, regardless of their current pay. It is therefore both the information and its full context that are needed for the correct understanding and knowledge to be obtained.

Removing context from information to produce a different understanding and conclusion is a trick commonly used by both politicians and advertisers (and many others). In the three invented examples below, the information is given in quotes, with the removed context following in brackets.

- "We have increased the budget by £100 million." (Context: The annual budget is £50 billion, so the increase is only 0.2%.)

- "Emissions from our transport have reduced by 50%." (Context: Transport emissions are only 1% of our total emissions, so this is only a 0.5% reduction of our overall emissions.)

- "We have recruited 10,000 new nurses in the last 12 months." (Context: We have also lost 10,000 nurses due to retirement, illness and other reasons in the same 12 months, so we have the same number of nurses, and they are now less experienced.)

Although these are all made up, the last one may be much closer to a real case. As a rather cynical rule of thumb, if a change is only a small percentage, then the absolute number tends to be used to promote it, whereas the percentage change tends to be used whenever it is significant. It is this misuse of information, stripping away the essential context that leads to the truth in the phrase "there are lies, damned lies and statistics", which has an uncertain origin, but is often attributed to either Mark Twain (1835–1910, writer) or Benjamin Disraeli (1804–1881, UK prime minister). Statistics are a pure mathematical construct and when used correctly, such as a national census or the studies of diseases etc., they are vitally important for our learning and understanding. It is this that gives them the credibility they deserve. However, when used incorrectly or without context, bad statistics can say almost anything, and they become worse than "damned lies". The book *How to Make the World Add Up* by Tim Harford helps to distinguish between them.[3] More generally, transferring, storing or stating information without the context creates another form of binformation, because we can't understand that information properly. Unless your intention is to mislead or misguide, removing the context defeats the object of having and using that information in the first place.

No context

Despite my critical words, there is one particular type of binformation, which has some or all of the context removed, which I quite like. Not in the way that I have described above, certainly not at work or when trying to do or fix something and certainly not all day, every day. The reason I like this type of binformation is because information without context has a more common and popular name: it is a 'puzzle'. As demonstrated below, the more context you remove, the harder the puzzle is to understand and solve. To start, all of the context has been removed.

> No context
> 52.30/13.25, 51.36/0.05, 40.25/03.45, 48.50/02.20, 41.54/12.29

That was fairly meaningless. Now only a small amount of context is added, such as a simple label or heading.

> Minimal context
> Location: 52.30/13.25, 51.36/0.05, 40.25/03.45, 48.50/02.20,
> 41.54/12.29

Although not obvious, with some context and effort you can now begin to understand what the information is. However, I'd still be very frustrated if I was expected to use this type of information directly in my job. Next, more helpful context is provided.

> Helpful context
> Location (latitude and longitude): 52.30/13.25, 51.36/0.05, 40.25/03.45, 48.50/02.20, 41.54/12.29

This is now a much easier puzzle, but you must still do a bit of work to get the answer and fully understand what the information is. Finally, with all the context provided the information is quickly and easily understood.

> Full context
> Location as latitude (North) and longitude (East) of European cities: 52.30N/13.25E (Berlin), 51.36N/0.05E (London), 40.25N/03.45E (Madrid), 48.50N/02.20E (Paris), 41.54N/12.29E (Rome)

This is no longer a puzzle, and you have everything you need. Again, this oversimplified example is only to demonstrate that without context it is difficult to know what the information really is. More realistically, in schools, business, organisations, government etc. where the data sets are more complicated, some context is easily lost by using short, ambiguous headings and labels like those below.

- Price (with or without VAT added).
- Cost (in pounds, euros or dollars).
- Data (last years' or this years').
- Results (from one age group, a varied group or the whole survey).

Providing information to others

Most of us are guilty of this quick, bland labelling when storing or transferring information. Losing some of the context makes it is easier for others to misinterpret the information or to understand it differently, and they definitely won't have the mind reading skills necessary to know what you really intended. Misinterpretation leads to confusion, which leads to assumptions, puzzling, discussions and delays, which are probably more costly in time than providing the information with its correct context in the first place (assuming the original provider actually knew the correct context). Perhaps your conscience is now judging how you provide information to others. If not, you can judge using the scale below.

a) Attempt to understand the full set of information they want or need and provide it along with the context you know is important.
b) Provide what you already have available, but with a few extra words of context explaining what it is.
c) Provide what you already have at hand, in whatever format, without any additional context.
d) Provide misleading information, to control or steer their understanding and decisions.

How much of a time-consuming, confusing puzzle are you setting for others to solve or, alternatively, do you just expect them to use the information blindly without questioning, checking or understanding it? In previous simple examples, the only context needed is a clearer label or column heading. In my own engineering work, using the word "speed" is just meaningless. Is it speed relative to ground, speed relative to the wind or speed relative to the nearest plane in the sky (which can be approximately zero or much faster than the speed of sound, depending on the direction they are flying)? In the case of the fire fighters' pay, the context was which survey group was used. In the case of the new nurses, the context is the rate that nurses are leaving.

Ideally, information should be passed around with the context with which it was generated, in order to understand it easily. However, this is much more difficult than it seems because context is difficult to define. Sometimes context is a simple label or heading, but sometimes it is more complex. For example, surveys taken at outdoor events might be heavily influenced by the weather conditions and surveys in town centres might be influenced by local carnivals or sports events at the time, producing unrepresentative or optimistic sets of information. Context is therefore a rather fluffy, undefinable, subtle thing and this is a very important distinction. Whilst computer tools excel (no pun intended) at storing, accessing, analysing and displaying well-defined, structured sets of raw information, they struggle to cope with a concept as ill-defined and fluffy as context. Although our brains use context all the time, this type of fluffy context is difficult or impossible for computer tools (that are programmed in a procedural way) to cope with. They tend to categorise things, make things binary, yes/no, good/bad or only work with specific choice of inputs like "7 days a week" or "5 days a week". They struggle with many of the fluffy subtleties and context of real life like "Mostly yes, but not on Tuesdays" or "It does do that, but only under these circumstances". By ignoring context, by trying to make things fit into neat separate boxes, many computer tools make it difficult to say what needs to be said, with context. An online mortgage application would not accept that someone could be both employed and self-employed and so it only allowed them to enter half of their income. Initially the computer tool declined the application adding significant complication and delay to the application it was supposedly attempting to simplify. Similarly, compulsory online medical forms cannot be completed by people who don't know the medical history of their biological parents, but the computer tools won't accept this, so what should they do, guess or lie? The list goes on. For anything that is not standard, neat, binary, quantised or categorised (which in the real world is an awful lot of stuff, an awful lot of the time), these types of computer tools make the simple task of transferring and recording useful (and correct) information more difficult and frustrating.

In this way, computer tools force us to lose or drop important context. If you are lucky, you may be offered a text box labelled "Comments" to add any important context, reasons or explanation (like a second income from self-employment), which the computer will ignore. If you are luckier still, your comments might even be read by a person who can cope with all this subtle, fluffy stuff. Where the context is known and is important to understanding the information, they should be kept together and often these "Comment" text boxes are the only option. If we leave them blank, then we are choosing to lose the context. In the absence of any other suitable text boxes, I have previously included important context in a box labelled "Requirement", so that others could understand the intention and reasoning behind it. I was then promptly told to remove this additional context for no other reason than "It is not the requirement". To me this was a choice of "no context" against "some context, just not in the best place" and I still know which I prefer. Other people obviously think differently or perhaps they just don't comprehend what context is and why it is essential for understanding information.

Computer monkeys

Today many jobs require us to enter, access or use computer information and, despite the various forms of rubbish binformation, the vast majority of it is correct, or at least very useful. The real problem here is not the human mistakes, the ambiguous labels or the complexities of context. The real problem is that our wonderful information tools, which are so amazingly good with raw information, are pathetically poor with the subtleties of context. They are very good at presenting us with information and answers, without us understanding the origin, calculation or context. This means that whilst we have lots of control over the raw information and have answers presented to us, the essential context and our understanding of information is quietly being squeezed, limited or abstracted away. Ultimately more and more people are entering, transferring and using information, with less context, comprehension and understanding of it. More and more types of information are being used blindly. This problem was once described by an engineer colleague of mine as "computer monkeys, feeding the machine". This is a bit harsh perhaps (but possibly excusable given the ranting nature of this book), but it does contain a strong element of truth. There is a huge amount of information being fed into computers, which is not well understood and can't be checked by those entering it. The same information is then viewed with little or no context and then used blindly by someone else. Neither person has good comprehension of the information or any ability to challenge the computer answer. This is effectively what happened when I tried to swap the blood donation appointments and whenever you hear those dreaded and frustrating phrases like "sorry but the computer won't allow me to do that".

In our miraculous Information Age, we concentrate on what our powerful collection of information tools can do for us. We become so concerned about collecting, storing, organising, accessing, transferring and displaying information, that we start to forget about the fluffy, subtle context we need to fully understand that information. Our understanding and use of information is increasingly controlled and limited by what the computer tools allow us to do. We often use and treat information blindly, whether that is accepting incorrect answers, blindly clicking "Accept all" to continue or becoming ever more resigned to and accepting of phrases like "the system won't let me" or "the computer won't allow me". We end up having to tolerate computer decisions, even when they are "bloody bonkers" and this is disrupting our use of information, the ability to decide for ourselves and the actions we can take.

Knowledge is power

These powerful, but still relatively recent, information tools allow people to quickly jump from information to decision, limiting or bypassing the understanding and knowledge parts of the chain. We start to lose the distinction between just having access to information (the physics book) and knowledge and understanding (knowing physics). Since the late 16th century, the phrase attributed to Francis Bacon "Knowledge is power" has been well regarded, but it has recently transformed into todays' more common phrase "Information is power". Information is wrongly becoming synonymous with knowledge. In this way, the tools of our modern Information Age have changed our relationship with information. After all, these amazing information tools are only "information" tools, they are not "understanding", "context" or "knowledge" tools. As we use more information blindly without understanding it, we make decisions and actions in ignorance. We don't know if what we are doing is right, we just accept and trust what the computer says. Knowledge is based on experience, understanding and the context of information. Knowledge involves an awareness of how good or suitable the information is and how it can or should be used. In short, knowledge and experience are the ability to use information well and that is so much more important than information itself. Without them, information can and will be used badly.

As in previous chapters, all this pessimism is only intended to demonstrate that these types of issues are real and to highlight the consequences of ignoring them. The correct use of information is an essential part of society, engineering and the advancement of technology, such as the national census, car engine management systems, jet engine life histories and preventing the spread of diseases, amongst many others, including the list of contacts in your phone. However, in many other aspects of our lives, an overreliance and dependence on computer answers can be "bloody bonkers" and erode common sense. The criminal conviction and financial ruin of over 700 sub-postmasters between 2000 and 2014 due to an error in the Post Office "Horizon" tool is a very stark example of where this ignorant or dogmatic belief that "the computer is right" can lead to.[4]

Whilst our modern information miracle allows us to share and access vast quantities of good information, the same technology also allows a similar proliferation of misinformation. In addition to the different types of binformation described here, we must also cope with the more deliberate Fake News. This term was first used around 2016, meaning "misleading information presented as factual news", which is the internet equivalent of fly tipping. We are adrift in this vast polluted sea, where our poor human brains struggle to cope with the quantity, quality, contradictions, context and lack of context of it all. It seems very ironic that, in the middle of an Information Age, people's opinions are becoming governed more by emotion and belief, rather than facts and truth, a phenomenon that was labelled "post-truth world" around 2016. Is it possible that our modern information miracle has so undermined the human ability to properly understand information that phenomena like a post-truth world may be starting to blur, undermine and diminish the role of information itself? If any, some, or all of this chapter is relevant, then our relationship with information is changing and it is affecting our understanding, our decisions and our actions. In some aspects of our lives, this can overrule our common sense and that is a worrying situation to be in.

"As attitudes shift to simply having and accessing more information, we move away from understanding the information we have."

06

THE PROCESS PIT

*"Precept is instruction written in the sand; the tide
flows over it and the record is gone; example is graven
on the rock, and the lesson is not soon lost."*
(William Ellery Channing, 1780–1842, author and moralist)

We all have to follow processes and procedures because they form a large and relevant part of how a civilised society operates. They ensure that things are done fairly, correctly and consistently for everyone, like getting married, taking exams or applying for jobs. We even follow processes when we learn to use a new piece of equipment or build flatpack furniture, because processes and procedures are just a list of instructions to do something in a prescribed way. To be a little pedantic, a process is considered to be 'what' you do, whilst a procedure is more 'how' you do it. However, this is a subtle and debatable distinction. If you are willing to give it any consideration, it quickly gets blurry and ambiguous again. Therefore, I lazily use the words 'process' and 'procedure' interchangeably, with a bias towards 'process' for two reasons: it is more common at my work and more importantly it produces a far better chapter title, as you will find out soon. Unfortunately, this is about as exciting as processes and procedures get, but at least they lead to one of the bigger and more controversial rants of the book.

Whether we notice it or not, large parts of our lives are governed by processes and procedures. They apply to countries, large organisations, smaller local groups, individuals, down to single items such as using a new coffee maker or disposing of batteries. They cover a full spectrum, from the things that we must do by law, need to do, should or shouldn't do, through to things we should avoid doing or must not do. They are everywhere, ranging from international travel, medical treatments, driving or setting up an account and that's before mentioning any processes you have at work. The table below attempts to show this immense range and scope of processes. The two outer columns, highlighted by thick solid lines, represent the legal processes (laws) that make civilised society possible and intend to benefit the whole population, like paying taxes and not exceeding the speed limit. The bottom row indicates all the user guide and instruction manual processes, which help us to use items like cars, TVs or washing machines, at least for those willing to RTFM (Read The F***ing Manual). The remaining large middle section contains all the processes that are not legal or mandatory but are created and used by choice for various reasons. Some to minimise waste, some to define a precise method of manufacture, some to define a good method of working etc. In other words, this large central block is concerned with guiding, constraining or controlling the everyday activities of people, groups and organisations and it is these everyday processes that this chapter concentrates on.

	Must (laws)	Necessary (needed)	Should (beneficial)	Guidance (suggest)	Avoid (prevent)	Must not (laws)
Countries						
Organisations			Everyday			
Groups			processes and			
People			procedures			
Items		User guides and instruction manuals				

increasing in number (vertical, left) — *Laws and regulations* (both outer columns)

increasing in number (horizontal, bottom)

Before continuing, note that the graduated shading indicates the increasing numbers of processes as it gets darker. The rows should be self-explanatory; there are more items than people, more people than groups etc. Although the number of laws in the first column may be large, different organisations will need or use different processes to meet that same legal requirement. In the centre columns, there are likely to be more things you want or prefer to do than those things you need to do. Finally, the things you should avoid or not do are everything else except the few things you are trying to achieve. In theory this list is endless, including not sticking knives into toasters, not putting metal into microwaves, not sticking pencils in your ear and definitely not eating batteries, mercury, lead or arsenic. Therefore, as you move from top to bottom and left to right in the table there is a trend of increasing numbers of processes, as the shading gets darker.

Writing a process

If processes and procedures are going to be useful and relevant, then the instructions or prescribed steps need to be clear. The examples below demonstrate how this becomes more difficult as the task becomes more complicated. The first example is a ridiculously simple, two-step process, which only has relevance to this chapter and other parts of this book.

A simple two-step process for the reader of this book

STEP 1) Read the sentence below.

> "This short sentence seems unimportant to you,
> but it is more important than you think."

STEP 2) Read the same sentence (in quotes above) just once more (so only twice in total).

END OF PROCESS

That was so simple and quick, please repeat this whole process once more, noting how the pedantic addition of "(in quotes above)" removes ambiguity over which of the 3 sentences should be re-read and how the "(so only twice in total)" is added to prevent the pedantic reader from being trapped in an infinite inescapable process loop. Hopefully this introduces the idea that it isn't easy to write a good, completely unambiguous process. The next process is for the slightly more difficult task of counting a pile of coins, assuming all the coins have the same value or ignoring the coin value.

A process for counting coins

STEP 1) Move all the coins to the left side (so there are none on the right).

STEP 2) Move one coin to the right side and count 1.

STEP 3) Continue to move only one coin at a time, only from the left to right side and count one more each time (i.e. 2, then 3, then 4 etc.).

STEP 4) When there are no coins remaining on the left side, write the last count on a piece of paper.

END OF PROCESS

This task is still very simple and something that 4-year-old children are taught to do. However, when writing it down as a set of instructions for someone else to follow, specific details need to be added. Details like enforcing "left to right side" help ensure it is not done incorrectly and "move only one coin" keeps it simple and easy. Again, it is difficult to write a good unambiguous process. This example also starts to demonstrate that the clearer and more explicit a process becomes, then (by definition) the more prescriptive and inflexible is also becomes. This one prevents an expert coin counter from moving and counting two or more coins at a time, even though that is a perfectly valid method.

The next example increases the level of complexity to doing simple household tasks, like hanging up washing, getting dressed or making a cup of tea. Now the process will need to include instructions like these:

- Get cup.
- Put tea bag into cup.

- Pour hot water into cup.
- Add milk and sugar.

But this set of instructions doesn't say what type of tea bag, how much water to use or indicate that milk and sugar are optional and variable in quantity. Having sorted out and covered all the different variances, the process for making a cup of tea would still need to include many of the less obvious instructions and details such as:

- Where to get the ingredients (tea, milk, sugar).
- How to use the kettle.
- Which way to hold the spoon and balance the sugar etc.

Extending the complexity further, now try to imagine writing the processes for repairing a car engine or building a house. The more complicated and variable the task is, the more difficult it is to write a good procedure for it. Instead, we rely on the human brain and a combination of knowledge, understanding, experience, skill and common sense to help do the task.

Processes are good for tasks that are the same each time, where they can be made very prescriptive and clear, like user instructions for operating a washing machine, applying for a passport or simple tasks like recording attendance. However, most tasks like making a cup of tea, repairing a car or anything involving people often have variations of circumstances, different choices and many different valid methods to achieve the same thing. So instead of spending lots of time creating huge sets of complicated written instructions that cover all possible valid options and choices, processes tend to prescribe only one or two chosen or preferred methods. This instantly relegates all the other valid and sensible options to be frowned upon as 'out of process', not because they are wrong or invalid but simply because they are not the option written down. In this way, written processes encourage or force us to view other valid, sensible options as unacceptable, which doesn't seem that sensible at all. It is also highly frustrating when you try to explain this to a 'jobs-worth' or 'process slave', only to be told "You have to follow the process". This is where the benefits of a prescriptive process are quickly devalued in the vast majority of activities where different people do different things, in different circumstances. In short, processes try to make things black and white in a world full of grey areas. Thankfully it is in these grey areas where our experience, knowledge, understanding and common sense work at their best.

In day-to-day home life we tend not to use many formal processes. We certainly don't write procedures for hanging up the washing, cutting the grass, climbing a ladder, washing the car or making a cup of tea, which tells its own story. At home we tend to limit our use of processes to one-off or occasional use, like building furniture, learning to use a new product or applying for something like a travel permit. In contrast to home life, working life and wider society are full of processes and procedures, such as working practices, quality, monitoring, efficiency, management and care of the public and employees, etc. This means that a large amount of our time is influenced or controlled by processes, all with the aim of making things fair, efficient, consistent and clear. The intent is to not make things more difficult. This prevalent use of processes and the huge scope they cover raises some more practical problems, like the sheer number of them, the time to write them and the access, awareness, use, maintenance and consistency of them. The rest of this chapter looks at these aspects a bit further, but, before that, now is a good time to repeat the earlier two-step process for a third time. Hopefully this two-step process meets all the criteria for a good process: it is clear, it is accessible, it is quick and convenient to use, and it is also relevant to reading this book (although admittedly this relevance is not yet known to you, but it will be towards the end of this chapter).

Time and effort

Writing processes and procedures can be time-consuming. Consider the time it takes to make a cup of tea versus the time it would take to write down clear instructions for someone else to do it. Similarly ponder a work example, where someone is using some tools at the top of a ladder. The activity of putting up the ladder and carrying the tools to the top would probably take around 30 seconds, whilst writing the process for this task would probably take at least 30 minutes, which is 60 times longer. You could easily increase this to 60 minutes if you wanted someone to check or review it for you. For those who think the 30 minutes is too big an estimate, consider some of the things it would need to contain for it to be both sufficient and useful for the user, the auditor or even a jury. The content would need to include:

- Checking the ladder before use.
- Suitable and unsuitable types of ground or surface.
- A person at the base and how to anchor the foot of the ladder.
- The angle of the ladder (not too steep or too shallow) and how to assess it.
- Maintaining three points of contact on the ladder.
- Type of tool holder to use so hands are kept free.
- How far to lean (or not lean) from the ladder when at the top etc.

I think there is 30 minutes work here to get some level of detail and good clear wording. So, for tasks involving variable circumstances (like using a ladder) it can take 50–100 times longer to write the process than to do the task itself. Less time would be needed for the simplest tasks with little variation. You might like to try writing a process for someone else to follow. It is not as easy as it seems. As you have already had several clues for the 'cup of tea' example, perhaps try something different like ironing a shirt, painting a picture or brushing your teeth. The main rule of this game is to follow only the written instructions and not to do anything else that isn't written down (like just getting the cup out of the cupboard).

For those who try this, you will find it harder to write instructions for children or inexperienced people than for someone who is more experienced. This exactly mirrors the use of processes in general, where experienced people already know what to do, whilst the inexperienced need more instructions, information and details. Not only are these more time-consuming to write, but also they simultaneously make the process longer, more prescriptive and less flexible. It is now possible to see a paradox: short concise processes are too vague and not much use to inexperienced people, whilst detailed prescriptive processes are inflexible and too constraining for experienced people. Whether 'short and vague' or 'long and prescriptive', the relevance of a process to you and your opinion of it will depend on your level of experience, from novice to expert. The compromise of the middle ground will still be too vague and unclear for the most inexperienced, who rely on processes the most, whilst being somewhat prescriptive for the experienced user. There are two solutions to this: continue to increase the level of procedural detail to match that of the least experienced or increase the level of knowledge and understanding of those doing the work. I'll let you guess which I think is the better solution.

Even after all this careful, considered effort to produce a clear set of instructions to climb ladders or iron shirts, it is almost certain that one of the first 10 people to use this process will have a situation that is still not covered. It might be an unexpected pleat, tuck or pocket in the shirt or the surface the ladder is leaning against. Processes are utterly useless at covering the variance and complexity of real-world experience. In this respect processes share a similar problem with many computer-based tools (that are all essentially procedural in nature as well). They can work well if it is only 'this' or 'that', yes or no, but can quickly struggle and fail when it is none of these, somewhere in between or whenever there is something unforeseen, unexpected or unknown (which in real life is very often). Thankfully this is where our old friend 'continual improvement' saves the day. We just improve (or change) the process to make it more suitable for this new situation, whilst perhaps simultaneously making it worse or incompatible with someone else's situation? Each new circumstance where the process does not quite fit produces yet another golden opportunity for an update and improvement and very soon the loop of continual unstable change sets in. The process is continually rewritten to bounce between all the various situations and levels of experience, which it is impossible for the single set of procedural words to cover.

Continuing on, now that we have a process that allows us to use a ladder, make a cup of tea and iron a shirt consistently, safely and efficiently, what about everything else we have to do? If we are to do all these other things correctly, then we need processes and procedures for them too. I have no idea how many processes and procedures schools, hospitals, the police or the civil service have, but a rough estimate (an order of magnitude calculation) for a large engineering company like the one I work for, with around 1000 different activities, suggests there needs to be around 5000 processes controlling how the work is done. On this scale, we are back into BINFORMATION territory, where the access, context, consistency and maintenance all affect whether all these processes can be used effectively together. It is highly frustrating and annoying to follow one process properly, only for someone to then tell you that another process says it must be done differently. This type of inconsistency greatly devalues processes and destroys the confidence and enthusiasm of those instructed to follow them.

Inconsistency can be reduced in two ways. Either by spending a lot of time and effort, doing the difficult task of getting all the details correct and consistent, or by quickly and simply making the words a bit vaguer. However, a vague process is more open to misinterpretation, defeating the object of having a process in the first place, because everyone will just interpret it differently. Unfortunately processes and procedures suffer from the problems highlighted in both the WORDS and BINFORMATION chapters (Chapters 1 and 5), especially when used in large numbers. This is not recognised by those who believe in the power of process, who think writing some words and storing them somewhere provides a good solution. The important steps of access (or awareness), interpretation, context, understanding and decision are all taken for granted. It is automatically assumed that everyone's actions will now be perfect and correct, in exactly the way they are not. As with everything in the real world, you never get something for nothing and there is no quick and easy solution here either.

This rough estimate of 5000 processes does not include any localised 'short lived' processes that people introduce on the spur of the moment. Someone may decide to introduce a process taking one hour a week, which on its own is easy to do and seems unimportant. Add another three of these over the coming months and you lose 10% productivity (4 hours from a 40-hour week). This use of localised processes may solve local problems, but they also accumulate. Like everything in the real world, they don't give you something for nothing and it is incorrect to assume they do. Despite all these difficulties, we have not yet reached the Holy Grail of processes, but we are about to.

Injury jury

There is one aspect of our lives which places more belief, trust, time and effort in the use of processes than anything else. This is something which every child has been taught about in school and every reader will have heard about, and it affects every one of us on a daily basis. By some it is seen as the single most important topic, but, in my opinion, it is the definitive example of good intentions turned bad. It is Health and Safety.

First, I must state categorically that I'm in complete support and agreement with the principle of Health and Safety to prevent accidents, injuries and deaths by using common sense, and hopefully no one disagrees with this. In my experience, the two repeated mantras of Health and Safety representatives are "Health and Safety is just common sense" and "Health and Safety is everyone's responsibility" and this is precisely what it should be. We should not use broken ladders, we should not leave things in a bad state for others, we should get help when we are unsure or when something is difficult, and we shouldn't put ourselves or others in dangerous situations. This practical, physical, active side of Health and Safety is predominantly just common sense, with a bit of education and understanding added in, and this is exactly how it should be.

Unfortunately, that is the simple, easy, common sense part over with. In complete contradiction to the mantra, Health and Safety is not "just common sense", much more is needed. This is the less promoted side of Health and Safety, the unmentionable part, the arduous part. It is the process part. The modern version of Health and Safety requires far more than just good intentions and the application of common sense. It requires process and plenty of it. It is relevant to note that we are now deep into the bottom right (dark shaded) corner of the table of processes, in the rows of people and products and the column of things we should not do. Here the numbers are at their maximum, where processes tell everyone what not to do, with every item, for every task, in every circumstance. In addition to the thousands of processes instructing us how to do something, we now also need processes to ensure:

- Every item of equipment is safe.
- Risks of using each item of equipment are known and reduced.
- Safe systems of work to ensure equipment is used safely.
- People are qualified and trained to use equipment.
- Processes to cover the different health conditions and needs of different people.
- Records of checks and inspections completed.
- Records of peoples' protective equipment.

Any activities which involve movement of people, crowds of people, mechanical movement, heights, use of electricity, chemicals, radiation or even just sitting on a chair at a desk all have Health and Safety implications and so need Health and Safety processes. Some of the terminology that you may recognise from this procedural quagmire follows: risk assessment, safe systems of work, PAT (portable appliance testing), inspection records, check lists, hazard analysis, COSHH (control of substances hazardous to health) data sheets, training records and PPE (personal protective equipment). If we assume that half of the 5000 engineering processes require five Health and Safety processes like these, the total number of processes increases to around 17,250, which is a full year's work for eight or nine people just to write them, assuming it takes 1 hour to write each process.

This application of "just common sense" has now led to the need to write down in process, procedure and instruction every action, of every person, of every task, for every item of equipment, in every circumstance, for every risk. Remember that earlier this was shown to be a bit difficult for something as simple as counting coins, climbing a ladder or making a cup of tea. On top of just writing them down once, all these checks and inspections take time and must be repeated regularly. These may feel like additional hurdles and obstacles, but again it is difficult to disagree with the goal of keeping people safe and it does seem sensible to check a vehicle is safe to use before using it, to spot and prevent a failure before it happens. This type of check may be done once a week and nothing may go wrong for 3 years, which is around 150 checks to spot a single potential failure 3 years on. That is a lot of time and effort, but maybe this is still common sense and all worth it to prevent a death. I don't have a problem with a process that says someone should not fiddle with the bolts on an aircraft during a pre-flight check, because, just like everyone else, I don't want the wing to fall off in the middle of a flight. The processes I think we could live without are the ones that instruct someone not to fiddle with the bolts on an aircraft because they may get some oil on their fingers and a bit of skin irritation. This is the point where we start to leave the world of common sense behind and start to enter the 'Process Pit' or 'Pro Cesspit' or 'Professional Cesspit', where the rules, regulations, need or preference to follow processes and procedures overtakes all common sense and begins to take on a life of its own. Before we enter this professional cesspit further, there is one more aspect of Health and Safety processes which needs mentioning.

Despite all the time and effort required to generate, review, use and monitor all these Health and Safety processes, their true purpose is only needed in the event of injury or accident. Following an injury or accident, a business must provide evidence to a court that they are not negligent, by showing how they tried to prevent the accident from happening. However, as you can never know in advance which accident is going to happen, you must do it for all possible accidents. The only way to do this is to write down processes and evidence for every human action, in every situation with every precaution. It sounds bizarre when you see it in these terms, but ultimately this is what it is. This is the part that the Health and Safety people cannot say out loud and never do, because deep down and intuitively they know that it is not common sense, and it contradicts their mantra. So, all this time and effort spent on processes is only really needed to demonstrate to an injury jury that in the event of an accident, some common sense accident prevention was being applied. Perversely, you have to break all common sense (by attempting to document all human activity into thousands of processes) just so that you can prove to a jury that common sense has been applied. HOW TWISTED IS THAT!?

The original intention to prevent accidents, injury and death and the subsequent reduction of these are both pure common sense. Modern-day Health and Safety is therefore like a common sense sandwich. Unfortunately it is filled with the largest, most repugnant, unpalatable of pile of rotten manure and bullshit you can imagine! This cesspit, this grotesque sandwich filling is increasing in volume, day on day, week on week, month on month and it is the outcome of a litigation culture, which has a chapter of its own in Part 3. The reputational cost and damage that a negligence claim can cause a business is worse than expending a huge amount of effort putting thousands of written processes in place. That is just the world we are in, but it does not seem like common sense to me.

Holy Grail

The last section is likely to raise some eyebrows and your opinion on Health and Safety processes may well differ from mine. They may be far more useful than I have insinuated and of course they are also a legal requirement, which importantly is not the same as being common sense. America has laws that allow people to carry guns in public, but that does not make it common sense. It is therefore worth reiterating that I am in full agreement with the common sense side of Health and Safety and the need to prevent accidents, injury and death. I just don't believe that documenting every possible working activity under all circumstances into wordy processes is a good, effective or efficient way to achieve it, and no one is going to convince me that is easy, quick or even feasible. To my mind it is an unachievable Holy Grail and if ultimately all this is only to cover the legal backside of an organisation after an accident, then Health and Safety processes are simply not common sense either.

In fact, the use of common sense, understanding and knowledge is precisely what I'm trying to promote and, to this end, there is an alternative, perhaps more common sense, approach to Health and Safety suggested in Part 4 of the book. The reduction in accidents achieved by Health and Safety is much more likely due to the education, culture change, understanding and actions of the people doing the work, rather than this large cesspit of WORDS, BINFORMATION and PROCESSES that have been created. That concludes the analysis of (or assault on) Health and Safety processes, so we can now venture deeper still into the professional cesspit, but before we do, now is a good time to repeat the simple two-step process for a fourth time.

The process pit

The process pit is the world where processes and procedures dominate, our common sense is repulsed and we are left in the stunned silence of sheer disbelief. The real-life examples below illustrate life in this process pit, where well-intentioned processes don't seem quite as good in the real, practical world. The first two remain on the subject of Health and Safety, before returning to some more general topics.

Wall integrity

"Check integrity of the walls". This is from a daily safety check list in a building less than 20 years old. This process said that each and every day the integrity of the walls had to be checked. Why daily? How quickly can a wall deteriorate? Do they realise the wall is three floors high? What does this actually mean? Check for any obvious cracks, do chemical analysis of the concrete or check the structural integrity of the steel beams? Does it mean check for any dents in the plasterboard or check the structure of the wall behind it? What did the person writing this process want to achieve? Did they hope to obtain some evidence that the building would not collapse today?

Use of hand gel

Like many hand gels, this one was predominantly alcohol based and contained some chemicals that would naturally contact skin and so there was a need to ensure it was safe. The Health and Safety processes were followed correctly, with the risk assessments and the correct COSHH data sheet obtained, resulting in the safe process for use of the hand gel. You may (or may not?) be surprised to learn, that this required wearing gloves to apply the hand gel! Note, this was not a simple instruction not to use the hand gel, just a process to tell people to wear protective gloves whilst applying it to their hands. It was pure madness.

Changing old pound coins

Sometime after the issue of the two-colour pound coins in 2017, my children found four old pound coins in their bedrooms and were worried they would not be able to replace them. In an attempt to dismiss their concerns and by way of introducing my young children to banks, I thought I would show them how simple and easy it is to change coins at the high street bank. I must have been in an optimistic mood and in this happy parental dreamland I temporarily forgot that banks also follow processes. The next 45 minutes went something like this:

- Stand in a queue for the service desk.
- When it was my turn, explain that my children wanted to exchange four pound coins (expecting a straight swap, and hence teaching my children how simple and helpful banks are).
- The reply was, "Certainly sir, we can help you, all you need to do is follow the process on the sign above that machine over there".
- The process on the sign said I had to do the following:

- Insert bank card and enter PIN.
- Enter the old coins you need to exchange into the machine.
- Take the printed receipt to the service desk.
- Having got the receipt I rejoined the back of the same queue that I'd previously been at the front of and when it was finally my turn for the second time, I handed my paper receipt over to the bank employee.
- The receipt number was then typed into a computer.
- Then using the same number, or a new number provided by the computer, the bank employee went to another machine which then issued four new pound coins, which were handed over to me.

My children left the bank happy, knowing that their new shiny coins were now safely held in their small hands. On the other hand, I left mildly baffled and frustrated. How could I justify my early assertion that it would be simple and easy? I couldn't, because some process had got in the way. This well-thought-out, well-intentioned, highly prescriptive process had been invented to make changing old pound coins into new pound coins simple and efficient. This process probably works quite well on a busy Thursday afternoon, for a shop owner that wants to exchange 400 coins, but it was a real pain in the arse for only four coins from a kid's piggy bank. Again, this is how the inflexible prescriptive nature of a process hinders or prevents the use of common sense. This wasn't money laundering or a business transaction, it was a kid's piggy bank, but the process could not distinguish between the different situations.

Euthanasia

This is a controversial subject and there is no intention to open a debate here. However, our current set of rules and processes prescribe that the following situation involving two people in hospital is the correct thing to do. An older person who openly wanted euthanasia had to be kept alive for several months or years at great financial expense to the NHS, whilst a young person was prevented from having a new drug treatment to cure their disease, because it was too expensive to buy. The processes in place said this was the best thing to do, but common sense just screams the opposite. Interestingly and controversially, neither was in the best interests of the individuals involved.

These are perfect examples where good intentions combine with processes to produce something utterly ridiculous, counterintuitive and in complete contradiction to common sense. This is how the use of processes can and does drown out, overtake or swamp common sense. Processes are not true understanding. Processes are not common sense. Processes are just a set of words that attempt (and nothing more than attempt) to define what should happen. A process effectively reduces an activity or choices down to a set of prescriptive, robotic, machine-like instructions, which partially or wholly replace the context, knowledge, understanding, flexibility and common sense required for almost every human activity, be that counting coins, making a cup of tea, repairing a car engine, testing an autopilot, teaching a class of children, nursing someone back to health or just exchanging a few coins in a bank.

The prescriptive nature of processes automatically relegates all other alternatives to being 'out of process', unacceptable, intolerable, inefficient, not allowed, not possible or even just plain wrong, regardless of how good, sensible or viable the alternative is. These judgements are not made on merit or the pros and cons of the alternatives, they are made instantly and automatically for no other reason than the alternatives just do not follow process. This procedural exclusion of sensible alternatives is why many simple things become difficult. It is also the reason why people just follow the processes blindly, not questioning or understanding what they are doing or why. Alternatively, they may decide to ignore the process completely by doing what they know and understand to be the correct thing to do. At this point, please repeat the two-step process for the fifth and last time.

Two-step process
Did you do the two-step process this time and what were your thoughts? "Not again", "Why do I have to do this?", "Why is this really that important?" or "I've done it before, I know what it is". There is no right or wrong here, but you will have done one of these four things:

a) Followed the process exactly as instructed every time.

b) Used your common sense to omit the part of the process that you thought was not sensible (such as not reading the sentence a second time.)

c) Override the process at some point and decide to stop following it.

d) Just ignored it completely every time.

As with all words, the written process itself does absolutely nothing at all, it is only your subsequent actions that matter. Collectively the four possible actions above prove two important points about what happens in reality, and this is the reason why the two-step process was "more important than you think". Firstly options b), c) and d) show how easy it is to not follow a process properly and quickly defeats the objective of having the instructions and processes to follow in the first place. If this can happen in a simple two-step process that is accessible, clear, short and convenient to use, what can you expect to happen in cases where the processes are less accessible, less clear, contradict other processes, invalidate better options or oppose peoples' knowledge, experience and opinions? The desire and willingness to override part or all the process just increases further. Secondly, those who decided to follow the process instructions exactly and reliably every time demonstrated how the process was completed without fully understanding what they were doing or why. To some extent these people switched off some of their reasoning, simply doing as instructed and, crucially, this is precisely what following processes can do. Following processes allows people to switch off their reasoning and common sense. This happens in call centres when they can't deviate from the script and procedurally continue to ask, "So when did you make the claim?" immediately after your statement "I haven't made a claim". (Why don't they listen and think?) Following a process is not a 'reason' to stop thinking, but it is certainly an 'excuse' to. "I've been told to follow the instructions, so I'll just follow the instructions". It encourages us to swap four coins for children in the same way you would swap 400 coins for a high street business.

For those who think that just reading two sentences is a ridiculous and unrepresentative example and that a clearer, more important process would produce a different result, then I completely disagree. I could have used a more important Health and Safety process for readers of this book, which suggested using sandpaper to round the corners of the spine, so that it hurts less if dropped on the sensitive part your foot or using a comb to soften edges of the pages to prevent paper cuts. Both would clearly involve wearing a face mask and using a vacuum cleaner so the dust is not inhaled, but no one would follow this either. Furthermore, if I were to put such an important Health and Safety process on the front cover or first page of the book to warn people, they would shake their head in disbelief, rightly think that I was a bit of an idiot and not buy the book in the first place. People do not actively look for opportunities to follow processes; in general they casually try to avoid following them, like drivers who speed and do not indicate at junctions.

It is clear what people truly think about processes, by freely choosing not to use them at home. If processes are so useful and efficient for doing things then why don't people write down a process to vacuum the house, clean the windows, tidy the shed or get the kids out of the door on time each morning. It is because in practice they are difficult and time-consuming to write and are almost immediately invalided by one or more real-world events, like a child snapping a shoelace, finding an insect nest in the shed or even just being interrupted by a phone call or knock at the door. However, in the more formal environments, such as at work, it is very different and processes are widespread, actively encouraged and promoted with phrases like these:

- "We should put a process in place."
- "They should be following a process, where is it written down?"
- "We need a process to manage this."

Can you recognise yourself saying these types of phrases? Why do people think yet another process will help at work, but not for themselves at home? It's because people are very duplicitous about processes and procedures. When people know how to do something they don't actively hunt for a process to follow, they just do it and say, "I do it this way" or "I don't need a process". The duplicity occurs when they struggle to do something, when suddenly the attitude changes to something like "There should be a process or instructions for this". To meet this kind of duplicity, we either need to read peoples' minds to know which processes they will need beforehand (which is an impossible task) or produce processes for everything (which is an almost impossible task), even though we know that most people will never find, access, use or follow them. This is the true cesspit of processes: the vast pool of processes and procedures that are written down and then pretty much ignored, because they aren't actually that helpful amidst the complexity and variety of the real world.

Processes help – don't they?

Processes aren't introduced to make things more difficult – the intention is to make things better or easier. This belief that a process can make things better is valid because in theory it is partly correct – but only partly correct, and only in theory. In principle a clearly written process that covers all circumstances and is followed with good robot-like reliability by all will result in the task being completed correctly, and so help overall. So, if one problem can be solved this way, so can the next and the next and the next, until we have processes to help us do anything and everything better than before. Unfortunately, this is another theory that suffers from false logic. It assumes that what is true for one process is true for all processes. If you put up a single warning notice outside a building, most people will read it before entering. Put up 5–10 warning notices and many people will ignore them, but still enter the property. Put up 100 warning notices and everyone will ignore them all, most will walk away without entering and a few may flee, thinking their life is in imminent danger. What applies for one notice or process does not apply for many or hundreds.

The belief that a process-driven approach can be successful for one task, such as getting a new air conditioning unit into a tight space in a roof void, is optimistic. The belief that this can be done for all tasks is just ridiculous because it is not the words or the processes that solve the problem and do the work. The problems are solved by the knowledge, experience, ingenuity, flexibility and common sense of people, precisely the things that processes constrain, restrict, or even prevent us from using. Hastily writing down just the right amount of vague magic words into yet another process does however provide a relatively easy, convenient, word-based, tick box solution to a problematic situation. It allows people to (falsely) claim "something has been done" and further promote the misconception that yet another bloody process has solved yet another problem. All that happens is the burden of the real problem is passed on to someone else, along with a few more inflexible procedural constraints.

In this context, the quote from the Roman philosopher Seneca "Be wary of the man who urges an action in which he himself incurs no risk" can be loosely interpreted as "Be wary of people who introduce processes, without having to follow them themselves". Our duplicity over processes has hit again; they are great for other people to follow but not so great when you must follow them yourself, as all of these people and many others can testify.

- Anyone who did not fully complete the two-step process all five times.
- All those who don't indicate when driving.
- All those who do not fully follow processes at work.
- All the politicians who break the policies and processes they announce.

Why do you never see those so-called Health and Safety people asking for safety barriers and risk assessments whenever they purchase flammable alcoholic liquids in the local pub after work, then carry them in unlidded fragile glass containers across a crowded room and put them on a table next to the naked flame of a candle, just hours after telling other employees that this is totally unacceptable behaviour? The hypocrisy is astounding! It is duplicitous for anyone to expect that others will reliably follow processes when they are not willing to do it themselves. This should not be taken as evidence that all these people are bad, as that would just reinforce the common misconception that processes are the solution to everything. What it actually implies and confirms is that written sets of words just aren't that good at controlling fallible human behaviour. In short, don't expect others to follow a process that you are not willing to follow yourself to the same extent. If you won't, or can't, then why should others?

Overreliance on process

Therefore, in complete contradiction to the common view that processes are an efficient, convenient and simple solution to lots of activities and problems, they actually suffer from these problems raised earlier.

a) They are difficult and time-consuming to write well.

b) The written processes are only words and do nothing on their own.

c) Depending on your experience they are either too 'short and vague' or too 'long and prescriptive'.

d) They are easy to continually change (improve?), resulting in post-change inefficiency.

e) It is difficult to keep large numbers consistent and up to date.

f) They provide an easy way to pass the real problem and burden onto others.

g) They restrict, demote or forbid many other sensible or valid options.

h) They are not followed reliably by many people.

i) They encourage us to 'switch off' and provide an excuse to not think or understand.

Having faith in lots of processes and their ability to work relies on this false assumption: "If it is written down and accessible, then anyone can do it". It ignores the need for interpretation of ambiguous words, assumes instant and perfect understanding, and discounts our fallible human nature.

Perhaps I have completely got the wrong end of the stick and perhaps processes are not there to help us do things at all. Perhaps their real intention is only to 'pass the burden' on to others or to pretend things have been fixed or improved. Perhaps they are only there so that someone who is unwilling or unable to understand your work or do it can then check if you have done it correctly, or perhaps they are simply there to provide evidence in court when needed. Whatever the real reason, it seems far too easy and common for the phrase "We need a process" to always be an acceptable answer. To me this just seems wrong. Perhaps those people who actively promote the power and usefulness of processes should not be overly concerned (or even be pleased) if their child's dentist were to leave a note on the chair saying "Thanks for coming in with your child today, sorry I'm not at work. Please just follow this 'Removal of a child's molar' process and everything will be fine." Perhaps they also think that processes are so good that, instead of having driving lessons and tests, we should just give everyone a set of instructions and let them get on with driving on the roads themselves. Having a process for something like this, and for countless other far simpler things, doesn't allow anyone or everyone to just get on with it. This is because many won't have the knowledge, understanding, skill or experience that is needed to really do the task, even if they have the willingness. However, issuing or having a process does allow those who already know what to do and all those who never have to follow it themselves to believe, assume or pretend that others can now just get on and do it.

Challenging the nonchalant "we need a process" attitude often gets a response like "The processes need to be flexible in order to adapt to the circumstances", which I've heard a lot, but is now recognisable as just more bland, empty nonsense that doesn't say anything meaningful. They can't be flexible without also being vague and open to interpretation, which just defeats the object of having a process to follow in the first place. If you are inclined to think this is all too pessimistic and pedantic and that we should "Use processes with a bit of common sense", as I've also been told on many occasions, then unfortunately you have missed the point entirely. I am fully promoting the use of common sense, knowledge, understanding and experience, in preference to the use of prescriptive or vaguely written processes. If the user needs to invoke some of their common sense to interpret, compensate, ignore or correct part of that process to get something done, then the process itself must be incorrect or breach common sense in some way, again defeating the whole purpose of having the process in the first place. A statement like "We should just use and follow processes with a bit of common sense" is just the same as saying "We must have processes and it is completely acceptable for them to be unclear, wrong, incomplete or not even sensible". What is the point of that? It defies common sense. Unfortunately, it is these very same promoters of 'flexible processes' who, at the first sniff of uncertainty, difficulty, problems or questions, will then grab for the nearest safe point of reference (a process), instantly forget their flexible, common sense approach and with their very next breath, demand "Have you followed the process properly?" This is yet another type of duplicity and hypocrisy.

Despite all the problems, processes are rarely introduced to purposefully make things more difficult, even if this seems to be the case sometimes. They are intended to make things easier, quicker, fairer, safer, more convenient or more efficient, so more and more jobs are becoming 'process driven'. They are certainly widely used in schools, hospitals, policing and engineering, where the defined steps and instructions are used to control or constrain the actions of both machines and people. Frustration is therefore understandable whenever all these important processes and procedures are difficult to access, unclear, hard to follow, not up to date, contradict each other or are not suitable for your set of circumstances. Unlike people, every machine and every piece of software does nothing more than unquestioningly and slavishly follow a set of instructions without any understanding of 'what they are doing' or 'why' and they do it extremely well. It is our human imperfections and ability to use free will that make people very bad at behaving like these reliable procedural robots. Whenever our actions, choices and behaviour are constrained and dominated by prescriptive processes, it goes against our human nature. Simply following instructions without question is a slave-like behaviour. Under these highly process-driven environments, where some of our natural human traits are inhibited, people can start to become:

- Fed up or bored of repetition.
- Frustrated at not being allowed to do sensible alternatives.
- Uncomfortable with acting like a robot.
- Mentally switched off.

This overreliance on or dominance of processes allows and encourages people to switch off, and to have less understanding, interest or concern in what they are doing or why. They become more like robots. In some cases, this may be the desired effect, to simply get a repetitive job done as efficiently as possible. More generally, blindly following a set of procedural words without any understanding or awareness, under a myriad of different circumstances and situations, is precisely how perfectly sensible valid alternatives are dismissed, avoided or even punished. Just as earlier chapters indicated how abstraction affects our understanding and decisions, this is how processes can abstract our actions away from the real aim, what was originally intended or what is sensible. Processes are not the solution, people are. A reliance on processes and procedures falsely assumes that everyone can do anything and will do everything, provided there is set of instructions available to do it. It assumes anyone can cook a good lemon meringue, complete online applications, and download and install the correct software on their computer. It implies that everyone can safely use any hazardous substance, that everyone can repair a car and, by extension, do other things we don't properly understand, like remove a child's molar, drive a car or fly a passenger jet, provided there is a written set of procedural instructions for it somewhere online. It is a very false assumption to make. This type of false belief and overreliance on process and procedure leads to a situation where more and more jobs are done by people who do not fully understand what they are doing and why. It is why help from knowledgeable, experienced people is in such short supply. It is why simple things (like exchanging coins or swapping appointments) become very difficult. Finally, for those who still believe in the power of processes, I have one last card up my sleeve.

Last card and final escape

This last attempt assumes that processes are as fantastic, reliable and efficient at getting things done as the advocates believe and that my opposing opinions are completely wrong. Under these circumstances, any business or management would want nothing more than for all the employees to rigorously follow all the processes precisely, all day, every day, to achieve the perfect, productive, efficient state that the business has been striving for. So, when the day comes that the employees claim that they are going to 'work to process', surely this should be greeted with delight and celebration. You should be able to hear the cheers, clapping and cries of joy from the management offices and hear the party celebrations long into the night. In the real world this doesn't happen. The cold, hard threat of 'working to process' is met with shocked silence, a shiver down the spine of the management and words in the board room that are a very close approximation to "Oh shit!" This is because even the management and the advocates of processes know (but do not often vocalise) that slavishly following process is not actually that productive, it is inefficient and doesn't work. They also know and realise that in many cases, processes constrain the human characteristics and behaviours that truly help get things done. What processes actually do is turn even the most enjoyable of tasks, like teaching children, solving problems, caring for people, arranging social events or building something, into arduous, tedious, prescriptive, repetitive, unthinking, robot-like tedium. An overreliance and dependence on rigorously following processes stifles understanding and constrains our awareness of what we are doing and why, whilst disabling our common sense at the same time (or "in the process!"). This is why people passively, casually and sometimes actively override processes when possible.

Before we finally crawl out of this disgusting pro-cess-pit, remember that some types of process are essential and beneficial. Firstly, there are the compulsory rules that apply to everyone and are necessary for a civilised society to operate, by keeping our behaviour within certain acceptable limits (not killing or stealing, speed limits, paying tax, births, marriages, passport documentation etc.). Secondly, the non-compulsory processes that help us complete very specific fixed tasks are genuinely useful for operating a new product, for precision techniques such as making hardened glass or cooking a very precise food recipe. Beyond these two constrained worlds of 'fixed rules for everyone' and 'fixed unchanging tasks' is the vast and wonderfully complex world of human activity. This is where our abilities, attitudes, knowledge, understanding, experience, situations and circumstances are infinite. Here it is impossible to write processes for our actions and, in my opinion, we shouldn't try to. Yet even amidst this continual flux, processes can still provide a useful guide or reminder of what to do. The problems only start when things stray beyond this helpful, suggestive, guidance role, when they start to control, constrain and dictate what is allowed or forbidden. The problems are caused when processes are used as a complete or partial replacement for true understanding or when they are written by those who know they will never have to follow them in practice. The value in processes is only when they do not prevent or hinder other rational, pragmatic, practical, viable alternatives or oppose common sense. Yet, once written down, that is precisely what most processes do. It is now written down, so everyone must do precisely that and only that. It is the unthinking and unknowing use of processes, to the exclusion of all other reasonable options and alternatives, that is the problem. It is the inconsiderate, unthinking 'jobs-worth' and 'process puppets' who can only slavishly enforce the strict written process, without ever having to follow it themselves. This is how something intended to make things better makes things worse and makes simple things more difficult. The optimistic belief in the power of processes and procedures suffers from the same flaw as making improvements. In both cases, the possible and expected benefits or 'gain' are accepted as guaranteed fact, whilst all the potential problems, consequences and 'pain' are ignorantly dismissed in a whitewash of bland words.

Processes and procedures are no substitute for our understanding, experience and common sense, but, far worse than that, they inhibit these valuable human skills to some extent. Collectively we are very bad at behaving like procedural robots, and this is why people tend to override, bypass, short-cut, ignore or actively avoid processes whenever possible. It is like forcing the 'large-round-peg' of human behaviour, through a 'small-square-hole' of prescriptive processes. Part 2 takes a brief look at a few human traits that make us unreliable and prevent us from behaving like robots, and how this affects the theories of Part 1.

"Processes can be followed without knowing what you are doing or why, and this is both the best and worst thing about them."

PART 2:

07

LIABLE TO BE UNRELIABLE

"Nothing is more unreliable than the populace."
(Marcus Tullius Cicero, 103–43BC, Roman statesman, lawyer, scholar)

Part 1 attempted to explain why several commonly held views and perceptions are not as true or effective in practice as many believe them to be. It is these perceptions that allow people to accept, compound and promote the collection of flawed ideas and theories like those below. They may sound great in theory but tend not to work in practice.

1) Continual dialogue and discussion are a useful and helpful substitute or replacement for making decisions, agreeing and taking action.
2) Our opinionated and contradictory feedback reliably produces improvements.
3) If we just improve this bit, then everything will be better.
4) Our decisions are right because we believe they are.
5) Just having information is the equivalent of understanding, knowledge and experience.
6) That everything will work well if we just follow the processes.

It would be easy to jump to the conclusion that these failings are caused by people. If we only behaved differently, a bit better, more reliably, a bit more consistently, then the theories would work. So, it is our fault. My view is that the theories are wrong because they ignore the unavoidable fact that people are just people. The theories fail because they attempt to dismiss how we really are. To put it another way, theories that ignore our natural human flaws may promise great things, but frustratingly deliver very little or not as much as originally expected, believed or claimed.

We are complex, varied, natural creatures with different needs, hopes, attitudes and opinions. We take pride in being individuals and we are rightly encouraged to be ourselves, stand up for what we believe in and say what we think (just as I'm doing in this book). People have many great qualities but being reliable, accurate, consistent and efficient are definitely not our collective strong points, especially when compared to machines. Therefore, this chapter looks at what makes so many of us unreliable. The following chapter then looks at what we can do to make things a little better, along with the bigger question of how our behaviours are influenced and driven, and how they change over time.

Round peg, square hole

Throughout Part 1 you may have noticed the collection of hints, suggestions and a few flagrant outbursts, on the common themes of understanding, decision making and actions. It is not WORDS or FEEDBACK or INFORMATION or PROCESSES that make things happen, it is only people's understanding, decisions, common sense, free will and ultimately actions that actually do anything. Saying you are going to diet and exercise will do nothing. Equally, writing down a diet plan will also do nothing on its own. Only doing exercise and eating less or better food will. To work well, the theories in Part 1 need our behaviours, decisions and actions to be collectively reliable, accurate, consistent and efficient, in exactly the way we are not.

1) The ambiguity of our language means it is easy to be misleading and difficult for us to be clear.

2) Our differing opinions and inaccuracy create unstable change and invalidate the theory that human feedback provides stable continual improvement.

3) We change things (or make improvements) without considering the full effect or detriment to others, so making things more difficult for them.

4) Abstraction and false logic make it more difficult to make correct conclusions and decisions.

5) Our varying levels of experience and understanding mean that information is not equivalent to useful knowledge.

6) The theory that a process will solve the problem is invalidated by both the vast variety of circumstances and the ability of our free will to override them.

The theories in Part 1 are attempting to force a very large misshapen round peg called 'natural human irregularity and unreliable behaviour' through a small prescriptive square hole called 'behave like a machine'. It is not a good fit; it isn't easy or natural and often it is very tedious and frustrating. The more we blindly follow processes, rely on information we don't understand or use unclear or misleading words, the less we understand about what we are doing and why. This lack of understanding makes our decisions and actions more abstract or detached and we become more unaware, unthinking or uncaring. We become a bit more like unthinking machines or robots, so it's no wonder that parts of modern life seem to defy common sense or are just "bloody bonkers". There is no suggestion here that all words, feedback, information and processes are totally useless: that is blatantly not true. However, a world where words say very little, where people's level of understanding is reducing and where people are increasingly made to behave like procedural robots is not one that I look forward to. If these trends are gradually increasing, then this seems like the wrong direction to be heading in. My thoughts may be analytical, but I'm very bad at behaving like a robot and I quite like being a lumpy (or grumpy) misshapen round peg. Furthermore, attempting to force misshapen round pegs through neat square holes can make even the simplest of things very difficult.

Not only are we different from other people, but everyone is also different day by day, even hour by hour. Our behaviour and actions are affected by a complex cocktail of attitudes, mood, health, tiredness, emotions, relationships, haste, distractions, stress, frustration, resilience, impatience, energy and motivation. One day you may be full of energy and concentration and do a good job, then the next you may be tired and prone to mistakes and do a really bad job. Not only is our individual behaviour a misshapen round peg, but it also morphs and changes shape throughout the day, week, month or year. All of this is a part of the natural complexity of being human, but it also makes our behaviour inherently unreliable, variable, and prone to mistakes and even contradiction. Collectively this is just the way we are and will continue to be. Despite this constant variation, some human traits form a stronger, more permanent part of our personality and have a stronger influence over our behaviour, decisions, what we do and why. The next two sections take a brief look at the human traits of laziness and selfishness.

The 'should', the 'glad' and the 'snuggly'

Everyone is aware of those people who just don't stop, and buzz around all day keeping busy. They pose a strong contrast to those who hardly do anything and avoid effort whenever possible. Across a large population, any characteristic such as laziness, income, weight or height will form a continuous spectrum known as a bell curve (Normal or Gaussian distribution) because of its distinctive shape. This natural bell shape is a result of few people having extreme characteristics, such as being very small or very tall, with lots of people being around average height. Often these continuous distributions are simplified and sliced to form several classifications, such as the familiar weight category classifications in the weight distribution below.

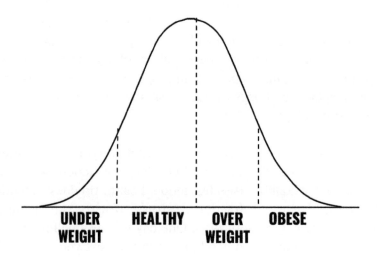

Below is a similar distribution for laziness is split into three categories, named in homage to the classic 1966 spaghetti western film, *The Good, the Bad and the Ugly*.[1] The percentages used below are for demonstration purposes only and based on nothing more than my experience, so feel free to use your own numbers instead.

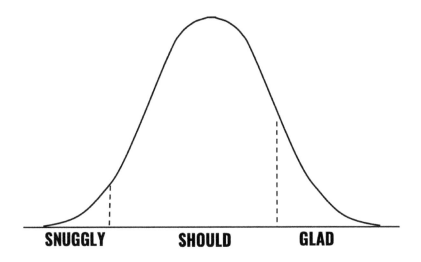

The 'should'
This is the biggest group, containing around 70% of people in the middle of the bell curve, who do what they 'SHOULD' most of the time. They are hardworking people who try to do things well and correctly, try to help people if it doesn't overly affect their own activities and try not to cause problems. However, this group of people will often limit themselves to what they are asked to do and how they are told to do it. It is unlikely they will actively try to pick up extra work or spend extra time doing a better job. If a task can't be done or is difficult, they may cut a corner or even leave it for someone else to do. In other words, they will tend to concentrate on what is asked of them, and do it reasonably well. This is how many people operate.

The 'glad'

This group of around 20% like to be active and doing something all the time. Like the 'SHOULD' group they are hardworking people who do their job well, but this group are also 'GLAD' to put in extra effort, they are 'GLAD' to help others, 'GLAD' to do extra jobs and 'GLAD' to do things as well as possible or in a different way if needed. As an aside, these people also tend to be bad at doing nothing and may find it difficult to relax.

The 'snuggly'

The final group of around 10% are those whose goal in life is to relax and do nothing, preferring to stay on the sofa or in bed. A work colleague provided a good example of this 'SNUGGLY' behaviour when they told me about someone who "would spend 3 hours trying to find someone else to do a job, that they could have completed within 20 minutes". Why do it yourself if you can while away the hours finding someone else to do it instead? This 'SNUGGLY' group tend to do only the minimum necessary, often poorly. You may also find they talk and complain a lot and rely on words to provide an excuse for not doing something. The lack of actions from this group mean they have little effect on the physical world, but for completeness they may have a detrimental effect by unnecessarily diverting the time, effort and actions of the other two groups – but that is a totally different subject and rant.

Despite these relatively arbitrary slices and percentage estimates, our laziness forms a continuous spectrum and so it is fair to assume that some degree of laziness will affect around 30% of the population – the 10% of SNUGGLIES and the bottom third of the SHOULD group. Whatever the real number is, this base level of laziness and unreliability is inescapable and any theories that ignore this reality are likely to be flawed.

Selfish bingo

We may not have selfish genes, but human nature has acquired a natural selfish behaviour from somewhere. Perhaps it is from our human ancestry, where those selfish enough to keep the food and shelter that was available survived. This is a trait seen in many animals, but interestingly not wolves, who share food relatively evenly amongst the pack. Perhaps this essential selfishness for survival was passed down or copied by future generations. However, once farming and rudimentary manufacturing methods were invented, essential food and shelter became more readily available, so our selfishness found other outlets and opportunities – selfishness for comfort, convenience or greed. Today in our modern consumer society, where most things are readily available with sufficient money and time, it is these that tempt our selfishness to the surface. We always feel the need for a bit more money and a bit more time. The Roman philosopher Seneca recognised this trait and summarised it with the following quote:

"Nothing satisfies greed, but even a little satisfies nature."

We happily grab at most opportunities to have more money and, as we become busier, we concentrate on making the best use of our important time and try not to waste it. As we rush a bit more, try to avoid delays and avoid being late, we become more tempted to jump a queue, park on the pavement or do only what we want to. Whilst concentrating on our own time, we have less time for others, making us a little more impatient and intolerant of others. Whatever form our selfishness takes, being impatient, greedy, intolerant or breaking a few rules, you can make a quick assessment of your selfishness using the situations below, in something akin to a game of 'SELFISH BINGO'.

- Rushing to the shortest queue before someone else.
- Blocking other people by stopping to check your phone in a doorway or aisle.
- Nipping through a red traffic light or cutting in front of another driver.
- Taking something from work, instead of buying it.
- Keeping an eye on the buffet table so you don't miss out on the last sandwiches.
- Grabbing the last '3 for 2 offer' before someone else gets it.
- Making excuses when it is your turn to do something (like help out at scouts or sport club).
- Lying to improve your chances of getting a job or promotion.
- Dismissing a person's valid point of view because you want to be proved right.
- Making other people wait unnecessarily at roundabouts because you don't use your indicators.

- Not helping someone who has asked for help.
- Buying a product because it is better than someone else's (keeping up with the Joneses).
- Changing something to make your life easier, without asking the people it will affect.
- Queue jumping at busy road junctions.
- Trying to avoid paying for something you should pay for.
- Claiming money for something just because you can, not because you should.

If a lot of these are applicable to you, then you might be thinking "but loads of people do this" and I would entirely agree. However, this only indicates that we are generally quite a selfish bunch. If the results of this trivial SELFISH BINGO, or any other more reasonable measure of selfishness, were plotted, it would produce another classic bell curve distribution, with a few very selfish people ticking most of them, a few altruistic people ticking very few and most people somewhere in the middle. This time I've split this continuous distribution into three slices using another crude estimate of 15% being selfish and 15% being altruistic, leaving the majority of 70% being varying grades of average in the middle. Again, these numbers are only for demonstration purposes, but if you find them unrepresentative or unacceptable then use your own numbers based on your own experience.

This type of selfish behaviour can be either an ingrained unconscious personal trait or a temporary conscious decision to concentrate on your own efforts for a while. I had to be consciously selfish to write this book, doing what I wanted for long periods of time instead of what my family wanted or needed. In many situations, there is conflict between helping others and doing what is best for yourself. This is a question only for your own conscience to deal with. Whatever the reason, the more consumed someone is with their own concerns, the more others will judge this as selfish behaviour.

Lift a finger

Some people are so selfish or lazy, they won't even lift a finger to help someone, literally not even lift a finger. How much time and effort does it take to help other road users by indicating at roundabouts? Just one small lift of one finger, taking only one second. Yet for some people even this is too much to ask. Giving some consideration to other road users by indicating at road junctions is a tiny effort, but instead some selfish or lazy people drive as if the road is only there for them and everyone else on the road is just an inconvenience to avoid, like another pothole. Indicating at roundabouts allows others to know where you intend to go and can sometimes allow other drivers to get on to the roundabout sooner and keep traffic flowing. Conversely, when drivers don't indicate you just have to wait there, in some ridiculous guessing game to see if they will turn left at the junction before you (meaning that you could have entered the roundabout sooner) or if they will go straight on past you (which means you should wait). Why do some selfish people drive with no regard for other users of the road? Indicating is never for the benefit of the driver or their own passengers, it is only ever for the benefit of other road users, so why do selfish and lazy drivers think they don't need to bother? At the risk of casting aspersions, I presume it is these same selfish drivers who don't indicate, who later complain that there were terrible queues at the roundabouts, because people don't enter the roundabout when cars turn left. They can't if people don't indicate their intentions, everyone must just wait and see what is going to happen.

We are not robots

Returning to the subject at hand, the combination of our laziness and selfishness affects what we do, how much we do and why. It affects our use of words, feedback, information, processes and logic (or lack of it) that we use to decide things. Combining the three levels of laziness (vertically) with the three levels of selfishness (horizontally) gives this diagram below. The whole of the top row represents the 20% of 'GLAD' people, with the whole of the bottom row being the 10% of 'SNUGGLIES'. The columns represent the levels of selfishness, the left column containing the 15% of SELFISH people and the right column being the 15% of ALTRUISTIC people. For those who are interested, the small oval shape is my own assessment of where I sit in this distribution, but it is probably better for others to judge that, not me.

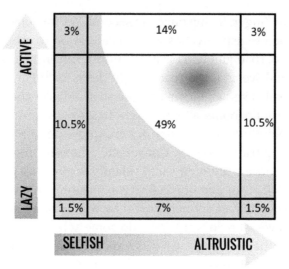

If you are willing to accept my rudimentary guesswork of the percentages, then the central block of people with no extreme characteristics of laziness or selfishness constitutes 49%, roughly half of the population. The curved shaded grey area towards the left and bottom of the diagram combines the most selfish in the left column, with the laziest in the bottom row, which is 23.5% of the population (don't count the bottom left 1.5% twice), along with those that have a reasonable but not extreme amount of both laziness and selfishness, which is about half of the central 49% or a quarter of the population. This implies that between a quarter and a half of the population will have some significant element of laziness or selfishness, so at any time we should expect around 25–50% of the population to not be doing what is expected, or to be unreliable in some way.

This is a significant percentage and provides some justification that as a collective population we are just not reliable enough to make the flawed theories in Part 1 work. We don't work or behave like machines and instead we use our free will to do what we want. We cut corners, use vague or misleading words, blindly accept numbers without checking them or don't follow a process. We are not robots. If you think most people are better than this, you have a much more optimistic outlook than me. I cannot comprehend how those people who are too selfish, lazy or ignorant to lift a finger and indicate when driving, even when there are processes, training, tests and rules to enforce it, will then be willing go out of their way or apply a bit of extra effort to help others. Equally I don't believe they will choose to spend time following a tedious process for the benefit of others. I don't believe that those people who are oblivious of other people around them and ignorantly block doorways, aisles and corridors whenever they get a notification on their phone, are then going to be aware or considerate enough of other people's needs when making changes or attempting so-called improvements. The fact is that an awful lot of people just do what they want at the time, depending on their ingrained levels of laziness or selfishness and the complex cocktail of feelings that affect our daily behaviour.

Those people most likely to behave like reliable, accurate machines are the very active, very altruistic people in the top right corner of the diagram, perhaps only 10% if my estimates are acceptable. The rest of the population (in which I include myself) will continue to help if they can (but not always), holding doors open (but only if not in a hurry), give to charity occasionally (but not all the time) and help at kids' clubs (but only because they feel duty bound to do it). They do so because they 'should', not because they actively want to, and they understand that it is for the greater good if everyone helps a bit. This large, flawed majority to which I belong will continue to be unreliable and fail to provide the reliability and accuracy needed or expected by flawed theories in Part 1.

Altruistic people

Many altruistic people on the right-hand side of the diagram enjoy or feel obliged to help others whenever possible. This ability to help others provides a nice sense of wellbeing, makes each day feel worthwhile, and adds a sense of something small but beneficial to the world by making someone else's day easier or better, like indicating at roundabouts. It is these altruistic people who will stop what they are doing to help others, who can be relied on in moments of need. They are the type of people we would like to have around all the time. Unfortunately, not everyone is able or willing to become one of these people, because of that stronger 'selfish something' we have inside and that complex cocktail of feelings and circumstances.

Regardless of your own personal views, history contains a lot of evidence to suggest that these altruistic, selfless people, who use their own time and effort to help, stand up for, protect or campaign for others (and not themselves), tend to be right in the long term. At the risk of grossly over-generalising, those altruistic people campaigning against racism, homophobia, smoking and, more recently, environmental issues, for the benefit of others, have all been proved to be correct in the longer term, despite having plenty of opposition at the time. It is my opinion that those who can see beyond their own selfish needs and try to help other people are the ones that tend to make the right decisions and do the right thing in the longer term. Is being more altruistic, more helpful and less selfish the answer to the problems and frustrations of modern life? This more optimistic question is considered in the next chapter, along with a look at some of the wider influences that affect our behaviour and actions.

"The less aware you are of others around you, the more selfish your behaviour will appear to them."

08

LIFTING A FINGER

*"We all have two lives. The second begins
when we realise we only have one."*
(Confucius, 551–479BC, Chinese philosopher)

Lifting a finger to use your indicators at road junctions is never for your own benefit, it is a selfless, altruistic act done solely for the benefit of other road users, albeit a tiny one that is expected and can be enforced with fines. By being aware of other road users and helping them in this small way makes things easier or better for them. This chapter looks at how being aware of other peoples' needs and trying to help them can make things easier, better for other people and reduce some of the frustrations highlighted in Part 1. It also looks at what drives and influences our behaviour, but it starts by looking at the difference between selfishly doing things 'for one' and a more altruistic approach of doing things 'for two'.

For two

What if every time you made a decision or did an action, it was done for the benefit of two different people or two different groups? How would being less selfish, always considering other people and making decisions for the benefit of others as well as yourself help prevent some the frustrations and problems of modern life? In this context, 'others' means those with a different perspective or needs and 'yourself' means any wider group with similar views to your own. To genuinely do something 'for two' and provide something that someone else wants, you need to be consciously aware of their needs and their situation, and attempt to understand the things that might help them or what they would appreciate. It requires some additional conscious effort, so except for those few naturally altruistic people, if you are not consciously aware of yourself considering others, then you are probably not doing it at all and you are probably thinking 'for one'.

The following two supermarket examples draw a stark comparison between considering others and not. The first few weeks of the COVID-19 pandemic were an exceptionally unusual time, which led to some exceptional behaviour changes. The first was from the selfish 'for one' part of our personalities, which gave no thought for others and caused a rush to stockpile toilet rolls, pasta and rice, resulting in empty shelves and leaving many people without. The second was a much more pleasant experience, although admittedly it would be difficult to be worse than running out of toilet paper. As people were much more consciously aware of others around them and their need for 2 metres of social distancing, the usual hectic supermarket experience changed into a very pleasant and polite experience, where the aisles were filled with phrases like "sorry, after you", "it's OK I'll wait" or "sorry am I in your way?" Unfortunately, a few weeks later it wore off and returned to the more normal state of rushing and moaning. This demonstrates how being consciously aware of other people's needs and actively trying to help can be far more pleasant than when people just do what is best for themselves at the time.

Applying this type of 'for two' attitude to the theories in Part 1 could produce the following effect.

- By consciously thinking or asking, "What does this person want and need to know?" and "What can I say so that this person will understand exactly what I mean?" could reduce the amount of useless empty, standard, presumptuous, contradictory and incomprehensible language that is used.

- More people would actively try to help others to do something, instead brushing them off with just another set of words like "You'll find it on the website".
- More people would consider "Who will this change have a detrimental effect on?" instead of the 'for one' approach of "How does this change help and benefit me?"
- Instead of jumping to the conclusion "It matches what I want, so it must be correct", more people would challenge the logic of a decision and consider other views or opinions.
- More people would try to understand what information and context is needed and make genuine attempts to provide both, instead of just quickly providing a file of information that is already available.
- More people would stop expecting others to follow the processes that they were averse to following themselves.
- Instead of dogmatically insisting that anything not written down in process isn't allowed, more people would acknowledge that other valid methods and sensible alternatives are acceptable; people would be a bit more pragmatic.

A fanciful idea

The suggestion that we should all be less selfish is not exactly a ground-breaking idea and the same message has been said many times before by many different people, so it probably has some truth in it. Yet, due to the bell curve distributions in the previous chapter, some people struggle to achieve even the lowest level of basic everyday altruistic behaviour, like in this list.

- Check where you are before stopping to look at your phone, so you don't obstruct those around you.
- Always put your litter in a bin or even pick up someone else's litter occasionally.
- Think of what little extra help you can provide, without being asked for it.
- Don't dominate discussions, let others give their opinion and genuinely consider if what you have heard changes your understanding or viewpoint, instead of immediately responding with your unmodified 'for one' response.

- Accept a mild detriment or some extra effort, knowing that it provides a bigger benefit to others.
- At the supermarket, let someone with only a few items get quickly served, instead of taking up lots of their time waiting behind your full shopping trolley.
- Use your indicators for the benefit of other road users at roundabouts and junctions.

Admittedly it is a rather fanciful idea to expect that even with the legal regulations, prolonged training, written procedures, guides and formal testing, people should then be willing and able to 'lift a finger' to help others by indicating at roundabouts. The suggestion here is not that people should indicate because it is written down in rules and processes, but simply because it is considerate, helpful and beneficial to other road users. Just as farcical is the idea that society would be better if everything was done with a 'for two' attitude instead of the more selfish 'for one'. However, the two supermarket examples do highlight how far our daily behaviour has strayed away from the more polite, helpful, pleasant behaviour that people are capable of, when they increase their awareness of others around them. They highlight how reducing selfish behaviour and being willing to 'lift a finger' more frequently makes things a little easier for others. Unfortunately, as with many previous attempts by different people to promote the same message, the main difficulty is converting these 'silent words' into 'real actions.' What is it about modern attitudes or modern life that reduces these more altruistic, helpful actions to an exception rather than the rule? A lot of simple things are becoming more difficult and frustrating, yet it is very difficult to believe or suggest that people maliciously try to make things more difficult for others. This isn't a very palatable explanation and is simply not true for the vast majority people most of the time.

People have many great characteristics. They like being individual, they like freedom of choice, they are inventive, creative, expressive, social, intuitive, sympathetic, caring and helpful. People generally want to help and make things better. They want things to be better for themselves, their families and others. With all these good natural instincts, impressive technology advancement and a continual desire to make things better, why does modern daily life often seem to be arduous? Why are the simple things difficult and over complicated? Why is there always more words and so little action? Why is there yet another hindrance or obstacle, rather than some active help? Why can't I swap appointments or get taps to work, in a society that is constantly promoting efficiency and convenience? Why does daily life not seem as good and easy as some want you to believe? Why aren't people less selfish? For the vast majority of the time people don't actively try to be unhelpful or inconsiderate, so why are things so bloody difficult at times? Our behaviour, choices and actions are not only controlled by our individual levels of laziness and selfishness or the distorting effects of being forced through small procedural square holes. Our behaviour is also the consequence of an incredibly complicated mixture of influences that have been the subject of psychological, sociological and philosophical studies for a long time. The next section takes a brief look at how our psychology also affects our behaviour.

A bit of psychology

What governs human behaviour has been an important subject of psychology for more than a century and there are many different theories.[1] Freud's psychodynamic theories suggest it is our stage of our development, whilst biological theories say it is down to our genes. Cognitive theories say behaviour is driven by our perceptions, whilst Maslow's humanist theory suggests it is driven by our free will and our hierarchy of needs, starting with food and drink, then safety, then belonging (or love), then self-esteem. The Pavlov and Skinner behaviourist theories suggest it is driven by our conditioning and society's reward system, whilst social learning theories say it is driven by copying and imitation of other people. It is fair to say it is a very complicated subject and all the theories have both good supporting evidence and limitations that suggest they are not fully correct. Collectively they suggest our behaviour is a complex mix of our age, genetics, personality, getting what we need and want, learning by association or reward and copying other people's behaviours, especially those that are rewarded or not punished.

One of the simplest demonstrations of how people's behaviour is influenced can be found in a video called "Dancing Guy" used in a TED Talk,[2] which clearly demonstrates how people tend to copy other people. If they do it, I'll do it. The more people exceed the speed limit without being caught, the more others will do the same. The more people refuse to use indicators at roundabouts, the more others will do the same. More pertinent to Part 1, the more people who get away with talking 'empty shite' all the time, the more people will do that as well. Therefore, in addition to our innate levels of laziness and selfishness, our choices, decisions, actions and resulting behaviour are also strongly influenced by the behaviour of those around us. We gradually copy and drift towards what everyone else does, what is accepted, normal or rewarded.

Changing behaviour

Although our day-to-day choices and behaviour are dominated by a little tussle between our own conscience and what those around us are doing at the time, the scope, long-term direction and drift of our 'behavioural norms' are more strongly influenced by what is possible and available, along with the rules and expectations that society places on us. Today our behaviour does not include travelling to the Moon for shopping trips, simply because it is not yet possible or available to us. Just as 40 years ago online dating wasn't possible or part of our behaviour, and initially it wasn't very socially acceptable, whereas now it is popular and very beneficial to many people. Similarly, over the last century smoking, drink driving and not wearing seat belts have all changed from being socially acceptable, to socially alienating.

Day to day, week to week, month to month little seems to change, everything is just normal, whilst over years, decades and centuries we move from one status quo to a new accepted norm. This is the problem with any 'normality': it is precisely that, it is just considered normal, and it is largely unquestioned and accepted as just the way things are. For younger people the current norm might be the way things have always been, such as using mobile phones, digital communication and the expectation to provide feedback on anything and everything from your coffee, fingernails or a lesson at college to your train journey home. It is all just normal. This doesn't make it worse or better than before, it doesn't make it good, bad, correct, valid or optimal, it just makes it normal and acceptable.

Being immersed for a long time in an acceptable, slowly changing environment does two things simultaneously. Firstly, it adapts and evolves our behaviour to match those around us, as we tend to copy them, whilst secondly making that collective behaviour more acceptable and just what everybody now does, like having more colourful hair and providing feedback. This prolonged immersion in an environment also makes it very difficult to see this normality from any other perspective than just being normal; it is difficult to see what it really is. You can't see the wood for the trees. A seat on a coach, a train or a plane are all a very similar environments and provide very little perspective, contrast or overview of what that environment truly is. Is it a mildly impressive coach that takes you a few miles up the road or a truly extraordinary flying machine that takes you halfway around the world at over half the speed of sound about six miles above the ground? Only occasionally do we get a different view or clearer perspective of the normality we live in. Dramatic changes, like the outbreak of the COVID-19 pandemic or making it illegal to smoke in public indoor areas, can awaken us from the slow gradual drift. They allow us to directly compare the previous status quo against something different. They allow us to see things differently, to compare and question both. Alternatively, you can simply listen to grumpy old men claiming that it "wasn't like this in my day".

An inquisitive and analytical attitude makes it easier to question things, to stand back, compare and contrast alternatives, and see a fuller picture and a bit more than just the accepted view. A questioning analytical mind makes it easier to see things for what they really are. If you can step back from the word 'feedback' and its connotations, you can see that it is just a collection of opinions. If you can step back from all the talking in a meeting room, you can see it is all just noise that doesn't do anything on its own. This is what Part 1 attempted to do, to question how much of this accepted normality is actually valid or correct. If using words to say nothing, making a process for every action or trusting answers from a computer screen that we don't understand all start to become 'the accepted norm', then this seems like a recipe for a lot of bad decisions and an unreasonable direction to be heading in. Therefore, Part 3 continues this alternative, analytical approach, to look at some important aspects of our society from a different perspective, to see them for what they really are and how they influence our behaviour. Along with some more moans, groans, rants and even a song, Part 3 looks at subjects like finance, technology and politics, raising questions like "How does the economy work?", "Do machines work for us or are we starting to work for machines?" and "How much democracy do we have?" Part 4 then combines these separate pieces in some kind of social jigsaw, looking at how they link and interact to provide an unconventional view on how our modern Western society operates and influences our behaviour, before ending with some much-needed optimism and a suggestion for an alternative version of society.

"Think of others before you act, then
act for the benefit of others."

PART 3:

THE INFLUENCES

09

FINANCIAL PLAYGROUND

*"Don't think money does everything or you are
going to end up doing everything for money."*
(Voltaire, 1694–1778, writer and philosopher)

I have never really understood finance or the economy, and this first became clear to me when I met my wife (this probably isn't heading where you suspect). Her father was interested in the stock market and investing was a bit of a hobby of his. At the time my understanding of the stock market amounted to "it is often beneficial over the long term if you have some spare cash doing nothing, but you could also lose a lot". To my mind, this translated as little more than educated gambling and so I had little interest in it. After several attempts to discuss his latest financial gains or losses, I soon realised I did not have a clue how this kind of finance or the economy really worked. This niggling puzzle that I had no real interest in sat in a dark corner of my mind for many years occasionally taunting me with whispers of "you still don't know how this works do you?" Becoming slightly irritated by my lack of understanding of such an important aspect of our society, I started taking opportunities to ask for explanations, but for over a decade no one who knew about finance could explain it to me in a way that I could understand. I finally got some kind of answer when a work colleague of mine was dating someone who worked in the London stock market – this was my big chance, finally I could get the answer.

The playground and Santa

The question I asked my colleague was this.

> "Can you ask your girlfriend to explain how finance and
> the stock market works, using words that a 10-year-old
> child would understand in the school playground?"

The answer I got was this.

Person A has a £1.00 coin and sells it to person B for £1.05 by claiming it will be worth £1.10 in 6 months. Person B then sells the same £1.00 to person C for £1.10 by claiming it will be worth £1.20 in 1 year. This continues with increasing price and duration. This means that everyone in the chain, except the last person, can profit from the sale of the same £1 coin. As long as the value of the coin grows as predicted then everyone remains happy. However, as soon as one person in the chain believes that it won't rise as much as expected, they think "oh damn" and try to get their money back. This starts a chain of everyone trying to get their money back, but it doesn't exist because all that actually exists is the same original £1.00 coin that started the whole thing off in the first place. All the extra value is just expectation and belief.

Just as the wording of my question requested, this answer is grossly oversimplified, but it strongly suggests that the stocks and shares market is based on little more than hope and belief. I had always thought there was some black art to finance that made it difficult for my analytical, logical mind to understand, but what I had just been told was that the world of stocks and shares, the financial markets, were just like believing in Santa. Lots of people (parents or traders) say lots of things that make it (Santa or trading) sound convincing that good things (presents or profit) will happen, until someone (10-year-old Sammy or a few unhappy traders) ask enough of the right kind of questions to realise something isn't quite right, then the whole thing (belief in Santa or confidence in the markets) collapses and vanishes into nothing. Although this very simple answer was the best I'd got so far, it felt somewhat lacking in substance to be a true explanation of how the financial markets and wider economy operate. It also raised more awkward questions, such as these:

What makes the share price value increase?
Where does this extra share price value or money come from?
Are these linked to economic growth?
What causes economic growth and how does it materialise?

These and other financial questions sat niggling away in the same corner of my brain for many more years, without any further answers, understanding or success.

Success at last

One Christmas, back when this book was still only an embryonic idea, I was shopping for presents and browsing through a bookstore when I came across a book called *Talking to My Daughter: A Brief History of Capitalism* by Yanis Varoufakis.[1] You can imagine the look on my face: "Is this it? Have I finally got the answer in my hand?" I quickly turned over the book to read the back cover, which confirmed that this book would help me understand the black art of banking and finance. This was it, finally I would understand how the economy works. I also found a second book called *Whoops!* by John Lanchester, which explains the 2008 financial crash.[2] I got both books for Christmas, read them quickly and have re-read them both since. If you have any interest in learning more about finance or if you have found any parts of this book remotely interesting, then I implore you to read either or both. You will be entertained, surprised and probably shocked. Armed with this new knowledge and understanding, along with a lot of further clarification, education and help from a retired economics teacher, my understanding of finance and the economy is now much better, but I still don't understand it fully. However, I do now understand why I couldn't previously understand it. I also understand why I will never be able to fully understand it. Furthermore, I understand why even the experts don't or can't fully understand it either. It is because the previous rather unsophisticated analogy with Santa was valid and the world of finance is no more fully understandable than the belief in Santa or any other belief system. Therefore, to provide one of the pieces to my jigsaw, my current understanding of finance and the economy is summarised below.

Finance and economy

The first question is what's the difference? The two books and additional education mentioned above made me realise that I didn't even properly understand the difference between finance and economy. I naively thought they were roughly the same thing, but they are not. The economy is an all-encompassing concept covering everything involved in using Earth's resources to satisfy people's wants and needs. Different kinds of moneyless economies existed long before the invention of money, and simple economies will spring up whenever and wherever people start to share, swap, exchange or barter goods, whether money exists or not. By contrast, finance is predominantly concerned only with money, and this makes the whole of the financial industry just one part of a much wider money-based economy (albeit a very influential one within modern capitalist-based economies).

The second question is where to start – banks, wages, share value, GDP (gross domestic product), tax, economic growth, profits – as everything seems to feed everything else. Money flows and spreads everywhere, everything is fluid and in constant flux. In short, it is very difficult to anchor it or find a firm foothold to work from. In the end, my understanding is built around the relatively familiar, understandable and firm foothold of the 'basic high street economy', which ignores all the complexities of shares, inflation, growth etc. for now.

Basic high street economy

This basic economy includes people buying day-to-day goods like coffee, phones, furniture and little fake fingernails from the businesses that provide them, where money flows from businesses to people (as wages) and from people to businesses (in purchases). Once the money from sales is inside a business, it is needed to pay the wages of employees, to buy consumable materials (such as more cloth to make clothes), to repair or replace old equipment (such as sewing machines) or to hold as reserves (as cash in the bank) to help cope with any seasonal variations or unforeseen disruptions. Any purchases that the business makes (in this case cloth and new sewing machines) are just sales to other businesses that then have their own equivalent outgoing costs to pay, including wages. Meanwhile, any cash reserves that are held in a bank are made available for loans to the public and other businesses, with the bank's profits being used to run and maintain the bank and pay employees. In this way, a fixed amount of money constantly flows through the economy from people to businesses, to banks, to people and back to businesses again. This type of basic economy highlights the original and essential role of money as nothing more than a 'carrier of value' to smooth or ease transactions. Money is just the lubrication of the economy, allowing it to operate more smoothly. This basic economy can also be thought of as a 'fixed' or 'static' economy, because for now it contains only a fixed amount of money (or lubricating oil) flowing through the economic pipes and cogs, so there is little or no possibility for growth. It cannot provide an increase in standard of living and if the population grows then we all get a bit less of the fixed amount of lubricating oil or money within this static economy. However, this is an economy where the rules of supply and demand can be applied well, because, regardless of how hard you try, there is a limited amount of coffee, phones, furniture and fingernails you can use, so the demand for these consumable items and services is always limited in some way.

National economy and taxation

Sticking with this 'basic' economy and still ignoring many of the complexities like shares, growth and inflation etc., we can introduce the concept of taxation, where sales, profits and wages are all taxed to provide money for the benefit of nation as a whole. In the UK this includes school education, the NHS, policing and defence etc., all of which are heavily controlled by the government. These are a type of government 'controlled' markets, as opposed to 'capitalist' or 'free' markets. Most nations of the world operate with a 'mixed' economy, where some things are provided by free markets (like fake fingernails) and some things are provided by heavily controlled markets (like education and health care), whilst something like energy markets may sit in the middle ground, operating as a free market but within some government constraints. Many communist nations tend towards using more controlled markets (perhaps for providing food, cars and transport etc.), whilst Western nations tend towards more of the free or capitalist markets. This introduction of taxation is a relatively simple addition to the basic or static market, as all the tax revenue is used to pay government employees or to build roads, buy ambulances etc. This means that all the tax money eventually ends up being used for more sales for some businesses, so this fixed amount of money continues to flow around as before, with access to a few additional taxation pipes.

Capitalist economy and shares

Many smaller or local businesses operate in this basic economy kind of way, naturally 'ticking over', providing for the local community and hopefully earning enough money for the owners and employees to live comfortably. However, many larger businesses also have shareholders, where part of the business is sold to people who want to buy and own a 'share' of a business. This is predominantly in the hope that they can either receive a 'dividend' (a share of the profits) or because they 'believe' (there is that magic word again) that the share price will increase in future when their shares can be sold at a profit, for someone else to own. A share price therefore reflects the current capital worth of the business (as you are buying a part or 'share' of everything the business currently has) along with a prediction of the future capital worth (you are hoping it will increase and not fall) and a prediction of future profits and dividends. Share price therefore reflects a prediction of how the capital value and profits of the business will change in future. In isolation this seems completely acceptable, and it is, but this approach does have several important consequences that cannot be ignored.

Firstly, this introduction of 'shareholders' and 'share price' changes the role of money in the economy. Instead of just lubricating transactions (as in the basic economy) money can now be used as a tool to make more money, in the same way that the buying houses can be used to make more money. This starts to create a scale or spectrum, starting with the consumable items like phones, fingernails and coffee, which reduce in value and become worthless. Next there are products like houses, art, vintage cars and land that we can buy to use and enjoy, but also hope they maintain or increase in value. Then there is buying shares which have little practical use other than an ability to just (hopefully) provide more money. As previously explained in the FALSE LOGIC chapter (Chapter 4), products which can hold or increase in value, like houses, do not correctly follow the standard market rules of 'supply and demand'. The demand does not necessarily reduce with increasing price; in fact increasing price is what now makes these products more attractive and so increases demand further. There will always be an unlimited demand for any product that provides the possibility of 'money making more money' and if other people see money being made, they will believe that they can make money too. This is starting to imply a kind of herd mentally, like buying multiple houses for profit, rushing to buy shares rising in value (think of the dot com financial bubble around 1998), and fleeing away from and selling shares going down. This type of profit-seeking herd mentally is a guaranteed way to exaggerate the response to any change and so induce or create some instability. Imagine what would happen driving a car if every time the driver turned slightly, everyone in the car tried to grab the steering wheel and turn it further the same way. However, beyond this rather academic monetary role change and a guarantee of inducing some instability, the introduction of shares and shareholders has some further practical consequences that are listed below.

- Businesses now need to generate more profit to pay 'dividends' to shareholders.
- There is a pressure to maintain or increase the share price of the business, predominantly by increasing the capital value or profits of the business (or growing the business).
- Shares create a flow or syphon of money towards those that can afford shares (money flows towards money).

In short, the introduction of shares and shareholders shifts the role of a business from just ticking over and providing something people want, towards growth and increasing capital value, profits, dividends and share price value. One catastrophic example of this type of shift was the 1997 merger between the Boeing company with its excellent engineering reputation and the McDonnell Douglas company that was more concerned with share price value. Ultimately it was this shift away from engineering principles towards concerns over company costs, profits and share price that was one of the contributing factors to the two 737 Max aircraft disasters, according to the TV documentaries on the topic.[3]

Finally, and in theory at least, a business does not need shareholders or a good share price to operate well. Although a large drop in share price would be unfortunate for all the shareholders losing money, it does not change the equipment, premises, employees, products, sales or profits of the business. The ability of the business to continue operating, producing and providing has not changed, it is only the level of belief that the shareholders' money can make more money that has changed. This highlights the disconnect between the current and shorter-term capability of the business and the longer-term share price predictions of what it will be able to do in future. They are two separate things and should be considered as such. In practice, however, this theoretical possibility probably doesn't happen very often. If the share price drops so low that the majority shareholding of the company becomes less than the capital value of the company (equipment, holdings, stock etc.), this will trigger an 'asset stripping' company to make a quick profit by quickly buying the cheap shares, for the sole purpose of then selling everything of capital value and shutting down the business. Forget the employees, the customers and the jobs in the community, now profit and money making has become the only important thing.

Growing economy

Economic growth is defined as an increase in gross domestic product (GDP), a measure of everything the nation produces and sells (both products and services), and this growth is essential for both increasing living standards and providing for increases in population. This growth cannot be generated by a fixed economy with only a fixed amount of money flowing, as there would not be enough money to buy the extra products and services. There would not be enough oil to lubricate these extra cogs and sales. There would be air gaps in the pipes and so these extra products would just sit as unsold stock. In short, the economy would begin to stutter and stumble. As indicated earlier, keeping shareholders happy also requires some kind of 'growing the business' to increase the share price, dividends, capital value or profits. So where does this economic growth and extra money or lubricating oil come from? The initial response is "from a bank loan", and this is partially correct, but this is also where understanding finance and the economy starts to become stranger and less intuitive.

Naturally, a business can take out a bank loan to buy a new machine, make more products, grow the business and increase sales and profits etc., and this money may come directly from a collection of customer cash deposits that the bank is looking after. However, banks are allowed to lend much more than just the money deposited with them and this is given the label of 'fractional reserve banking' and is based on a percentage called 'cash reserve ratio' (CRR). For example, if the CRR was 100% then the bank would always need to hold 100% of its customer cash deposits in reserve, in case they all wanted it back immediately on the same day. The bank would never be able to lend anything to anyone and would be nothing more than a large piggy bank made of concrete, steel and glass. However, if the CRR is 10%, the bank can now loan out 10 times its level of cash deposit reserves, so if £1 million was deposited by customers and held in reserves, the bank can then loan out up to £10 million. This extra £9 million is created from nothing more than fresh air and is labelled 'credit creation' (of £9 million) in the finance industry. This extra £9 million can then be used to increase production and sales, before being paid back at some point in the future – but paid back with what? If this extra lubricating oil is paid back and removed from the pipes, air gaps will form, and the economy will begin to stutter and stumble. This is where the national banks (like Bank of England or European Central Bank) step in. The 'credit creation' allowed more products and services to be available for sale, effectively increasing the national GDP, which needs some extra monetary lubrication. Therefore, the national bank supplies the economy with enough extra money to lubricate (or service) this increase in national GDP. Perhaps you would like to take a guess at where this all this extra money comes from... correct, it is from nothing more than fresh air again.

As a little side-act and complication to this main feature, the bank's credit creation can easily fuel increasing inflation, which the national banks have the role of controlling using nothing more than the base interest rate. The theory is that if interest rates are high then people will save instead of spending and so keep inflation under control. However, this desire to save and not spend also slows some of that essential lubricating money flowing through the economic pipes and reaching the business sales figures and so reduces profits.

Full economy

Finally, there is the full economy to consider, which includes the national debt, bonds and more financial wizardry. When the government does not have enough tax income to fund something such as the unexpected COVID-19 outbreak, it must obtain more money from somewhere. It can borrow from the national bank and in doing so add to the national debt. This time there are no prizes for working out that this loan also materialises out of fresh air, simply by typing a '1' followed by lots of zeros into a computer. The same is true for 'quantitative easing' and all other new money that is pushed into the pipes of the economy. Alternatively, the government can use some of the money that already exists in the economy, by issuing and selling bonds for the public to buy. These bonds guarantee a fixed interest rate and your money back at the end of the bonds' fixed term, which is just like the government acting as a deposit bank for a while. As with most things in the financial world, the ownership of these government bonds can also be traded and sold on to others at a market price that varies according to other competing interest rates available elsewhere, such as the high street banks. That just leaves the extra wizardry of what could be called 'higher finance' including hedge funds, futures, options, pension schemes and, as strange as it may sound here, selling debts for profit.

Both futures and options are types of 'derivatives', which essentially means that they attempt to predict the future. If you believe that the price of oil will increase from $100 to $120 in the next 3 months, then you can buy a future or an option to buy the oil at an agreed price of say $112 in 3 months' time. If the oil price does rise to $120, you win. If the oil price does not rise above $112, you lose. Whilst a future is a fixed contract that must end with the purchase at the agreed price, an option is just a fixed payment which buys the privilege (or option) to choose whether to purchase at the agreed price of $112 in 3 months' time or not. If the price goes above $112 then paying for the option was worthwhile, whilst if the oil price is lower than $112, you lose your option payment but can then buy the oil at the current lower price. These type of derivatives are not limited to commodities like oil and can also be used for the following:

- Commodities such as minerals, cocoa and grain etc.
- Currencies such as changes in exchange rates or interest rates.
- Financial stocks such as changes in share prices and debts.

If you only have an interest in buying grain or oil then this type of commodity derivative is probably your best option, but if your investment aim is only to make more money (like a pension scheme) then all this prediction can be risky, which is where hedge funds can help mitigate some of the risk. Hedge funds gather cash from many traders (often called investors, but it is more accurate to say traders) to trade or invest in a wide range of products, so if some go up and some go down then you hopefully still make some money. For something like a pension scheme, which must pay huge quantities of money, to many people, over many years, any opportunity to grow or increase the total money pot available is essential. This makes share prices, with their tendency to increase in value over the long term (albeit punctuated with several financial crashes) and hedge funds to mitigate some of the investment risk, very attractive options. In this way, pension schemes are entirely dependent on increasing share prices and economic growth and without them simply won't be able to afford to pay people's pensions. It would then be left to the government to pick up the pieces, look after the people and foot the bill. Therefore, the government also has a strong vested (or invested) interest in economic growth and share prices etc.

At this point it is worth highlighting that many 'stock derivatives' work on predicting changes in share price value, just as 'commodity derivatives' work on predicting the price of a commodity like oil. Therefore, stock futures are actually 'a prediction of a prediction of profit'. To put this into some context, it is like balancing a vertical stick, on top of a vertical stick, on top of a pebble; it is like a three-ball plant in snooker when all three balls are well separated; or it is like an accumulator bet – the outcome is massively uncertain, and almost anything could happen.

In short, the full complicated world of finance (or at least this type of higher finance) is built around prediction, uncertainty, belief and confidence about what might happen in the future and that is definitely not the strongest of platforms on which to build the foundation of your economy and society. In fact, it is an inherently unstable platform, one that is susceptible to disruption and prone to unstable cycles of boom and bust. This is all exaggerated by people's natural herd mentality which can help when things are on the up (with steady economic growth and confidence) but is also disastrous when things turn downwards (recession and uncertainty). The one thing people have in common is that they don't like losing their money, so, just like in the simple playground explanation at the start of this chapter, a loss of confidence and belief can very quickly turn into a financial crash.

Financial crashes

Consequently, the world of finance is not really the finely tuned, balanced, optimised system that it is often portrayed to be. It is a strange, unstable, belief-based world, which feeds from an unlimited pool of fresh air and is difficult to understand or visualise. Maybe my brief overview has helped a little, but to help visualise this ability to crash more clearly requires a more physical analogy. The world of finance (and by extension the economy) is more like a precariously balanced inverted mountain, which could topple (or crash) at any moment and the only thing keeping it stable is that fragile supply of hope and belief. In the real physical world, an inverted mountain balancing on its tip is likely to fall and it would require large numbers of massively powerful physical machines (instead of belief) to control and maintain the balance. It is then possible to visualise the following situation.

> Whenever the wind turns in the wrong direction, the mountain will start to have a wobble. To stop the wobble, you need a huge amount of extra power for machines, to stop the mountain from falling over. If the mountain did fall over, it would need an immense amount of power to pick up the mountain and put it back on its tip again.

If you think this analogy is completely ridiculous, replacing the few words listed below creates a new situation (with original words in brackets to aid the comparison).

"wind" with "confidence and belief"
"mountain" with "economy"
"a wobble" with "uncertainty"
"power" with "money"
"machines" with "business"
"falling over" with "crashing"
"pick up" with "restart"
"tip" with "feet"

Whenever the confidence and belief (wind) turn in the wrong direction, the economy (mountain) will start to have uncertainty (a wobble). To stop the uncertainty (wobble), you need a huge amount of extra money (power) for businesses (machines), to stop the economy (mountain) from crashing (falling over). If the economy (mountain) did crash (fall over), it would need an immense amount of money (power) to restart (pick up) the economy (mountain) and put it back on its feet (tip) again.

Does this now sound a little more familiar? Does this sound like something you may have heard the financial experts reporting in the news in 2008? Is it now slightly more believable that the economy is an inherently unstable system? Is it now easier to accept that the world of finance is so contrived and detached from the real world that it has no realistic physical equivalent?

Incidentally, a major contribution to the 2008 crash, apart from fragile confidence and this chronic instability, was a reliance on two types of BINFORMATION. Firstly, the financial models were wrong (and probably always will be). Engineering and scientific models of car braking distances, aerodynamic forces of aircraft or planetary orbits etc. are repeatedly tested and validated against physical reality. Conversely, financial models don't have this luxury and they are attempting to model the behaviour of a belief system with the unpredictable whims of people in a constantly varying global environment. No wonder they were completely wrong. Secondly the context of the financial information was lost, abstracted away or, to be a little more accurate, purposefully hidden. The monetary value of toxic debts was dissolved away into complicated monetary cocktails of shares, futures, debts, hedge funds and portfolios. The origin and all context of the monetary value was abstracted away, until it became nothing more than yet another number on a screen. The whole finance industry, including the experts, blindly sailed headfirst into the 2008 crash, because the reality of the situation had been completely abstracted away and there was no way for common sense to intervene. It is possible that a few people did actually know that a crash was likely, but the alarm wasn't raised. Maybe they had too much to gain personally and so effectively let the rest of the world take the pain for their own selfish and very significant financial gain. Following the 2008 crash, the financial industry was resurrected once more by wiping out all unpayable debts and generating another massive injection of cash from that infinite supply of fresh air by simply typing a 1 and another shed load of zeros into that magic financial computer.

Frankenstein and Santa

In any vaguely real situation, having access to such an unlimited supply of help is just not possible, and yet this unstable broken financial system has used the magical properties of fresh air to resurrect itself or nurse itself back to health many times in the last 100 years alone. If the financial system was in any way consistent with physical reality, it would have died in the 1930s' financial crash, with no possible rescue or resurrection. It would have remained dead and been replaced with something better or at least different. In the real and physical world, we do not tolerate this continual repeated cycle of failure. We would not tolerate a bridge, road or building that regularly collapses, we don't tolerate cars or computers that continually break down or are unreliable. If your phone, car or home behaved like the financial system, you would consider it unacceptable, get rid of it and replace it. Instead, even after the most severe financial crashes and blatant demonstrations of all its flaws and problems, we just keep rebuilding our entire society on this unreliable, unstable financial platform. For some bizarre reason we just keep resurrecting the same financial monster over and over again, like some kind of financial Frankenstein.

Therefore, instead of the financial industry being analogous to a belief in Santa, it is closer to a belief in a kind of 'Frankenstein Santa' that just keeps returning to life after each death. However, unlike our belief in Santa (which only happens once), after each financial crash and resurrection, we all start believing that exactly the same financial system is now in good working order again. I'm acutely aware of my lack of proper understanding on this subject. I know that my overly simplified explanations, my naïve opinionated views and my idea to condense the whole of the financial world into the single grotesque caricature of a Frankenstein Santa monster are unlikely to be overly convincing. Therefore, those wishing for clearer, more detailed, candid expert views of this weird financial world should read either or both the financial books mentioned earlier.

These opinions contrast sharply against the more common perception that the financial system is a robust, stable, finely tuned, well-balanced system that is based on sound mathematical and scientific theories. Promoting this more idealised perception is possible because both finance and the economy are complex, difficult to understand and disguised behind many layers of jargon and complicated mathematical theories. Two of the assumptions on which many financial theories and the financial computer models are based are "the market is always right" and "consumers are sensible". Both these maybe correct sometimes or be partially true, but Part 1 showed how attempting to apply specific theories to complex environments can often be wrong. However, there are more fundamental problems with these assumptions. Firstly, I cannot comprehend how something which does not understand and cannot even acknowledge the existence of human values or suffering can make the right decisions for people. Secondly, I would never classify the greedy, gambling, spontaneous, herd-mentality, error-prone and unreliable nature of people to be sensible. Furthermore, neither of these change the fundamental fact that, underlying all that financial jargon and maths, there remains that unstable fragile platform of prediction and belief. It doesn't matter how good your house is, you still shouldn't build it on sand. Hopefully some of these financial misconceptions are now just a little less common than they used to be. However, one thing that is even harder to accept than my rather ridiculous Frankenstein Santa analogy is that those who maintain and promote this idea of a robust, reliable, stable financial system are also the ones receiving the biggest financial bonuses and rewards for doing so.

Dependence and detachment

All of this is the reason why, for so many years, no one could explain to me how finance and the economy work, because in any real, practical, physical or logical sense, it is no more explainable and understandable than a Frankenstein Santa, a religion or anything else built on a platform of human belief. But at least I now know why I can't and never will understand it. I also understand why even the experts don't and can't fully understand it either. This modern capitalist financial system is a human invention, built on an unstable platform of belief and confidence, fuelled by fresh air and a belief, desire, need or greed for money to make more money. This human creation has evolved and grown over the many decades, it has changed or distorted the original role of money and it has become totally detached and abstracted from the real world that spawned it. It has grown and evolved into a separate 'money making world' of its own, on which our economy, our government and our society has become totally dependent, just like an addict who is dependent on drugs. This is why economic growth is considered so important for our society, why it is always in the news and why economic recession (technically decreasing GDP) is considered so bad. Over the last couple of centuries our society has become increasingly dependent on economic growth: the pension schemes need it, the economy needs it, the government needs it, and our jobs and employment need it. We and our society have become hooked, dependent and addicted.

We are caught in a never-ending loop of economic growth, where growth depends on confidence, which depends on share prices, which depend on increasing profits, which depend on increasing sales, which is a higher GDP and economic growth. Astute readers may now be realising the fundamental problem. When enough growth is obtained in one year, more is required the next year and the next and the next and there is no escape from this loop that we have become trapped in. The immediate consequences of this for businesses are tackled in the next chapter and then Part 4 looks further forward and considers the longer-term future.

This detachment of the modern financial world from the day-to-day reality of the real world is highlighted in this table of differences.

	Financial world	Real world
Fuelled by...	Fresh air and belief	Materials and energy
Limits and constraints	Unlimited	Physical laws and time
Taxation	Rare or low	Common or high
Debt	Promoted and profitable	Avoided and costly
Instability	High and accepted	Avoided
Attitude to risk	Rewarded	Avoided
Consequence of failure	Just restart	Stop or change

These stark differences help to highlight just how detached the finance industry has become from the real world. After all, none of us go hunting for an unstable Wi-Fi signal, none of us like having a car that fails (or crashes) regularly, and businesses are legally obliged to have risk assessments for fitting a new light bulb, whilst in the finance industry taking risks is rewarded. The 'real world' and 'world of finance' truly are worlds apart. Perhaps this table, combined with relatively huge salaries and bonuses available in the finance industry, will just make things unintentionally worse by advertising several reasons to go and work in this fanciful world of finance.

Furthermore, perhaps these stark differences are also the reason behind the public's distaste, dismay and even disbelief in the operation of the modern financial system, something which was captured perfectly by one of my favourite TV clips, filmed at the start of the 2008 financial crash. A news camera on the streets of London zoomed in on an upper floor of a finance building, where some finance workers were holding a makeshift banner which read "SAVE OUR JOBS". The person operating this camera did a brilliant job, as they zoomed away from this banner to zoom in on an equally makeshift banner held by the crowds in the streets below which simply read "JUMP YOU BASTARDS". To my mind, nothing epitomises the general public's level (and total absence) of sympathy for the financial industry than this little TV gem.

Money, profit and value

This monstrosity of a modern finance system is not how it all started. The original concept of money was an intermediary (or lubrication) between transactions, so that people who wanted some cloth didn't have to carry chickens, grain or fruit around with them to barter with. Money was invented or conceived as just a 'carrier of value', a role which some of the earliest coins did quite literally, such as Electrum coins that were made of silver and gold by the Lydians in 600BC.[4] Today everyone knows how exceptionally well money continues to fulfil this essential lubricating role.

For money to be this universal carrier of value it must allow a pile of bananas to be directly compared with a block of cheese, a plastic toy to be compared with a book and food to be measured and treated in the same way as transport, energy or education. To do this money must be completely abstract in nature. In finance, this placing of abstract monetary value on something is called 'commoditising' and it is the only way that the financial system can see, understand, value, measure or judge anything. Even something as fundamental as time itself must be commoditised. Even though time is the same for every single person, is freely available, and can't be touched, changed, moved or controlled in any way, it is still commoditised and given different monetary values in the form of wages, based on what actions we do during that time. That rather philosophical point will be left hanging so that those wanting to think about it a bit more can give it some consideration, but it will be raised again in Part 4.

In the world of finance, anything which does not have monetary value, say a butterfly, a tree in a field, the pain in your leg, your local woodland, or your love of singing at the top of your voice in the shower every morning, are all simply worthless. All these things are important to people every day but have absolutely no value whatsoever in the world of finance. This is the crucial and fundamental difference between 'value' (monetary value) and 'values' (what people want and need), and this important point is something which Mark Carney concentrates on in his 2020 Reith Lectures.[5] There is naturally plenty of overlap between monetary value and human values, such as food, transport, homes etc., but equally there are many human values, like concern for the climate, that financial decision makers find very easy to ignore until commoditisation has occurred. This is precisely why a monetary value was put on carbon dioxide (CO_2) emissions, so that the financial world would have to stop ignoring then. Unless our human values can be attributed with a similar kind of arbitrary monetary value, the financial world will not be able to comprehend, judge or value them and so will continue to completely ignore them. Nevertheless, using such an abstract single monetary value of measurement still seems a strange, oversimplified and a very inhibited way of measuring things like the state of our climate, a walk in the woods, education or hospital care, unless of course you are only interested in one thing... money alone (and not what it represents), in which case it works perfectly well.

This is not the only way that the abstract concept of money affects our decisions. Once the original role of money started to disguise products and services behind an abstract number or value, it started to stretch and weaken the firm link between the real world and value. It became easier to charge 6 instead of 5, or 95 instead of 90, and money started on a track towards its second role of being used to just make more money. Initially this was only at the expense of others needing to pay more, because back then people were neither clever nor stupid enough to think that an infinite pool of fresh air could also be used to create wealth for them. However, the idea that 'money makes money' quickly caught on and under the impetuous of human greed it steered money towards a second 'money making' and 'profiteering' role. This eventually evolved into the more capitalist economy of today, with its large and powerful finance industry that concentrates solely on making money from money.

Just as monetary value and commoditisation affect our decision making, so does this second role of money, subtly shifting and twisting both our perception of value and our decisions, as shown in the simple example below.

> You are hungry and have a small amount of money with which to buy some vegetables, which you could eat raw or cook in a meal (such as nice vegetable stew) and so meet your current hunger needs. Alternatively, you could cook the vegetables and then sell the hot meal to someone else for more money and then be able to buy both vegetables and fruit much later.

This second monetary role subtly sways the emphasis away from "What is needed or what can I have now?" towards "What can I gain or make in the future?" At this point money stops being a simple carrier of value and becomes a core part of our decision making, where a 'current need' must compete against a 'potential future monetary gain'. So, what happens with the choice of "Do I buy £500,000 worth of hospital beds today or have £700,000 to spend next year?" In this way, the two different roles of money affect our decision making. Firstly, the 'carrier of value' role abstracts our decision away from any unknown human values that have not been commoditised. Secondly, the newer role of 'making more money' tempts us away from what is needed now, towards what might be gained in the future. It's no wonder our economy is struggling to tackle climate change and other important issues like long-term care. There is plenty more about this in Part 4.

Stepping back

Both finance and the economy have evolved a lot over the centuries, but our current capitalist-based mixed economy, with its dependence on growth, its complex finances and its large financial institutions, has now existed for many decades. This means that most of us were born into it. It is all we have ever known or experienced, it is the way it has always been, and so we just accept it as normal. That makes it more difficult to see what it really is. It is only by stepping back from the normality and escaping all the complexity and confusing jargon, that you can start to see what is really happening. Hopefully this chapter goes a little way in doing that.

Over the centuries, the economy and finance have changed the role of money from its humble beginnings as a carry of value to lubricate transactions, into an increasingly influential form of abstraction in our decision making. Today money subtly diverts us away from our human values towards the more important task of using our money to just make more money. This newer second role rationalises charging others a bit more, forces prices to be as high as possible, and promotes and justifies profiteering as the right thing to do. It is this need for profit that generates another barely believable business practice, 'planned obsolescence'. This is purposefully making the product less usable or less reliable, so forcing customers to buy more in future. This practice started with the light bulb industry, when sales of light bulbs started to drop. The first light bulbs were just too reliable, they hardly ever broke, so nobody ever bought new ones. Bizarrely, the financial answer was not, "Great, look at this fantastic really useful reliable product that is now available", it was "Shit, we are never going to be able to sell enough of them, lets makes it worse than it is now so it breaks easily – that's a great idea and will really be appreciated by people". Many more modern versions of this unhelpful, unintuitive, almost unbelievable practice to purposefully make something simple more difficult exist. They include selling products where you cannot change the battery (you must buy a new one when the battery dies) or purposefully slowing down computer software, making your device frustrating slow and difficult to use, until in exasperation you are forced to buy another one. This is how the need for profit and growth distorts decisions and makes life more difficult. In even worse (less legal) situations it leads to rip-off prices, cutting corners, fraud, suspicion and mistrust. In short, profit entices the selfish side of human nature to the surface, whilst simultaneously feeding our mistrust of others (they are doing this just for the money). As money operates at all levels, this applies equally to the local odd job man as to large corporate businesses. This doesn't mean they are all profiteering; it just means those who are tempted to do it are financially rewarded for it. None of this prevents the better side of human nature, nor does it prevent altruistic behaviour, charitable donations or helping people, but it does put up some very stiff opposition to those more charitable altruistic decisions and behaviours.

The role of money as a carrier of value to lubricate transactions is essential. Money itself is not the problem, money is not the "root of all evil", as is often misquoted. The original form is more correct, which says a "love of money" is the real problem. The problems come from profiteering and just using money to make money. Regardless of how good, bad, beneficial or evil the financial system is, it has become a hugely powerful influence within our capitalist economy and society. Therefore, the following chapters look at how different parts of our society cope and behave in this strange financial world and its relentless need for growth, profit and more money.

"Using money as a common measure does not mean it is common sense to measure everything with it."

10

BUSINESS AS USUAL

"Corporations have neither bodies to be punished nor souls to be condemned, they therefore do as they like."
(Edward Lord Thurlow, 1731–1806, lawyer and politician)

Since the start of the Industrial Revolution in the mid to late 1700s, businesses have flourished and thrived. The availability of coal, iron and steel allowed the development of the steam engines, which provided power on a large scale, leading to mechanised transport and the generation of electricity, which ultimately led to electric motors and lights etc. In just a few centuries, businesses and the market-driven economy have brought us through the Industrial Revolution, albeit via workhouses, the poverty of millions and several financial crashes, to produce an explosion of businesses which sell us all the modern products and services we are familiar with today. Whether they are essentials like food, clothes, medicines or phones, luxuries for comfort and entertainment like TVs, games, cosmetics and another bike, or even those things we would be better off without like kitchen appliances we never use, cheap DIY tools that don't work, another year of wasted gym membership or gambling, we are reliant on businesses to provide them. It would be reasonable to assume they exist only to provide us with these products. This chapter looks at what a business is and the role of business in society.

What is a business?

If making and providing products and services for us is the prime role of a business, then a car manufacturing business could decide to branch out and start making motor bikes as well, then mopeds, then bicycles, then metal scooters. From here it could make plastic scooters and then other plastic toys. There is nothing stopping a car manufacturer from doing this; they could choose to make almost anything, yet none of them do so. From this perspective it appears that what they produce is not the prime role of a business. Perhaps the prime role of a business is paying wages so we can pay for our food and shelter, live comfortably and prevent us from going hungry or cold, but then it is very rare for a business to voluntarily raise wages. The reasons why businesses tend not to dramatically change product lines or be over-generous with paying employees is because they are constrained and driven by finances, ultimately in the form of making profit. So, is making a profit the underlying fundamental role of a business?

Successful businesses make a profit, which allows reinvestment to buy new machines or research new technologies for new products. From the start of the Industrial Revolution, this reinvested profit has been the driving force behind the technology advancement that provides many of the real beneficial improvements. The rest of the profit is spread between paying wages, reserves for a rainy day and providing dividends or bonuses to shareholders. Even in much smaller family businesses, there is still a need to generate enough profit to support a few people or a family. An unprofitable business can be kept operating for a limited period by financial support, like loans from a bank. In a few cases, longer-term financial support may come from an altruistic source such as rich owners of football clubs that use their own money to keep afloat the club that they have supported all their life. Similarly, a family may support its own business producing the cakes, baby clothes, pottery, art or wooden ornaments etc. simply because they enjoy doing it as an activity and aren't as reliant on the profit. In these cases, does the once-profitable business stop being a business and become just a pastime, a passion or a charity that needs some financial support? In most cases, a business that is still making and selling the things we need and want, but not enough of them at a high enough price to generate a sustainable profit, will eventually die, be bought out or be taken over by a healthier business. Many would accept therefore that the underlying fundamental need and role of a business is not what it makes or sells, or who it employs and pays, but is to generate profit. Any business that is able to sell vast quantities of rubbish, at very high prices with a very low salary bill, would be considered a great business (and many would want to know the secret of how they were doing it).

During the day-to-day operation of a business, profits can be increased in four ways.

- Increasing prices.
- Paying employees less.
- Selling more.
- Reducing costs.

Increasing the sale price is easily achieved and businesses will do this whenever possible, especially if competitors' prices will allow it, and to this end some businesses have occasionally been accused of price fixing between themselves for their mutual benefit. There is also the urge to always sell a bit less product for a slightly higher price, as the Victorian shopkeepers did. It still happens today when chocolate bars decrease in size, but not price. However, in a competitive market both these methods are constrained. Paying employees less may be another dream situation but in practical terms it is also not an easy option. Employees will leave to find other jobs and those who remain will become demotivated. This leaves 'selling more' and 'reducing costs' and it is these two areas, where businesses apply a lot of time and effort, that are considered next.

Selling more

We are all very aware of the method used to promote sales. It is those annoying persuasive things that our favourite TV, radio and videos keep interrupting (I know it is supposed to be the other way around, but it does sometimes feel like the programmes are interrupting the adverts). Adverts must be persuasive and influential, as their sole purpose is to persuade more people to buy more things. This is aided by that magical word 'improved' and its close relatives 'new', 'upgraded', 'latest model' or 'next generation' products. Adverts don't have to prove that the product will make things better, they don't have to prove we need them, they only need to make us think, believe or feel that we do. Adverts don't sell a product; they only sell a dream or a hope. Buy this breakfast cereal and your children will behave like angels all morning, buy this time-saving product and you will have time for a full and exciting social life, buy this car and you will be able to spend all week driving the most scenic roads in Europe and not stuck crawling along the M4 five days a week. Adverts use a collection of enticing messages:

- Escape your current lifestyle, you deserve it, treat yourself and enjoy it.
- This will save you time and make things easier for you.
- This product gives you more, don't accept less.

Collectively and in the broadest possible sense, these messages tell us to want more (be selfish), do less (be lazy), have more (be greedy). Before you object too much to yet another crude oversimplification, there are of course adverts for exercise machines, trainers, gyms, health foods and drinks etc. which do encourage a healthier lifestyle, but on balance (and why I purposefully said "in the broadest possible sense") there is encouragement from adverts to want more and do less. It is under this strong advertising influence that our behaviours change and become re-normalised. A recent example of this is the obesity problem, which can be viewed as going from rationing to obesity over two generations – a shocking way of looking at it.

Reducing costs

This section describes some of the bigger cost-saving methods a business can use, before the next section explains some of the subtler, smaller, continual attempts to save money under the label of 'efficiency savings'.

Machines and technology

From the beginning of the Industrial Revolution, businesses have reduced costs by developing and using machines and new technology to replace the human workforce. Although machines have running, maintenance and repair costs, they do not need to be paid each month so often prove to be both cheaper and more reliable than people. They can also do things that people simply can't, such as lifting heavy objects or manufacturing computer chips, which is explored further in the next chapter.

Customer service

Reducing the number of employees is not limited to the manufacturing industries. Many businesses replace relatively expensive customer service employees with a collection of automated lines, websites full of FAQ (frequently asked questions) pages and plenty of 'do-it-yourself' online processes. All these cost-saving changes (not improvements) turn a personal, helpful, knowledgeable customer service into a much more frustrating self-service, where the burden has been passed on to us. It seems very strange that so many calls are met with the words "Your call is important to us" and yet so few seem to have enough employees to answer it. I'm just glad that the emergency services don't have similarly high business standards of customer service for their important calls. The opposing view says that without good customer service a business could not survive, but there is a flaw in this opinion. Ironically, pre-purchase customer service, otherwise known as the 'sales department' always seems to have people available to help and it is only after a sale, when the profit has already been made, that things become more difficult. A business can survive without good post-sale customer service and returning custom, provided its adverts can encourage enough new customers to replace the disappointed ones. Within business, there is very little room for anything that does not directly help to generate profit.

Training

Most businesses put a lot of emphasis on training, whether this is due to law, skills and education, precautions against litigation or just good intentions. Training is both necessary and beneficial. Inevitably this leads to a lot of training courses, which like most things in business must be done at relatively low cost. The cheapest forms of training are online and classroom-based courses, the worst of which involve listening to the trainer do little more than simply read the words from the presentation slides. If that is all they are going to do, just send me the words – I can read too! Even when the trainer is more skilled, much more engaging, with stories and examples that are a joy to listen to, this type of classroom training has a flaw, which is best encapsulated by the following observation by Confucius:

> **I hear and I forget.**
> **I see and I remember.**
> **I do and I understand.**
> **I reflect and I learn.**

Reducing training to its cheapest, most cost-effective form of just listening or watching is perfectly acceptable to raise some new awareness or provide some initial familiarisation, but beyond this it quickly strays into the realms of listening then forgetting and it is of very limited practical benefit. It does however provide a very quick and cheap way to say training has been completed and to 'tick a box'. This is the procedural, theoretical, abstract approach to training. Training is needed, training has been provided, everything will now work exactly as expected. The reality is different. In a month or two many will forget they even had this type of dull training. They will be no more capable, knowledgeable or informed than they were before, an outcome far removed from the original intention (any sense of déjà vu here?). It is comforting to know that some Health and Safety roles, which have high levels of legal responsibility over people's safety, must be filled by a 'competent person'. It is much less comforting to know that an untrained incompetent person can apparently be turned into a trained competent person by spending two caffeine-fuelled days listening to an uninspiring verbal drone. I'm just glad that airline pilots, train drivers and electricians are not trained to be competent in this way. Becoming a truly competent person needs lots of real practical experience and local knowledge, not just a set of verbal or written information. Conversely (and as another aside) words are free and easy to produce, so selling words alone can be very profitable. This explains the growth of the consultancy, advice and training industry, which all sell words for profit with almost zero risk or consequences, which is nice work if you can get it.

Efficiency

In addition to these large cost-cutting methods, costs can be reduced by the day-to-day operation of the business becoming more efficient. Below are some very brief descriptions of common efficiency improvements (or changes?).

Stock levels

Buying and holding materials, parts and stock is a way of tying up or wasting money that could be invested to make more money. Financially it would be more efficient to buy and hold less stock and only buy when needed. However, the consequences of not having enough material or parts readily available are a nightmare for an engineering team. A shortage of items creates delays at best, but may lead to different items being used, retesting or design changes.

Component cost

Reducing the production cost of a product can be achieved by replacing expensive components with similar cheaper ones. The key word here is "similar" because any electrical, material or performance change could affect reliability or result in expensive design changes and retesting, putting a lot of extra effort on the design and quality teams.

Processes

Wherever people's work cannot be easily replaced by a machine, a business will try to find ways to make employees work more efficiently, by introducing all those super-efficient and perfect processes discussed earlier. As our work becomes more procedural, we shift away from thinking, helpful, flexible, innovative, but inherently unreliable, 'personal', to much more efficient, unthinking, perfect, process-following, machine-like 'human resources'.

Quality assurance (QA)

The need to maintain (dare I say improve?) quality often goes against this drive for efficiency. The extra checks, recording, testing, reviewing etc. all take time and effort, so can reduce efficiency. That is why good quality assurance (QA) needs to be pragmatic and practical. I have met some very pragmatic, very helpful, very practical QA people who are willing to look at the work, records and evidence to assess where it fulfils the quality criteria and where it doesn't. In other words, they use their common sense to judge whether things have been done as intended and their attitude is to help, support and guide you to produce a good product. This is an efficient, practical and helpful way to provide QA. Unfortunately (in my experience at least) this type of efficient, pragmatic QA person is quite rare. Much like their Health and Safety colleagues mentioned earlier, it is more common that they are the finger-pointing, less than helpful, unthinking process slaves, who prefer to highlight that "You haven't recorded the changes you have made to your record of the 'review of the design changes', which were reviewed and recorded in the previous 'design review' based on your initial record and review of actual design change proposal" (you might need to read that a few times to understand it). Equally they may state something like "This document is not in the correct format and font" even though it clearly contains all the necessary information and evidence, in a clear and structured way. These types of people are either unwilling or unable to do the real work, but, in total ignorance of the real problems, are somehow given authority to say whether other people's work has been done correctly. It is this slave-like adherence to written process, generating extra obstacles and difficulties, which doesn't help efficiency one bit.

Coping with contradiction

Hopefully these few brief descriptions highlight some of the many contradictions that exist within businesses, and they can be distilled down to this:

- Cost of customer service wages **versus** providing customer service.
- Cost of training **versus** need for training.
- Cost of holding stock **versus** delays making products.
- Cost of components **versus** design, test, performance and reliability.

- Just doing what is needed (process) **versus** unreliable people.
- Quality **versus** time and effort.

Adding a few more similar, and hopefully recognisable, contradictions gives:

- Quickest time **versus** highest quality.
- Machine-like efficiency **versus** new ideas and innovation.
- Lowest price **versus** best product.
- Low wages **versus** motivating employees.

In fact, the world of business is full of contradictions and this condensed list helps to highlight that the main sources of these contradictions are time and money. The common view of this financial pressure and influence is that it encourages, motivates and drives high performance, and the essence of this is true, but that is only the good side. The other less beneficial side is that it is also the source of constant contradiction and tension within businesses. Businesses sit in an unenviable position, bridging between two very different worlds. On one side is the real physical world occupied by employees, customers, products, services, delays, failures, problems and the laws of physics. On the other side are executives, directors, board rooms, profits, cost base, order intake, shareholders and that unstable, abstract, incomprehensible world of finance. Instinctively, this seems like a precarious position to reside and perhaps explains why the world of business is often considered to be 'difficult', 'volatile' or 'cutthroat'.

Stuck in the middle of this precarious bridge between these two different worlds are the managers, for whom being awash with contradictions makes it difficult to even discuss things without looking like a bit of an idiot or a liar. For example, if a manager said "All we need to do is increase productivity, whilst reducing spend, at the same time as introducing changes to the design without it affecting the reliability" people would simply laugh at them. It sounds impossible because it is impossible. So to overcome this problem, managers use 'business speak', which turns the previous ludicrous suggestion into "We need to optimise output, utilising effective cost-management systems in parallel with continual capability and quality improvements". This is much easier to agree with and accept, but only if you were totally ignorant of the fact that this is just meaningless tripe and instead of making someone look like an idiot, it now makes them look like a pretentious idiot. This type of business speak hides the reality; it is another form of abstraction that inhibits both our understanding of the real situation and our common sense. It leaves us wide open to making a bad decision, such as thinking that a laughable, impossible suggestion is now perfectly reasonable and possible. I described my short 5-year stint in a management role as needing the ability to say two contradictory things in the same sentence and make it sound believable. This was only one of the reasons that I was not a particularly good manager and stopped doing it. However, a large proportion of professional managers do rely on and continually regurgitate this type of meaningless tripe an awful lot of the time. As explained in the 'Meetings' section of WORDS chapter (Chapter 1), these people learn that clear statements are easy to question or challenge and so it is much easier to use meaningless, empty statements that people find hard to disagree with. Words are ambiguous enough on their own, without these people purposefully making the situation worse and strengthening the reputation of management as being just a talking shop. As a rule of thumb, the less understanding, experience and control a manager has of the situation, the more business speak they use to cover up their own shortcomings and inability to explain clearly. Business efficiency is not the result of this puerile business speak, more monitoring, more performance indicators, more data collection or yet more processes. Hopefully this book will help to make all this nonsense just a bit less believable and acceptable in future. Remember we are not very good robots and true efficiency comes from the understanding, knowledge and experience of people.

Trapped in a maze

The constant financial pressures within the competitive, volatile, professional, efficient world of business creates incentives to continually cuts costs, save time, improve quality and reliability, sell more and be more efficient. This is a breeding ground for changes and solutions that are nearly always described as "initiatives", "teamwork" or "improvement". However, the conflicting and contradictory needs and aims of the different parts of larger businesses means that the changes which are beneficial for one area are often detrimental to other areas.

It is simply not possible to optimise all or even any of them and the best that is both theoretically and practically possible is a compromised centre ground. However, in an environment where everyone is expected to achieve optimal performance, maximum efficiency and continual improvement (there is that awful phrase again), any suggestion of being satisfied with a compromised centre ground is ridiculed, frowned upon and rarely acceptable ("this person does not want to improve and is satisfied with mediocrity") and so the never-ending attempts to escape these internal contradictions, conflicts and frustrations continue.

If only they could see the inescapable real-world maze they are trapped in, where change after continual change leads right back to where they started, where creating a quick navigation route through the maze for one group only produces blockages and obstructions for others, and where the incessant generation of processes and route maps through this maze only leads to dead ends and wrong turns. I once heard this described as "Company policy is obstructing company policy". If only they were aware that a new glossy name, logo, label or buzzword does not change the amount of work that needs to be done or the amount of real, practical problems to be overcome. If only they could see the reality that in an environment of contradiction, 'acceptably good' is about as optimal as the real world will let you get. If only they could recognise that 'reasonably good' is actually very difficult to improve, instead of ridiculing the suggestion that change is not necessary or could even make things worse. If only they could recognise that none of their words, opinions or repeated attempts to 'continually improve' will win against the complexity, constraints and reality of the real world and the law of diminishing returns. It seems like more and more people prefer to keep themselves busy fighting this unwinnable battle, highlighting more areas of change and improvement, suggesting more ways to be a few percent more efficient, by promoting ever more complicated and time-consuming methods of monitoring and recording metrics. All of which leaves fewer people and less time available to do the actual work, something more practical and helpful than just monitoring and recording. However, all this extra effort does enable them to accurately monitor all the work that isn't being done and that of course provides plenty more opportunities to talk more garbage and think of more changes, more information to record and more process improvements, which can all make things better. It can be a full-time job! All these futile attempts at improvement only help to give the impression that they are controlling the situation or coping with the contradictions, when it is much more likely that the real situation (the lack of sales, technical problems or time delays) are actually controlling them.

Food for thought

Like so many other subjects, the whole subject of business is incredibly complex, and it must be reiterated that a few more cynical pages cannot pretend to provide the full picture or solve any problems. However, hopefully they do provide some more food for thought and highlight how financial pressures create contradictions with the real physical world, cause internal conflicts within businesses and influence our behaviour. Just as adverts encourage us to want more and more, spending a lot of time within this type of business environment makes us slightly more prone to do some of the following:

- Use empty, bland language to abstract and hide real problems.
- Be more machine-like, switch off and just rely on processes and procedures.
- Resort to trivial 'tick box' exercises to claim tasks are done.
- Continually change things in the hunt for tiny improvements.
- Focus our use of time and money on our own purposes instead of helping others.

Little by little, what is necessary, promoted and acceptable in businesses and finance is nudging our own behaviours in the same direction, to the extent that our own personal human success is now measured in business terms (not in more human terms as indicated in brackets).

- How much money you have (not how nice you are).
- The things you have got, own or done (not what you have provided to others).
- How much you can gain (not how much you help others).

The simple phrase "You're smart, why aren't you rich?" encapsulates this modern attitude, which inherently assumes the main purpose in human life is to be rich, the same underlying principle of both business and finance. However, it is also these same financial pressures on businesses that have continually driven and provided many of the hugely beneficial technology advancements that our society enjoys. This is one of the main arguments why our society needs to have profit-driven businesses and this very important point should not be forgotten, as it is raised again in Part 4.

"Whilst businesses promote innovation, teamwork and flexibility, most work is manacled and constrained by rigid process and contradiction."

11

WHO DECIDES?

"Technology is a useful servant, but a dangerous master."
(Christian Lous Lange, 1869–1938, Nobel Peace Prize winner)

From the beginning of the Stone Age when the first flint stones were used as cutting tools, the ingenuity of humans has developed increasingly complex tools and machines to help us. Whether this was ploughs for farming, ways to transport water, the use of candles and dripping water to measure time, using fire beacons to communicate and produce straight lines over huge distances or using furnaces to help bend metal, they were all developed with the aim of making life better and easier for people. Centuries of technological advances in tools, machines and science brought us into the Industrial Revolution, when further inventions such as radio, light bulbs, cars, batteries and washing machines etc. all helped to make our lives easier and better.

However, not everyone was fully behind this technological advance. Some thought that some technologies would destroy certain essential skills, in the way that farming destroyed the skill to hunt and industrialised farming destroyed the skill to grow our own food. Some even thought that the introduction of industrial ink manufacturing would destroy people's ability to make ink and so prevent people from writing. Concerns like these may have been valid at the time, especially for grumpy old people who are less welcoming of change and believe "it's not the way things should be". Generally, however, all these advances helped us, and we certainly didn't go short of food or stop writing. We simply didn't need those skills any longer.

A modern version of this apprehension is the opinion that overuse of computing will eventually lead to a reduction in the ability to write with pen and paper. This prediction may become true eventually, but only because that skill or ability will no longer be needed. Perhaps voice recognition technology will write and translate for us when we speak, but only once the problems highlighted in the BBC Scotland comedy sketch "Voice activated elevator" are solved and automated voice recognition phone lines become more reliable.[1] In hindsight, these fears about the progression of technology seem mildly amusing and they definitely don't stop or hinder further technological progress. Today, there are very few people who would want to stop using ballpoint pens, cars, phones, TVs, washing machines, lawn mowers, hair driers or computers. As claimed in the IMPROVEMENT chapter (Chapter 3), it is these technological advances that genuinely provide the real improvements that benefit people's lives.

The Industrial Age

The beginning of the Industrial Age marked an important change in the use of machines. As they started to exceed the power, speed and endurance of people and other animals, they could work harder and longer, whilst complaining and costing less. The development of machines was now for the benefit of factories and production lines and not solely for the benefit of people. Very quickly, machines took over much of our physical work and people were left to find other, more intelligent types of work, such as operating and repairing machines or becoming salespeople to interact with customers, to sell the large supplies of cheaper products that the machines now made.

As this trend continued, more accurate machines could replace the more skilful crafts and trades, such as knitting, pottery, carpentry etc., resulting in more career changes. Importantly, these more accurate machines could also be used to make precision parts for even more complex and accurate machines and, relatively quickly, machines also overtook our ability to do things accurately and precisely. Initially via complex arrangements of cogs in clockwork movements, followed by various primitive mechanical calculating machines, through to the pivotal and complex electrical Bombe machine designed by Alan Turing, which was used to crack the German Enigma code in the Second World War, machines were designed to do increasingly complex tasks. Ultimately this led to the advent of the computer. Therefore, by the end of the Industrial Age, but before the advent of the computer, machines had already overtaken humans and animals in terms of:

- Power
- Endurance
- Speed
- Reliability
- Accuracy

Over a couple of centuries, this advancement of technology replaced skilled workers with better and better machines. This was not wrong, and more was to follow. After the Industrial Revolution the next generation of machines, namely computers, were now set to overtake the human capabilities of:

- Memory (information storage)
- Analysis
- Basic decision making

Computers

Since the advent of the computer, machines have become capable of some intelligent work previously reserved for the cognitive abilities of people, like storing, retrieving and analysing information. Everything this amazing box of micro-electronics does is the result of long, complicated lists of instructions, previously called computer programs or procedures but more recently called code or software. Without software, computers do nothing. It is the software that allows computers to follow very complex procedures very quickly, making decisions based on lots of information, carrying out different actions, in very much the same way people do. This means that computers now control very precise, complex machines autonomously all day, every day, 24/7, without human intervention, such as those used in car manufacturing production lines.

This level of automation, sophistication and control is becoming increasingly obvious in our daily lives, as we witness the advent of driverless cars. Driving is a very complex task which combines, vision, judgement, perspective, potential dangers, self-protection, the safety and awareness of other road users, the simultaneous use of multiple controls and perhaps even some degree of politeness to other road users. The ability to drive takes people several weeks, months or even years to do well and, for many people, driving a car may be the most complicated control of a machine that they experience in their lifetime, yet many think they can do it one-handed, whilst using their phone and forgetting to indicate. The driverless car machine will soon do all this for itself, including using both the phone and the indicators. Driverless cars will ultimately make driving both easier and safer for us all (as most car accidents are caused by human error and distracted drivers). They will allow us to safely use our phone, read a book, work or even drink alcohol whilst being driven. Ultimately, like many other technology advancements, it will make our lives better. It will lead to more career changes, with drivers of taxis, white vans and lorries amongst those soon to be looking for different jobs, and eventually we will lose the skill of driving.

Artificial intelligence

Two of the more recent trends in technology advancement and the evolution of machines are nano-machines and artificial intelligence (or AI). The miniaturisation and accuracy of machines has developed to the point where we can now manufacture simple nano-machines which are less than 10 millionths of a metre (or 1/100 of a millimetre) in size. This is only mentioned for interest and completeness, as this section concentrates on the revelation in computer software known as AI or 'neural networks'. These greatly increase the ability of computers to make more subjective judgements, such as those needed to play complex strategic games. The AI software inside Google's DeepMind AlphaGo can already beat world champions at the traditional Chinese strategy game Go.[2] This type of AI algorithm can learn by itself, by repeatedly trying something over and over again, using some external confirmation that it is right or wrong, be that from a human, the real world or a game score, in exactly the same way that a child or person would learn. The creation of these neural networks within computer software is an amazing feat of scientific and engineering ingenuity and will ultimately produce many benefits for people and industry alike.

At the time of writing, AI is already being used to help to spot and diagnose cancer from scans and pictures,[3] but this will only be the start. Relatively soon, AI will be used to do many of the more subjective, intelligent jobs that machines are not yet able to do, and then more skilled people will need to find different types of jobs. These and many other aspects of AI are explored by Professor Stuart Russell in the 2021 Reith Lectures.[4] Some experts suggest that the care sector (caring, interacting and helping people in need) is one area of work that is unlikely to be overtaken by AI technology soon. It is likely to be a growth area for human employment in future, but this has its own affordability problems, which are explored further in Part 4. For the moment, however, AI is still in its infancy, and it is still relatively difficult for AI to do something a 3-year-old child is capable of, reliably recognising whether a picture contains a dog or a cat.

As with most things in the real world, AI does not give us something for nothing. There is a problem that the AI experts are acutely aware of and are already actively trying to research and solve. Just as it is impossible to know how a person learns or decides something inside their brain, it is equally impossible to know how an AI algorithm learns or decides which moves to make to win the game. Whilst we can at least ask a person about their reasoning and decision, it is categorically impossible for us to understand the context, criteria, judgements or reasoning behind any AI decision or answer. We have no idea how these phenomenal neural networks produce very good and sometimes very bad answers. The experts are therefore trying to work out how we can obtain an insight or understanding of the criteria, judgements and decisions of AI. They want to make AI decisions more transparent to us. This is very different from more traditional styles of computer software (or code), where, given enough time and effort, people can explicitly check, diagnose, debug, fix and fully understand each and every instruction, decision, operation, result and mistake of the software, if needed.

The BINFORMATION chapter (Chapter 5) attempted to explain how our traditional use of computers changes our relationship with information. As the information we are presented with and use is more abstracted, we have less context and less understanding of it. In a similar, way using

AI changes our relationship with judgements and decisions, as all the important criteria, choices and context that were used in the decision are now completely removed, hidden or abstracted away. We are left with a totally abstract decision or judgement, with no way of knowing if it is good or bad. When AI fails to recognise a dog in photograph, our common sense says "Ha – you got it wrong", but in more abstract situations, like a move in a strategic game, there is no way of knowing if a particular move is a very good match winner or a horrendous game loser. We have absolutely no way of knowing, understanding or checking whether an AI decision is good or bad. This makes AI decisions a pure form of BINFORMATION, where all possible context, explanation, criteria, reasoning, judgement and understanding are removed. The AI answer could be better than any human could achieve or the worst possible thing to do, but we simply have no way of knowing, understanding or judging. We have nothing but blind trust in the decision. Just for completeness and context, we are already losing our ability to fully understand how these wonderfully complex machines (computers) work and operate, as demonstrated every time the expert computer engineer offers you the solution to just "switch it off and on again". If we don't fully understand the operation, then it also becomes difficult (or impossible) to fully control it.

A tipping point

This brief history of machines brings us right up to the current day. For a few hundred years we have been building machines that exceed our own capabilities, for the benefit of people, industry and business, and it has worked incredibly well. Initially, whilst machines were only overtaking our physical abilities of power, speed, endurance and accuracy, they were still truly under our control and slavishly did what people designed them to do. However, since the advent of the computer this balance seems to have shifted slightly and to some extent people are now controlled by the machine, for the benefit of the machine. The machine is becoming the master. We are expected to do what the computer wants, how it wants it and when it wants it, such as:

- We follow machine instructions.
- We must wait for the machine to 'update' itself (it does not wait for us).

- We must do things the way the machine wants.
- We can only choose from the options the machine offers.
- Computer tools dictate what data we record and in what format we see it.

Today, the unquestionable technical efficiency, performance and capability of modern-day computing is tainted by the practical, everyday frustrations of continual updates, sign-ins, robot checks, crashes, reboots, incorrect data formats, changes and non-existent links etc. These irritations raise the question whether the machine is working for me or whether I'm waiting for, working for, coping with and following the instructions and demands of the machine. I certainly don't ask for updates, and I categorically do not want all my personal options to be reset, so that I'm then forced to set them all up yet again following every bloody update. It feels like I'm swimming against the tide of what the computer wants (or more accurately, what the computer software company wants). It is like I'm gradually becoming a slave to a more dominant machine that always gets its own way. When accessing some online accounts, I must prove that "I'm not a robot". I already know that I am not a robot, the time and effort I spend doing this is little puzzle is quite clearly not for my benefit and is blatantly for the benefit of the computer.

Although computers are continuing the role of machines to make our lives easier, modern computers expect more from us. The increasing myriad of software applications that need us to conform to their prescriptive, repetitive, procedural demands is for their benefit, not ours. Over several decades the accumulative effect of all this is to nudge, encourage or (in my case) drag people to conform to a more machine-like behaviour and begin to just accept this as normal and correct. Perhaps my opinion that machines are there to help people and not the other way round is becoming outdated and old fashioned? As indicated in Part 2, me and most other people are not very good at behaving like machines, so the more we are forced to continue conforming to the demands of the machine, the more uncomfortable, irritating, tedious and frustrating our lives seem to become.

To some extent we already blindly accept that the computer is in control. We already have the sentiment that "The computer told me this, so it must be right" or "The computer won't let me". In future, as the use of AI increases and this acceptance of computer control and answers continues, how much will we really understand about the information, reasoning, judgements and decisions that computers provide? Who or what is really going to decide and how? Since the start of human evolution people have been in control of decision making, choices and the subsequent actions. These decisions have not always been made with the best intentions and it is valid to say that many decisions are badly made or wrong, because of false logic, chasing selfish goals or putting profit before people etc. However, at least these human decisions can be questioned or investigated and, more importantly, explained and justified by those who made them. This is very important if you are trying to understand how and why a subjective judgement was made. If necessary, the decision makers can even be held to account and punished. However, when AI starts to make judgements and decisions on our behalf, all this will be lost. It will not be possible to assess or judge how good or bad, right or wrong, valid, biased or reasonable each decision is. Surely that is a tipping point in human evolution.

The future

For those starting to feel uncomfortable with these latest technology advancements, be reassured that you are just the latest in the long line of people saying, "This is not the way things should be". You are only concerned about the uncertain future and a fear that the worst could happen (which is perhaps not helped in any way by the content of this book?). You are not alone; some AI experts are also genuinely concerned whether AI could lead to a dominance of machines or even the destruction of humans.[5] In the same way that we can look back and smile at the unfounded pessimism of those who thought we would starve or be unable to write, future generations will probably find today's concerns equally amusing. It is incredibly difficult (or impossible) to argue against the facts, that the machines and tools we have today are for our benefit and make life easier, and very few people would argue that we should halt or reverse technology advancement or stop using our phones. As all previous technology advancements have done, AI will also continue to provide great benefits to a lot of people, help businesses and continue to alter people's jobs and roles in society, whether they like it or not. All this has been going on for centuries and is completely acceptable, so why has the subject been raised here?

There is a fundamental difference between all the historical technological advances and the advent of AI. Until now, machines have only helped us physically, but all reasoning, judgements and decisions have essentially remained human (even if computers sometimes prevent us). The next set of human skills that are going to be overtaken or replaced are our understanding, judgement, complex decision making and reasoning. Is this really the next set of skills we want to lose or hand over? Without any understanding, context, criteria or reasoning, how will we know if AI judgements and decisions are good or bad, right or wrong? AI will provide huge benefits across a wide range of applications, but, just as computers can abstract information and change our relationship with it, AI could equally abstract our understanding, judgements, reasoning and decisions. That is a very dangerous situation to be in and again there is a bit more on this in Part 4.

The message here is not to stop using machines, computers or AI, but, as our real world is only shaped by the judgements, decisions and physical actions of people and machines, then understanding the reasons, criteria and judgement behind those decisions is both critical and essential. In future, how will decisions be made and by whom?

"The abstraction of information weakens understanding, the abstraction of judgement and reasoning is just incomprehensible."

12

THE SEWER SYSTEM

*"Most of the dishonest lawyers are the product of
dishonest clients, the demand creates the supply."*
(Morris Salem, 1873–1922, lawyer and author)

Although it is not clear from the title, the subject of this chapter is the legal system, which sets and enforces the laws and rules we live by. It is therefore very influential and it is just as important to a civilised society as a good sewer system. Unlike much of the original sewer system, which is now 100–150 years old, the legal system has evolved a lot since its dubious beginnings and the era of judging people to be guilty of witchcraft for steadfastly refusing to drown. Things have got a lot better since then. Despite a few blatant miscarriages of justice, an occasional politically swayed outcome and the protection of friends in high places, overall, the legal system can claim to be doing a reasonably good job of keeping law and order, just as businesses can claim to be doing a good job of providing us with the things we need and further technological advancements. Despite this, the legal system is not perfect, so in-keeping with the recognisable pattern of previous chapters, it is these less than perfect parts of the legal system that are considered.

True motives

It is easy to highlight some of the common practical problems that we experience with lawyers, such as the slow, time-consuming and expensive nature of their work. Getting paid very well for each hour of work or letter written provides financial rewards them for being slower and very little incentive for them to speed up. The extreme case of Jennens vs Jennens was a family dispute over an unsigned will for an immense fortune.[1] It was fought for 126 years from 1789 to 1915, resulting in the entire inheritance estate being spent on the lawyer's fees and the family ending up with nothing. Although this was as much the fault of the feuding family as the lawyers, it does highlight the lack of incentive for lawyers to resolve issues quickly whilst they are being paid. More recently, a friend from university was so incensed by the slow progress of their divorce and the mounting cost of all the letters, that he went to his solicitor's office, only to discover that his wife's solicitor worked a few doors down the corridor.

I know there is a need to record things formally in legal cases, but this at least raises a few suspicions, concerns or questions on their true motives. Is it to help their clients and customers receive justice and settlement or is it just to earn and profit as much as possible? Although lawyers should be paid for their legal services, until recently they were not allowed any direct financial gain from judicial judgments or to receive a share of any financial settlements. It was only when the Criminal Law Act of 1967 decriminalised both 'maintenance' (essentially meddling in others' legal affairs when they don't affect you) and 'champerty' (similar but also getting a share of any proceeds) that things changed. The emphasis shifted from independent lawyers who help people achieve justice for fixed payment, towards lawyers who encourage people to take more financial claims to court and get a direct share of any financial winnings.

Blame and claim

Fast forward a few decades to the present day and we now have a justice system that aggressively promotes a "no win, no fee" and "where there's blame, there's a claim" culture, in the form of adverts in hospitals and claims against employers, schools, hospitals and councils. Whilst some of these may be valid claims of real negligence, such as when a building collapses, the majority are little more than opportunistic attempts to claim large sums of money from an accident or mishap, where the person was a bit lazy, distracted or careless. Claims can be made against loose kerb stones, faulty ladders, loose wiring or poor flooring and some or many may think "and rightly so", but to put this into some perspective, this results in the need to check and monitor every kerb stone, every pothole, every ladder, every floor tile, every electrical appliance, every chair, desk, shelf and cupboard etc. It is an immense task and simply impossible in any real practical sense. If you think this is a false statement, try an experiment at home. Everyone in the house needs to live for one month without any kind of accident occurring, no stubbed toes, no spillages, no trips or falls, no cuts or grazes, no burns, no stepping on objects on the floor, no dropping things, no breaking anything, nothing falling out of cupboards, no bumping into people etc. Then if an accident does occur at home, all you need to do is write down a few choice words in the back of a notebook, call it a process, tell people to read it and it will magically stop the accident from ever happening again. These are the conditions that businesses, hospitals, schools and other organisations are attempting to work under and, if they don't, a claim can be made against them.

Is there not some level of common sense that says people can be self-aware and cautious enough to protect themselves from the type of personal accident that is now called "someone else's negligence"? In the three hypothetical situations below, it is quite possible for the person making the claim to be perfectly capable of doing more difficult, riskier activities in their own time.

- The person claiming against a loose kerb stone will happily walk on rocky hillside paths in the countryside.
- The person claiming against a faulty ladder at work will clean gutters at home without a harness or without checking a ladder first.
- The person claiming against poor flooring might have floor coverings in a worse condition at home.

What makes these competent people, who are specifically chosen and employed for their experience, capabilities, intelligence and ability to do the job, suddenly become idiotic imbeciles the moment they enter the workplace? The moment they step through the work entrance they become incapable of doing the simplest of things like carrying and lifting, climbing ladders, using tools or even just walking around without tripping over or bumping into things. They must first be trained, told how to do it or given written instructions. Perhaps they do remain fully competent and capable of doing these things, but are just encouraged and incentivised to make large amounts of money by claiming that they weren't taught, told or trained how to do it properly? If any of this is true, then it is a very large step away from the role of the legal system to provide justice for the benefit of all and it is a very large step towards a greedy profit-making legal business, willing to blame anyone, for anything, for cash. It is the litigation culture we are familiar with today.

Protection by process

The increasing levels of litigation claims paid by various organisations, like businesses, hospitals and schools, means they will naturally try to protect themselves against such claims. If someone is going to claim against a broken ladder, then they must prove that all the ladders are regularly checked. They must implement and correctly follow a valid ladder-checking process, so they are not considered to be negligent. This needs to be repeated for the immense number of items and situations that any accident-prone person might encounter in their daily work, which, expressed like this, shows just how utterly ridiculous and impossible it is. These types of process are not introduced because they are useful or beneficial in their own right, but as a kind of defence against claims. They naturally join forces with the cost-reducing and efficiency processes from the BUSINESS chapter (Chapter 10), to create the PROCESS PIT described in Chapter 6.

However, there is an important difference between these two types of processes. The cost-saving and efficiency processes act in such a way that there are no related or further consequences (engineers call this 'open-loop'). On the contrary, once the 'legal protection' processes have been implemented, they immediately provide a second method by which the legal system can make a claim. They can claim if there is no process, but, once in place, they can also claim if the process isn't followed properly. The more processes there are, the easier it is to prove non-compliance against one of them, so the more claims are made and so the more processes are put in place to protect against claims, further increasing the likelihood one is being followed incorrectly. This is not 'open-loop', it is a self-feeding 'closed-loop'. As explained in the FEEDBACK chapter (Chapter 2), wherever a 'closed-loop' system exists there are three possibilities: a well-designed stable feedback control system (as in engineering), instability and continual oscillation, or continual unlimited decay or growth in one direction (like microphone feedback). Here the closed-loop effect is always pushing in the same direction and so constantly creates the ever-more legal protection Health and Safety processes.

The litigation part of the legal system is caught in a never-ending, highly profitable, self-feeding loop, which is a great financial benefit to lawyers and an enormous 'pain in the arse' to many businesses and employees. Large numbers of people are forced to waste huge amounts of time and effort, doing something which neither works nor has real benefit. The situation is actually worse than this, as there is also an amplification involved (in engineering terms the 'loop' contains a 'gain' factor). The more times litigation claims are seen as financially profitable, the more people will want to start making claims or become litigation lawyers themselves, so amplifying and speeding up the effect further. If you don't think this is correct, whilst the number of police officers has remained relatively steady between 2006 to 2022 at around 140,000 (with a small dip between 2012 and 2020),[2] the number of practising solicitors has increased dramatically, tripling between 1980 and 2011,[3] with similar increases between 2012 and 2022 and reports of maximum numbers in several more recent online sources. They must be getting their work from somewhere. Just as I suggested that the financial system is unstable, I also believe that this financially driven, litigation arm of the legal system is trapped in an unstable, ever-growing loop that increasingly affects us all. From this perspective, the existence of an endlessly growing litigation loop might not seem sensible, but, as explained in Part 2, this litigation behaviour is already becoming accepted and normalised, and is already viewed as correct by many.

Pointing fingers

As litigation culture becomes normalised and more people see the financial rewards of pointing fingers and blaming others when things go wrong, more will be tempted to do the same, in worse cases exaggerating or even falsifying claims. How many people would really make claims against their hospital, school or business if they were not enticed by four, five or six figure cash rewards? Without this financial temptation, how many people would be willing to accept that an accident was mainly due to their own human fallibility and was not really the result of a negligent lack of a process?

It seems fundamentally wrong that the hospital staff who work hard to save your life or aid your recovery can then be blamed for not doing things quite right. These NHS staff are some of the least selfish people, they are overworked, many are underpaid, and they are trying to help you through a difficult situation that is not in any way their fault. What part of common sense says you can then blame them for sometimes not quite following a process precisely? To me this just seems incomprehensible. I think a more common-sense approach is to ask the following question: "Are you in a worse situation after their help or treatment than you would have been without any of their help or treatment at all?" Only if the answer to this question is YES has your situation been made worse by their intervention and only then would you have some sort of claim against those trying to help. This litigation culture, this sense that you can be blamed or sued, creates a type of deterrent against offering to help others. Every first aid course I've been on in the last 15 years, someone (not me) has asked the question "Can I be sued for giving first aid?" In all honesty, it is a rather sad situation to question whether you can be blamed for trying to save a life or help someone.

Little shits and big arseholes

The first time I became aware of this type of lawful injustice was in a martial arts lesson, when someone training started to gloat about their (fake) whiplash claim. The contradiction of claiming for whiplash injury, whilst openly fighting people in funny white suits, led to the conclusion that it was pure dishonest, selfish greed. Unfortunately, being much younger at the time and not yet in my "SAY IT ALL" phase of life, I did not say anything, but I did dwell on this disturbing compensation claim for a while, until the crude collection of thoughts coalesced into the poem or song lyrics below, which then ultimately led to the unusual title of this chapter.

THROW THE SUE-ERS IN THE SEWERS

I've heard some words that sound absurd,
There's cash to be had, when you trip on a kerb,
Whether distracted or using your phone,
Take no blame at all, the fault's not your own.

(CHORUS)
Throw the sue-ers in the sewers, it's where they belong,
For blaming others, for their own wrongs.

Hide your shame and find someone to blame,
It's "No win, no fee", so go make your claim,
Lawyers of this type, will respond in haste,
And your chance of profit won't go to waste.

How much did they say that you could be paid?
How much can you earn, now your morals decayed?
You do not need to falsify your alibi,
As the words "duty of care" are all that apply.

Throw the sue-ers in the sewers, it will suit them well,
To visit the place, where their morals dwell.

How low can you sink, now you don't have to think,
When you don't use your brain, you can just claim again,
Now that others must care for your safety and health,
Because you're no longer responsible for yourself.

Throw the sue-ers in the sewers, along with all their gloats,
So their inflated egos can keep them afloat.

(RAP SECTION)
Does your mirror, say it's clever to cash in on your own error,
Look yourself in the eye, try to deny that it's undignified,
It's a shame your claims try to shift the blame to a different name,
You're on the make, from your own mistake, for your own selfish sake,
Ten grand in your hand, if you can reprimand those who offered you a
helping hand,
Your immoral plight, this false fight, just can't be right you piece of shite,

Indeed, your selfish deed sows the seeds that feeds society's greed,
This flow will continue to grow as more get to know how low they can go,
Whilst lawyers applaud the flaws, they've caused, in the laws,
And the congress profess that an excess of process will fix this mess (that's progress?)
As the devastation of litigation, spreads across the nation,
It's irrational that it became vocational, national, even fashionable,
People fear your insincere career when they hear this verbal diarrhoea,
Don't participate, hate this trait, we can't wait or hesitate,
The solution is a population revolution against this moral pollution.

> Throw the sue-ers in the sewers and hope they sink,
> As the taste of other people's shite, might make them re-think.

A few greedy people started this fire,
And now we're all waist deep in their quagmire,
It's an easy way to get the money they desire,
But there is nothing in this method to admire.

Continuing the theme of this fortunate homophone (sue-ers and sewers), if the sue-ers can be described as 'little shits' that belong in the sewers, then the collection of blame and claim lawyers that produce these little shits could aptly described as the big arseholes.

Foundation stone

Over the last half a century, the legal system, an essential foundation stone of a civilised society that maintains justice and reinforces right and wrong, has become blurred and distorted under financial pressures and influences. It has developed an unrecognisable and unreasonable version of justice (a litigation arm) that promotes crude finger pointing and blame, whenever our natural human fallibility and flaws result in an event that we used to call an accident.

The justification or common perception of this blame and claim approach is that it makes businesses and organisations be responsible and improve (that bloody word again), and it prevents them treating employees badly. This intention is partially true, but it is also fuelled by greed and the large financial gains encourage selfishness, blaming others, proliferation of processes and in the worse cases raw dishonesty. It also makes day-to-day life of the average honest majority more difficult and frustrating. For one of the fundamental pillars of society to be pushing the public in this direction seems to be wrong. Analytically it is wrong, intuitively it feels wrong, it contradicts our common sense (or at least my version of it) and yet litigation has become an established, accepted, normalised, common and growing part of modern Western society.

"Isn't it strange how financial injury claims rarely affect the ability to continue doing enjoyable physical activities?"

13

A BIT OF DEMOCRACY

*"There are no necessary evils in government.
Its evils exist only in its abuses."*
(Andrew Jackson, 1767–1845, US president)

My knowledge of politics is only slightly better than that of finance; I struggle to understand either of them in any meaningful way. However, as democracy and government undoubtedly have an important influence on the population, below is a terse account of my limited and blinkered view of politics.

Democracy

Democracy, voting and free elections are essential and very important parts of our Western society and are far better than any undemocratic alternative. However, I do question how truly democratic a 'first past the post' system with a general election every 4 years really is. Many constituencies in the UK will always elect the same party, making a democratic vote for any other party in these regions immediately redundant. Collectively, these constituency results then determine which one of the few large political parties is elected, normally with a majority. For the next 4 years, this effectively reduces the influence of just under half the population to zero. All the spoken words, statements, interviews, finger pointing and questions of the opposition parties towards the elected are all a close approximation to zero influence, especially if you accept the underlying premise of the WORDS chapter (Chapter 1). Meanwhile, the winning party and Prime Minister select a cabinet of like-minded individuals, who can then judge and decide how and where to spend money on behalf of the entire population for the next 4 years (which touches a raw nerve for those in the north of England).

Having no second place, this first past the post system promotes a 'win at all costs' attitude. It encourages all those pre-election claims and promises of reduced unemployment, lower taxes, more nurses, hospitals and police, higher economic growth, better schools and more, that are intended to sway voters and swing the election. These claims can take one of two routes and as they must be announced openly in public to gain votes in the first place, it is easy to see them for what they really are later. They can turn into actions that benefit the population or remain as yet more misleading sets of words, for the sole benefit of the political party or politicians. This type of manipulative, selfish, political behaviour and false promises is probably one of the main contributing factors in the reducing levels of trust in politics and lower voter participation.

To put this method of general elections into perspective, it is a bit like having only two or three TV channels and having to choose one of them to watch for 4 weeks without being able to turn over. You have a fully democratic choice of which TV channel you choose (which party governs), but you have very little democratic control over which programmes get shown (or what the government decides to do). In engineering terms, our vote is 'independent of' or 'de-coupled from' what the government decides to do. So, despite having a fully democratic voting system and living in one of the most democratic nations on the planet, we actually have very little democratic control over what happens in reality. There is more of this in Part 4. Incidentally, there is absolutely no suggestion here that we should have elections (and potentially change the government) every month or so, as that would be utterly preposterous, completely unworkable and a nightmare for everyone.

In theory, democracy means that decisions follow the will of the majority of the population; after all that is what democracy is and how it works isn't it? However, our version of democracy condenses a single democratic vote once every 4 years into the hands of a few like-minded people that can then spend 4 years choosing whether to make decisions for the benefit of the population, the nation, the planet, their own political party or their own career. In other words, it is yet another example where practical reality does not really match the words or the intention. In reality, we only have a little 'bit of democracy' with almost no 'democratic control'.

Government

Having used our little bit of democracy to concentrate the nation's decision making in the hands of a few like-minded people, the government are then faced with an almost impossible task. Opinions vary widely across the population and so, regardless of the choice, decision or action, someone will always oppose or criticise. Attempting to appease and suit everyone (or even just the majority) is far from easy and this is precisely why human feedback produces continual change, rather than providing reliable real improvement. This makes the government's job of deciding incredibly difficult, which ultimately generates long delays and heavily compromised and unclear decisions, which approximate to some heavily watered-down imitation of the original idea or intent. Generally it takes the government a huge amount of time to decide anything, keeping themselves busily employed, endlessly reviewing and debating the complex and infinite range of options, whilst achieving relatively few actions, which only meet a fraction of the public's preferences. It is generally accepted that for every government, there is a mismatch between their overly optimistic, pre-election, vote-grabbing claims and how much they can or do actually achieve in reality. The biggest fundamental problem of government is they do not convert their words into action. All this makes it difficult for me to see that the UK political system is operating well and efficiently. However, if I were to sum up the government in a single word it would not be 'inefficient', because the role and work of government is incredibly complex, but in terms of providing what a lot of population need, I would probably use the word 'ineffectual'.

Politicians

That was my positive view of democracy and the government as a whole. My view of politicians is far worse. From collectively being ineffectual, taking politicians as individuals we can add in hypocritical, insincere, egotistical, greedy and selfish, along with several other less-than-complimentary adjectives. The justification for this opinion is based on real examples, such as the expenses scandal in 2009, regular MP pay rises that are above national average, breaking the laws they make, old school networks, large financial donations, not returning from personal holidays during national or international crises, contracts awarded to friends, lobbying scandals, employing family members (do the adverts for these jobs including the clause "must live within 15 metres of the MP's house", so that only family members can apply for them?) along with many other self-rewarding, well-paid sideline activities.

They have bemoaned the cost of providing free school meals, whilst their own canteen absorbs over £5 million of taxpayers' money each year. I am not stupid, I can do the sums, I know the cost of providing millions of children with free school meals costs a lot more than providing nice meals for a few hundred politicians, but for me it is a question of morality. Would it be right to provide all MPs with sports cars, just because it is cheaper than providing every school child with a bike? If free school meals are truly unaffordable (which I don't believe for one second) and the politicians really were that concerned (which I also have significant doubts about), then their answer should be "Look, we simply can't afford millions of free school meals, but we recognise this and the least we can do is to fully pay for our own food, instead of letting the taxpayer foot the bill for it".

All politicians will claim to be busy and work hard and I honestly believe them, it is how they proportion their work that I question. How much of that work is genuinely for the population or nation, how much is for the benefit of their own political party and how much is in their own self-interest and making money? I find it very hard to accept that someone who actively avoids answering questions, breaks rules, accepts financial benefits or attempts to cover up scandals is genuinely working for the benefit of the population. I also don't believe that benefiting the population is best achieved by misleading people. These common types of political behaviour are much more aligned with protecting their own self-interest and their own political party, than working for the benefit of the population. I may not have a high opinion of politicians, but they are all incredibly clever, capable people who have out-manoeuvred, out-thought (or out-fought?), out-bought and out-talked others to get to the positions they have reached. Unfortunately, it seems that all too often they use their intelligence and effort to further the selfish goals of their party and themselves, rather than benefiting the nation and population as a whole.

They seem happy to contradict themselves, often within just hours or days. Criticising companies for not paying tax, whilst doing everything they can to avoid paying tax themselves. Telling people not to travel or have parties during COVID-19 lockdown, then breaking these new laws themselves. Instead of being apologetic or embarrassed, they behave as though the contradiction is perfectly acceptable. Their hypocrisy is dumbfounding, as though they consider themselves to be above the laws and rules they set: "Everyone else should do this, but not me because it is mildly inconvenient for me personally, therefore I don't think it should apply to me." Seeing politicians break the rules they have set and then using dismissive words and excuses to wash over a problem or inconvenience will only entice others to try the same thing: "if they do it, then I'll do it too". This is yet another example of how an important, significant, highly influential part of society is subtly affecting and changing the behaviours of the population in a detrimental way. The behaviour of politicians influences the behaviour of the population, in just the same way that the behaviour of financial institutions and businesses influences the population. Unfortunately, these influences always seem to be in the same direction: look after yourself, get what you can, mislead others for your own gain, get more money whenever you can, get your own way and talk yourself out of problematic situations rather than changing your behaviour. The list goes on and on.

Prior to 1911, MPs weren't paid – they volunteered their own time and effort – but, as this excluded everyone who could not support themselves financially, politicians' wages were introduced to allow anyone to become an MP. This may still be valid today, but being a politician is now a very highly paid job with a lot of additional benefits and it is now much more common to hear the justification that these high MP salaries are necessary to "attract the right kind of person". Is the right kind of person someone who is only willing to have the nation's best interests at heart and help other people if they are very highly paid to do it? Surely the high salary can equally attract those individuals who just want lots of money to talk bland, misleading garbage for 30 years like 'career politicians', as well as those high-performing people who have the nation's best interests at heart. In most forms of employment, with standards on breaking rules, honesty, professionalism and financial corruption, the behaviours of many MPs would require some form of formal disciplinary action, not respect, admiration and reward. This again undermines their claims that they fulfill this important and privileged role in the genuine interests of the nation and not just themselves. If their true interests really are the nation and the population, then they have some extraordinarily unusual and wholly inappropriate ways of showing it.

A few hours' work

In just a few pages, I have questioned the level of democracy, the effectiveness of the government and the morality of politicians. Not bad for a few hours of work! In line with the ideas in the WORDS chapter (Chapter 1), these personal views have been based on the actions of politicians and governments, not their words. If the judgements had been based predominantly on the words and speeches of politicians, then they would be a remarkable collection of people who save the population from all sorts of ills and dangers, preventing disaster after disaster, solving all sorts of local problems, and be the smartly dressed superheroes that their egos probably believe they are. Unfortunately, being a realist, not a fantasist or optimist, my judgements are not made on words but on actions and reality, and those tell a quite different story.

Despite all this, there is still an essential role for government to protect the national interests, to provide the safe environment and infrastructure that the population needs, encompassing education, policing, hospitals, prisons, transport, utility supplies and communication infrastructure. This essential role of both government and democracy (and maybe even politicians as well?) is raised again in Part 4, where the separate topics of Part 3 are combined into a kind of jigsaw, producing some approximation of a full picture of our society. This picture is then used to highlight and explore some more important interactions, influences, loops and contradictions that exist across our society.

"The biggest insult I could be given
is to be called a politician."

PART 4:

THE FULL PICTURE

14

THE JIGSAW

*"It is dangerous to be right in matters in which
the established authorities are wrong."*
(Voltaire, 1694–1778, writer)

Just as you should not judge a team by one player or judge a car purely on the gear box, tyres or engine alone, it is equally wrong to judge our society purely on its government, lawyers or financial operation, even if they are all far from perfect. In these three cases (and with just about everything else) it is necessary to look at how the individual parts combine, interact, influence and operate together as a whole. Therefore, this chapter aims to fit together the various pieces of the society jigsaw, to highlight and understand some of the interactions and characteristics of our society. This is something sociologists and philosophers have been doing for thousands of years and their various ideas and discussions could fill many books and multiple PhD theses. Therefore, a single chapter of a flippant and disparaging book of this type cannot provide any level of detail. The approach here is to look only at the main structure or skeleton of society, using a more analytical, engineering approach to understanding complex systems, interactions and finding some more of those self-feeding loops.

Understanding complex systems

Within engineering there are several methods and tools to help understand the interactions of complicated systems, like cars, planes, phones, rollercoasters, washing machines and even toys. Often diagrams are used to help see the interactions more clearly and provide a better picture of how the influences spread to other parts of the system. This approach helps to highlight the 'loops' or knock-on effects, which might otherwise go unnoticed when considering only one or two components individually. The diagram below shows how part A directly influences part B and part B directly influences part C, but if part C then has an influence on part A, it creates a 'closed loop' interaction. In a closed loop chain, any single part can influence the operation of any other part or all the other parts, and so affects the operation of the whole thing and the overall stability of the system.

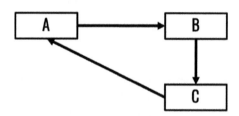

This type of closed loop effect was introduced in the FEEDBACK and SEWER chapters (Chapters 2 and 12), where it was explained that any closed loop interaction can produce one of three different behaviours.

1. An unstable or runaway effect (like a microphone feedback screech or the litigation loop).
2. A continual unstable change effect (like the customer feedback blue, red, yellow example, changing shop layouts or the repeated business restructuring every 5–10 years).
3. A stable effect with a self-limiting behaviour.

It is also important to note that not all of these interactions are the same strength or influence. For example, when people eat out at a pub in the summer, the influence of the weather will have a strong influence on (or is 'strongly coupled' to) whether they eat outside or inside, but perhaps only has a small influence on (or is 'weakly coupled' to) what they choose to eat. This idea was introduced in the DEMOCRACY chapter (Chapter 13), in which I insinuated that our democratic vote has little influence or control over (so is 'weakly coupled' to) what the government chooses to do.

As the immense complexity and subtlety of a human society is difficult to comprehend, let alone attempt to present on a flat page, only a grossly oversimplified, almost superficial, basic skeleton of our society is provided here, but even this is sufficient to highlight some more subtle influences, interactions and loops within it. However, in the true spirit of suspense and just like any other jigsaw, the pieces must first be fitted together, hopefully to provide a recognisable picture of the society in which you live. If not, then all is not lost, because this 'society jigsaw' diagram is still required later, to compare against a rather different version of society described in the ALTERNATIVE SOCIETY chapter (Chapter 16).

Society jigsaw

Society is a construct built to provide what is needed for the whole population. Although people have very different concerns, opinions and preferences about almost everything, at the most basic level people are all the same and really only need three things: sustenance (food and shelter), safety (environment and justice) and stimulation (activities, entertainment and social interaction). The government provides the safe environment in the form of police, hospitals, education, regulations and defence (labelled as 'infrastructure' here), whilst lawyers provide us with justice by penalising those who break the rules. Businesses and other similar organisations provide both our sustenance, in the form of homes and food, and our stimulation and entertainment, in the form of TVs, games, toys, sports, theatre etc. (labelled 'products' here). Therefore, the jigsaw starts with just these three main pieces, providing only what people need (shown as the dashed lines).

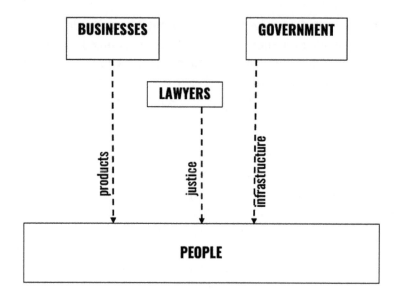

It is fairly evident that these things are not obtained for free. Therefore, the next diagram adds in the familiar monetary transactions, such as wages, purchases, tax, bank loans etc., which are indicated by the thin solid lines. The large, dotted box indicates the collective types of employment (banks, business, lawyers, government) and the pair of arrows towards the bottom left corner indicate the exchange of wages paid for this employment. Two further interactions are added to the government box (towards the bottom right corner) to represent people's votes and the essential support and safety net that government provides society, using the recognisable (but possibly now outdated) term 'state benefits' for those people less able or willing to work.

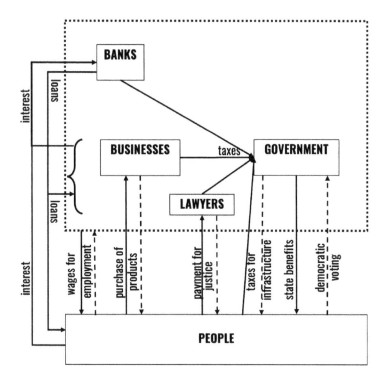

The next diagram adds in the role of the large financial organisations (again within the large, dotted employment box), where the belief and confidence of the population fuels share prices and money is used to make more money. The interactions of these financial organisations with the wider society, including stocks and shares, government bonds, bank debts and investments, are all shown as thick solid lines. The thick lines on the far right (labelled 'investments') represent how those people with some spare cash available can also participate (benefit and lose) in some of these financial games. Finally, and most bizarrely, this full version of the diagram also emphasises that whilst the lubricating money is cycling around these economic pipes, all new money actually comes from fresh air. This is still shocking to type or read; it is totally counterintuitive. It is these types of phrases that really help to enforce how detached and different the financial world is from the real physical world.

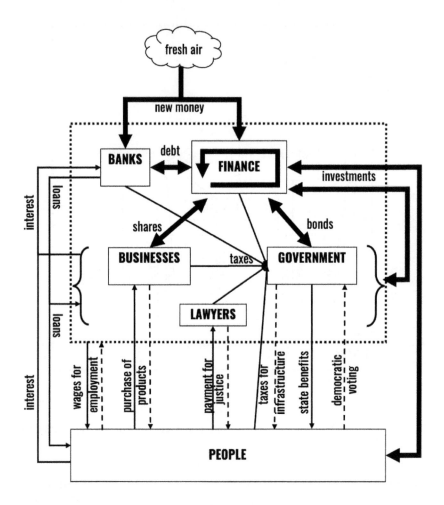

The list below provides a brief indication of a few types of interactions missing from this grossly oversimplified (but already busy and complex) diagram.

- Transactions from one business to another (which would be extra details inside the BUSINESSES box).
- Government and bank purchases from business (which would be extra lines like the purchase interaction between PEOPLE and BUSINESSES).
- The second-hand market where people sell to other people (which would be extra details inside the PEOPLE box).

- Donations to charity that boost the essential (but limited) infrastructure provided by the government. In the context of this diagram, CHARITIES could be seen as like the GOVERNMENT box, but the tax input would be replaced by voluntary donations and the infrastructure output would be more based around care and research.
- Any non-financial interactions.

So, on the premise that this is a recognisable picture of our society, it can now be used to look at some of the significant interactions and influences of society in a wider context.

The contradiction layer

The precarious bridging position between the real world of PEOPLE and the strange world of FINANCE can now be seen in the diagram. However, it appears that this layer is occupied by both businesses and the government. Government has a different role to business. Government attempts to provide the safe environment and infrastructure that the population needs, whilst managing the national debt, not raising taxes (too much), struggling with a limited income and gaining votes by persuading us what a brilliant job they are doing. A role not short of contradictions itself. Whilst businesses use their 'business speak' to cope with and abstract away their internal contradictions, politicians prefer to publicly avoid answering questions by using standard or contradictory words, supported by all that statistical BINFORMATION that is so prevalent in political speeches and answers. Life in these precarious bridging positions, sitting between the two very different worlds of finance and physical reality, promotes, or necessitates, the use of this temporary word-based coping mechanism (called bullshit), whenever the contradictions might be awkward, difficult or embarrassing. It is no coincidence that the vast majority (but not all) of the bullshit we regularly hear is generated from within this precarious bridging position, labelled the 'contradiction layer' and shown as the shaded (or shady?) area in the diagram below.

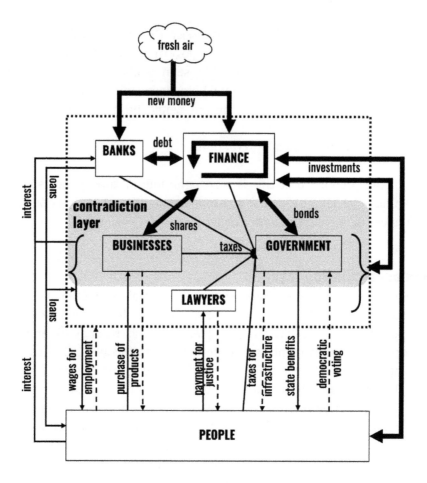

Part 2 described how our behaviour is strongly governed by the attitude "If they do it, I'll do it" and so this poor use of language gradually spreads through society, becoming increasingly accepted and normalised. This is not the usual complaint about the natural evolution of language, which started long before the times of Shakespeare and has continued ever since. This is highlighting and complaining about two giant foundation stones of society, slowly but systematically stripping away the useful tangible content of language, leaving a bland mush, with so little content that it says nothing. That is a very different complaint. Worse still, the normalisation and acceptance of this effect means that some people are starting to confuse this 'talking drivel' with being useful, informative and helpful, or as a valid substitute for deciding, doing and taking action. If you were so inclined you could make a whole career out of endlessly talking the same drivel over and over again, which unfortunately some choose to do. It is easy for words to disguise or cover up contradictions, skirt around problems, avoid taking action or even hide the truth completely, but in doing so they provide a gross abstraction from reality. It seems that the existence of this 'contradictory layer' is the source of, or at least a major contribution to, the problems described in the WORDS chapter at the start of Part 1 (Chapter 1). It also seems wrong for these two important giants of our society to need or choose to behave this way.

Employment and purchasing products

The diagram shows the two main interactions between PEOPLE and BUSINESS. One is people's purchase of goods and the second is payment of wages for work. Both the BUSINESS AS USUAL and WHO DECIDES chapters (Chapters 10 and 11) looked at how using machines is often more efficient and profitable than employing people, who then become redundant and must look for other work. In isolation this seems an acceptable side of progress and it has been going on for centuries. However, the diagram now indicates that wages and purchasing form a 'loop' or interaction that is not immediately obvious from looking at things in isolation. If enough people are out of work, then collectively they will not have enough money to buy the products being made by the machines. As fewer people work, they earn less and collectively they will buy less, companies will be less profitable and stop producing, until the balance of products and affordability is re-established. Seeing the loop in this way highlights a natural self-limiting characteristic; this is an inherently stable loop. Unfortunately, this natural self-limiting stability can be bypassed or destabilised by our concerned, sympathetic, caring friend called the finance industry. Using that convenient pot of fresh air, they can externally fuel this the loop with growing personal debt, so maintaining sales and increasing bank loan interest payments. However, this is only a temporary solution. Continually increasing personal debt means that people must then earn even more, by demanding more from their future employment to pay back the borrowed money with interest. Either that or the cumulative debt becomes unpayable (like subprime mortgage loans in 2008) to produce another financial crash (but no worries because fresh air can fix that again as well).

The value of time

In addition to collectively paying employees enough to buy products and services, there is continual pressure to make profit, increase sales and grow. This can only happen if collectively businesses continually increase wages, as people can't buy more if they don't earn more. This is a loop where collective wages and collective sales chase each other in a never-ending profit-making game, like a dog chasing its own tail. This self-feeding, unlimited inflation loop has existed for centuries and is not a major problem, especially if you are willing to accept that it is just the way the economy works, but there is a less obvious, more subtle consequence. This continual collective increase of wages that we are familiar with (just compare your wage with that of your grandparents) raises the monetary value of our 'time at work', which, combined with a pressure to reduce production costs, means that the sale price of any product or service becomes increasingly dominated by the wage bill or the cost of employees' time. To put this more succinctly, the monetary value of our time is progressively dominating the cost of things we buy. This is why a product that costs only £3 in materials is then sold for £40, why it costs £200 labour to fit a £10 oil filter at the garage, why teaching is expensive even though many subjects require very few materials so in theory could be taught for free and why it costs something approaching a second mortgage to pay for full-time childcare. This is also the reason why it is cheaper to just throw something away and buy a new one, rather than pay more for a time-consuming investigation and repair, even if this seems counterintuitive in the practical world.

Worryingly, we already live in a society where 'time is money' and this affects our decisions and how we use our time. It is common for people to choose the highest paid jobs available, as opposed to those they might be more capable of, find more fulfilling or enjoy more. Often the higher-paid jobs are those that generate most profit; you can earn more for serving coffee than caring for someone. It affects how much of our (expensive) time we spend helping others, unless they are willing to pay for it. It also makes us more impatient and less tolerant of those who waste or use up our time – it is like they are costing us money. Finally, this increasing 'cost of time' creates a clear incentive to locally minimise wage bills, ideally by creating unpaid employees or volunteers, who spend their own free time (free in both senses of the word) doing some of the work that businesses used to pay trained employees to do. If you haven't guessed, these 'unpaid volunteers' are the customers, you and me. We are increasingly forced to battle through the computer obstacle course of unrecognised passwords, incorrect data formats, reading pages we don't understand, repeatedly entering our data and hoping the computer won't tell us in red text that it knows we have done something wrong, then coping with the fact that it won't give us any clues as to which part is wrong or why. Many of us are capable of battling through this irritating kind of "Just give them an online process and let them work it out for themselves" approach, but it is a hell of lot more effort and more frustrating than having the help of a customer service employee who knows what to do and does things quickly first time. What is wrong with the traditional approach of knowledgeable people helping those who are less knowledgeable? Oh yeah, I forgot, it costs money. It is only our modern Information Age that makes all these online processes and 'unpaid volunteers' possible. They may save money, but they also make some very simple things so bloody difficult, generating a lot of continual unnecessary frustrations. To summarise, the increasing cost of our time results in the following:

- Throw away and replace, rather than time-consuming repair.
- Get others to do it at their own expense.
- Don't spend time helping others.
- Reduce the time it takes to doing something (do the minimum).

There is no natural limit or threshold to the cost of people's time. This inflationary loop is not self-limiting and so the cost of people's time will continue to increase without limit, as footballers' wages adequately demonstrate. This is just another indication of money's detachment from reality. If we are not already in this position today, the cost of people's time will eventually dominate the cost of all products and services. Extrapolating this even further, to its full extent, nothing will have any monetary value except human time. All other costs will be insignificant compared with the rising cost of any human time involved and yet, ironically, in the real world 'time' is one of the things that is freely available to everyone; it cannot be controlled or altered and is the same for everyone (unless your job requires you to work near a black hole or travel at speeds close to the speed of light). Intuitively it seems quite perverse that some abstract and possibly arbitrary monetary value placed on time should then dominate the price and availability of everything, influence important decisions and decide what is done and when. Yet we are already a long way down this track and accelerating in that direction. We just don't see it, because it is normal and just 'how we do things'.

Taxes and infrastructure

This section concentrates on the government, which predominantly operates using tax revenues as an input to pay for the national infrastructure and state benefits that it provides as an output. The financial benefits and pressures to pay as little tax as possible constrain the government's tax income, whilst the desire to be re-elected makes it very difficult to (openly) raise unpopular taxes to pay for more. This is the government's life in the 'contradiction layer', trying to convince us they are providing more for less. Other than covering up this contradiction with political words, some more practical attempts include making some of those amazingly easy and practical efficiency improvements (again, read as continual changes), which include cutting back on some non-essential things, passing the burden of effort and workload onto the public or by finding ways to make some profit by charging more for some services. These are precisely the things that businesses are very good at, so as it becomes harder for the struggling government to afford to provide some services and infrastructure, then businesses step in and rightly claim they can do it better than the inefficient, ineffectual and over-bureaucratic government. For some businesses, this means that minimising the amount of tax they pay has a double benefit. It keeps more money in their own pockets and, by restricting the government's ability to deliver what is needed, it also indirectly generates more business opportunities for them. This starts a slow but gradual drift towards businesses providing more of the national infrastructure and services that were once provided by the government, with examples in the UK including water supply, gas supply, electricity network and railways etc. Whether this is a good or bad thing is a politically polarising topic (and certainly not a subject for here). However, as long as the need for profit and growth is stronger than the penalties for not paying taxes, then the financial forces and influences which cause this continual drift will continue, with businesses taking over the more profitable services, like the undercurrent in a lazy-river loop in a swimming pool. This undercurrent or loop is now starting to affect what is happening to the NHS (the rise of private hospitals and medical schemes), education (via student loans) and the care services (selling equity in your home to provide care). It is a slow drift away from providing what people need, towards what will maintain or increase profits.

Incidentally, around 2010 there was a suggestion of a form of Robin Hood Tax of around 0.05% on financial transactions (the thick black lines in the diagram, excluding the personal investments) that could raise around £100 billion per year to alleviate or prevent this funding problem, an idea promoted in an advert with actor Bill Nighy.[1] That means that, in 2010, the value of the transactions (the thick black lines) equated to around £200 trillion in the UK, and it will be much more now. Such are the power and influence of the financial industry and the desire to not pay tax, that it was never implemented. Similarly, some political parties have hinted at a 1% income tax raise purely to provide additional funds for the NHS, but again this has not been implemented – such is the aversion to pay tax.

Haves and have nots

The thick black investments arrow, on the right side of the diagram, is the syphon tube which diverts the monetary value of stocks and shares towards those that already have some spare cash available to trade or invest. This syphoning of money towards money is replicated to a lesser extent on the left-hand side, where spare cash can sit in bank accounts gaining interest. Furthermore, those without are much more likely to borrow money and pay interest on their loans. Therefore, it is always possible for those with money to make more than those without and this drives the increasing divide between the haves and have nots. This does not mean the poor are getting poorer: they have been getting steadily wealthier for a century or more. Afterall, some of that extra fresh air that gets converted into money and pushed into the financial pipes must reach the poor eventually. It's just that more of it gets syphoned towards those who already have spare money to invest, it is not distributed evenly, so the gap between richest and poorest widens (at least in raw cash terms). There are of course exceptions – rich people can gamble and lose, small investors or poor entrepreneurs can win big and become rich – but these are very much the exceptions to the rule. This widening gap is also an unlimited loop. In a society with an economy that is reliant on the ability of money to make more money (growth), there is simply no way for the have nots to ever close the gap. Regardless of how many politicians, philanthropists, optimists or charities make claims of wanting to do it, regardless of how many solutions are proposed and regardless of how many futile attempts are made, the financial interactions of our current society simply cannot and will not allow it to happen. There is more on this topic in the next chapter.

Conglomerates and corporations

This effect is copied directly into the business world, where the large business corporations are the 'haves' and the 'have nots' are smaller businesses. The incentive for large businesses to make more profit is an incentive to gain new technology, gain skills, grow and buyout or takeover smaller businesses, or simply remove competition from the marketplace. This gives larger businesses a huge advantage over smaller businesses. In the same way that the haves can always accumulate more than the have nots, larger businesses can always grow more by accumulating or swallowing smaller businesses. In most cases, this constant consumption of the little fish by the bigger fish means that large businesses maintain a position of dominance and can continue to grow without limit, or at least until the rules of monopoly and mergers start to apply. Those that wield sufficient power do not, will not and cannot go as far as to say, "You can't grow" or "You can't make any profit", so the very best they can do is to slow down these effects, letting them continue at a slower rate. This ability for the big fish to stay big and get bigger leads to more huge multi-national conglomerates and corporations that are increasing in size, power and influence.

The existence of these huge multi-national corporations means that there are three main giants of our society: business corporations, governments and financial institutions. Or if you want to label them with derisory, story book names: The Demanding, The Deceitful and The Detached, respectively. These three giants, whilst entirely dependent on each other, are also in a three-way power struggle, which is considered further in the next chapter. For now, the attitude and response of governments to the 2008 financial crash and their inability to collect sufficient taxes from some of the largest corporations, which control many of the biggest business deals and a lot of the national employment, suggests that savvy gamblers would not bet on governments winning this three-way power struggle.

No limits

From these five loops (from the previous five sections) and the litigation loop (from Part 3), all except one are growing, self-feeding loops and the one that isn't (employment and purchasing) can be bypassed by increasing personal debt. This is not too surprising as, like many things in our society, these loops are driven financially by the unlimited need for economic growth and fuelled by an unlimited supply of fresh air. Therefore, the cost of our time, the size and power of corporations, the number of services provided by profit-making businesses, the gap between haves and have nots and the amount of litigation will all continue to grow without limit, simply because there are no limits. There is absolutely no concept of "that is enough" and the only answer is "MORE". If you sell 100,000 cars, you are expected to sell more next year. Nobody ever says, "That's enough profit for this year". Nobody says, "That's enough crisps", they say "How can we sell more crisps?" Nobody says, "This product is reliable, so you won't need insurance", they ask "How many more products can we sell insurance with?" Just as everyone is getting used to the idea that three blades are enough for a good shave, they persuade people that four or five blades are now needed. On which pre-Christmas campaign will we be persuaded that six blades are now needed to have a proper shave? In fashion, this season's colour may be yellow, but to encourage us to buy even more clothes in a few months' time, the colour will change to turquoise, magenta or purple. As soon as you have your expensive car, house, bike or phone, someone is encouraging you to buy a newer, bigger or better one.

This is another fundamental contradiction. Our society is being driven by uncontrolled, unlimited forces that conflict with the limited resources available to us. This wasn't a problem over a century ago at the start of the Industrial Revolution, when production, products and population were all much lower. However, as commercialisation, consumerism and population have all grown, these contradictions are easier to recognise, especially by the younger generations. Today recycling materials is considered the solution and on a planet of limited resources with high consumption this is absolutely necessary. However, the next chapter, which looks further into the future, shows how 100% recycling provides only a temporary solution; it only temporarily disguises the fundamental, underlying contradiction; it only dilutes and delays the real problem. Whilst financial pressures mean that many of the short-term battles continue to be won by profit and the need to sell just a few more profitable items, the long-term war will be won by the real physical world, as all the collective longer-term consequences will eventually be realised. It is this contradiction that drives conflict into our decision making, straining our intuition and common sense. Do we really need five blades to shave or only to maintain profits and growth?

Functional flow diagram

The society jigsaw diagram used so far shows how the individual parts fit and operate together but does not show what is going on. A similar parts diagram for a car, with the engine, gear box and wheels, would not show that fuel is burnt to spin a shaft, at different speeds, to rotate the wheels. Therefore, the next diagram peels back this parts layer of the society jigsaw diagram, to reveal a more functional 'what is going on' layer below. This layer shows how the influences and consequences of the loops described above spread and interact with each other and us. In this diagram, the 'loops' can be found by following the arrows, each of which should be translated as 'promotes', 'encourages', 'leads to' or 'generates' etc.

If you wish to spend time following the arrows you may find yourself looping round the same track several times, suddenly realising the existence of an interaction (possibly self-feeding) that you were previously unaware of.

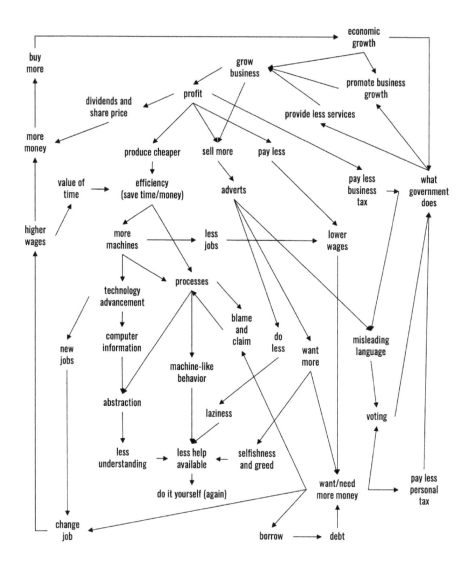

Effect on people

This very brief but broader look at our affluent, efficient, convenient, comfortable, caring, democratic society attempts to show how these interacting loops affect and alter people's behaviour and contribute to the everyday frustrations and problems. It shows how they make simple things more difficult and how their unlimited nature allows their influence to grow over time, gradually shifting and moulding our behaviour into a new accepted norm. Below is a short, amalgamated summary and reminder of all the topics from Parts 1, 2 and 3, which provides some context and a foundation for the next two chapters, which look at the future of our society and potential alternatives.

Finance

- Finance and money became increasingly detached from reality.
    - Human need (and greed) combined with the ability of money to make more money, ensure that profit making became a driving force within society and the economy.
    - The finance industry aims to maximise both profit and growth, evolving into a complex, self-feeding, unstable, belief-based system.
    - Finance has no concept of limits or 'that is enough'.
    - This detachment of finance from physical reality creates a 'contradiction layer'.
    - Profit and finance teach us that "money is good, and more money is better". It teaches us to be – and rewards us for being – greedy and selfish, and encourages us to obtain as much money from others as is legitimately possible.
- The drive for profit has commercialised (commoditised) large sections of society, distorting the role of money.
    - Money and profit both abstract the value or worth of something (they concentrate on monetary value, not human values).
    - The drive for more profit and growth creates an unlimited loop of more sales, more money and higher wages, which continually increases the monetary value of time ('time is money').
    - The commoditisation and increasing value of our time distorts how we use it. We become less tolerant of those using or wasting our time, as it becomes linked to wasting our money. It corrupts the fact that time is freely available to everyone, whilst money isn't.

Business

- The desire and drive for money and profit ensured that scientific discoveries and new technologies led to the Industrial Revolution, the advancement of machines and advent of computers.
  - Machines and computers have provided huge benefits and convenience for most of the population.
  - The huge success of machines and computers led to engineering and scientific theories of 'feedback' and 'improvement' being applied more widely across society, where they are less applicable and help to generate constant unstable changes, which frustratingly haunt every single day of our lives.
- The drive for profit and efficiency leads to using more processes and procedural methods.
  - Reliance on procedural methods and process promotes (or excuses) 'switching off'.
  - Reliance on procedural methods and process limits our understanding, so abstracting our actions away from what we are doing and why.
  - Reliance on process excludes and prevents alternative valid, practical solutions.
- The advent of computers means we have far more information, but less context and understanding of what that information means.
  - Use of computers abstracts our understanding of information.
  - We now use more information blindly.
  - Computers enable the 'passing the burden' approach, replacing knowledgeable personal help with frustrating do-it-yourself online processes.
- The combination of machines, processes and computers means that more of our behaviour is being squeezed through small square procedural holes. We are encouraged to be more robotic and slave like (just do what the computer wants, the way it wants, when it wants – the machine is master, so do as you are told!).

Law

- The desire for more financial reward (profit) within the legal system has led to a litigation culture, where lawyers can directly benefit financially from encouraging people to blame others.
  - Litigation led to the overuse of process as a form of defence, where just about everything we do is written down as evidence and protection against being sued.
  - Litigation encourages us to blame others instead of taking responsibility for ourselves.

Government

- The desire for profit and money makes it difficult for governments to raise sufficient taxes to provide infrastructure and services.
  - This creates a continual undercurrent, where businesses replace government as the provider of infrastructure and services.
- The political 'first past the post' system may be democratic, but it provides very little (or no) real democratic control over what is decided or done (our vote is disconnected or de-coupled from the decisions the government makes).

People

- Those working in the 'contradiction layer' experience the inconsistency between finance and reality and attempt to cope with it by disguising it, ignoring it or abstracting it away behind ridiculous 'business speak' or 'political talk'.
  - This empty or standard language removes the useful content from language.
  - The acceptance and normalisation of this meaningless empty waffle allows people to constantly regurgitate it (with the worst culprits falsely believing it provides a constructive, valid and helpful alternative to decisions or doing something).
- The business drive for profit and growth floods society with adverts, convincing people they need, want or deserve more, that life will be better if only they spend more money. We are

continually encouraged to want more, to be greedy and to be selfish.

Hopefully, this rather stark, bleak perspective of society is recognisable from the content, examples, hints, suggestions and rants made so far. You may even accept it as a grim view of the society we live in. None of these negative influences are the intention or direct consequence of our society, they are only the unavoidable side-effects of how the main cornerstones of society interact and work together as a whole, forming self-feeding loops, undercurrents and behavioural drifts. These less-than-pleasing influences are not commonly promoted. They are not the ones that government, businesses, banks and lawyers choose to describe the way our society works. They maybe unspoken and hidden, they may be difficult to see, but they are also accepted and normalised. Yet hopefully these rather bleak conclusions are at least a recognisable part of real everyday life. Alternatively, they could just be the incorrect opinionated views of an outdated, increasingly frustrated grumpy old man. Again, that is for you to decide.

Meanwhile, these social influences will slowly and subtly continue to steer our behaviours. The dominant financial and economic influences will continue to reward profit making, paying people more for jobs that generate money (finance, sales, advertising) and less for those that help people without profit (nurse, teachers, emergency services, social and care workers etc.). We will continue to be enticed away from the lower-paid jobs, subduing our natural more altruistic instincts to help and think of others, towards the more selfish attitude of "I'll just serve coffee, if it pays more than helping old people". In short, our society and economy seem to be nudging and encouraging us towards the selfish (left) side of the selfish/laziness diagram created in Part 2, as shown by the large central arrow in the modified version below.

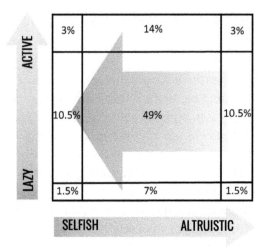

If this is true, then it answers the question raised in Part 2, "Why aren't people less selfish?" It is because our society does not actively encourage or reward people for being less selfish, whilst in contrast it does entice, encourage and reward selfish attitudes. Once again, intuitively this does not seem to be the right thing to be doing.

Trying to do the right thing

Not only are there relatively low financial rewards for trying to help people, but also it is becoming increasingly difficult to help in even the smallest and simplest ways. My first personal experience of this was in the late 1990s when I attempted to give a few dozen leftover inflated balloons to a junior school for the children to play with in the playground at lunchtime. More recently, around 2015, donating a lockable metal tool cupboard in very good condition to a school seemed to be an impossible suggestion. How ridiculously stupid of me to think that I might be able to do something that seemed right, to help, to do something good or nice for people, when all these processes, records, checks and risk assessments are put in place to help make it all so simple, efficient, quick and easy to do. If only I'd been willing to spend a few weeks filling in forms, making statements, getting things checked, recorded, reviewed and signed off, then all those lucky junior school children would have had dozens of deflated floppy bits of rubber to enjoy one lunchtime and a perfectly good metal cupboard might not have ended up as scrap. The problem is this: as soon as someone asks questions like "Is it safe or suitable?" it becomes very complicated, very quickly. A quick visual check just doesn't cut it these days. This makes the whole thing very time-consuming, which often translates to very costly (time is money) and before too long the easiest and cheapest thing to do is just scrap it. Once again, money wins and common sense loses. Many people naturally want to help, but with a little influence and a helping hand from our convenient, caring, affluent, efficient, modern society, it all ends up being a laborious uphill struggle, until they eventually reach the point where they decide to stop trying and simply not bother anymore. Once again, our behaviours are slightly shifted towards a new accepted norm of "Don't try to help, it's too much hassle, just throw it away".

The majority of altruistic work is therefore a battle between our desire and willingness to help others and the effort of swimming against the flow and tide of society's influences (money, profit, processes, litigation etc.). Although a few leaders of the largest charities do earn significant six figure salaries, most of these more helpful, charitable roles rely predominantly on the altruistic side of people's nature to fulfil them. The various charities and voluntary causes, which collectively employ around 1.5 million people, with around 7 million (presumably part-time) volunteers,[2] operate despite our society and economy, not because of it. They are based on the good side of human nature and arguably they provide more genuine benefit to people than those various aspects of society insultingly described in Part 3. Many individuals rely heavily on these charitable activities and volunteering work, but how would finance, businesses, machines, lawyers and government react if every single charity, volunteer group and campaign was removed or stopped? The answer is, very little: they could just carry on as normal – just as you might react if your favourite café closed, the busker you enjoy listening to stopped playing in the local market or your favourite convenient little car park was closed. There might be less cancer research, fewer palliative care hospices, more people stuck at home without the care and support they need, a few more churches with leaky roofs, and unemployment might be higher, but the government, businesses, lawyers, banks and finance would all continue operating in exactly the same way, barely noticing. Our current version of society enjoys the benefits and availability of altruistic charitable work, but it certainly doesn't need it or rely on it to operate and so it doesn't need to actively reward it either.

If our version of modern Western society encourages and rewards a lot of selfish, greedy and misleading activities, whilst doing very little to actively promote and reward 'helping other people' (which is different from just selling them something) and 'doing the right thing', then it all seems profoundly incorrect. It contradicts any concept of common sense, yet it happens all day, every day and is considered a completely normal part of our society. It is not the good side of human nature that decides, it is money.

Money decides

It would be both strange and wrong to judge the weight of something by its shape, the speed of something by its colour or the taste of something by its size. It is simply incomprehensible to judge or measure something using a scale that is detached or independent from what it is measuring and yet we do it every single day, whenever money decides. Money is an abstract construct, which over the last century or two has become increasingly detached from physical reality. It is a poor way to measure health, education, environment, transport, wildlife, pollution, safety etc. yet we use it to decide, or at least strongly influence, whether to build a new school, close a nursing home, drill for more oil, buy medicine for a patient, build a bridge over a busy road or just to add an extra topping to your coffee or pizza. Asking why we use money to measure and decide such things is a profound philosophical question, with many glib answers like "It always has done", "It just has to be", "Money is real, isn't it?", "What else can we use?" or a much more definitive but equally uninformative "Money decides everything – stupid!". These are not reasoned arguments or explanations, and they don't provide any evidence for why money is a good way to measure, judge or value things like education, care, saving lives or even just helping people.

Those with some knowledge or understanding of the financial world may provide slightly more sophisticated responses like "The markets decide" and "The market is always right", which is even worse. The world of financial markets is so unpredictable and complicated (profit, share value, interest rates, inflation, tax, exchange rates, investments, derivatives, futures, portfolios, hedge funds etc.) that not even the experts fully understand it or know how to control it. Just like the sports cars they buy with their monthly or quarterly bonuses, if they knew how to control the markets, then they would not crash. However, just like driving too fast in sports cars, they do know how to drive the markets hard and exploit them until they do crash. The financial markets are so unstable and unpredictable that they allow a business to double or half in value, even though it physically remains the same. This not based on reality but on belief, like a kind of religion – but at least religions have the decency to stick to their beliefs and not change their minds at the mere hint or suggestion of a change or a dip in share price. Anyone or anything with the ability to change their mind so dramatically, to be that unstable or unpredictable, should not have control of the TV remote, let alone people's jobs, health, care, transport or the environment. So, whilst it is bad to let an abstract monetary value decide for us, it is worse to let a detached inherently unstable, uncontrollable, incomprehensible, financial belief system decide things for us. How can this unstable financial market system know what is good for people? Of course, it can't. It can't even comprehend, judge or measure our 'human values' so why does it get to choose what is good, what is possible, what can and can't be done, which jobs to keep and which to lose? Deep down, people know what is good for people, so why shouldn't people decide what is good for people?

Isn't it ironic that a society with a financial system specifically designed and optimised to generate wealth and profit does not have enough money to look after those people who need care? This is not because the system is bad at generating money – it is incredibly good at it and there is plenty of it about. It is because the more recent role of money (to just make more money) means that is not worth investing or wasting money on things that don't help to generate any more money or any direct profit back. We therefore must fight against the tide of finance to keep the NHS going, to have enough teachers, prison places or care homes. More recently we even need to fight against finance and debt to get educated at university. Whilst profit-driven economies promote greed, selfishness and profiteering from others, and extend the gap between haves and have nots, they do not have a great record for looking after those who need help the most. A profit-making society does not encourage people to look after others, it encourages people to compete against each other. These are the harsh but true consequences of living in a profit-driven society. From this perspective, money and profit are not the provider of all things good, they are the constraints and shackles that prevent people from deciding and doing what is right. Whilst many people truly believe money is the solution, what I'm suggesting here is that money and profit are actually the source of the problem, simply because they have become so utterly detached, abstracted and out of touch with both the real physical world and the better side of humanity and human values.

Over the centuries do-gooders have fought for things they believe to be right. Despite the initial opposition, those things that are the right thing to do, inherently correct or just plain common sense are nearly always accepted eventually. Significant things in this category include: abolition of slavery, fight against racism, women's rights, gay rights, mandatory seat belts and banning smoking in public indoor areas. Not everyone agrees, but the vast majority do. The reason these arguments were won is because the underlying basic principles were correct, it was common sense and it was almost impossible to continually argue against them over the long term. The same is now true with the argument over the environment, providing care for those who need it and free education. It is almost impossible to argue that we should commercialise education, not care for people, waste the Earth's resources or risk an environmental collapse, and yet a society driven by finance, profit and money seems unable, unwilling or incapable of deciding to do it.

Who should decide?

It is not only money that influences the decisions we make. As indicated earlier in Part 1, there are several other problems that also distort how we make decisions, such as these hopefully familiar examples.

- "I didn't really understand what they meant, so I just did this."
- "The results from the feedback say we had to change this."
- "That approach seems sensible, but the process says we have to do this instead."
- "We can't just leave it like that, we have to improve it."
- "The computer told me this, so it must be correct."
- "I couldn't be bothered reading and understanding all that, so I just agreed with it."

Along with money, these various effects join forces to form a toxic cocktail that limits and abstracts our understanding away from reality. They disable the ability of our common sense to shout, "This isn't right", allowing and encouraging us to switch off a little bit. Sometimes this might be justifiable to do; it is often easier to switch off and just accept, rather than think, understand, judge and decide for ourselves what is best to do. Time pressures, efficiency demands and the lazy and selfish parts of human nature don't help much either, so there is no blame or finger pointing here. We have all done it and it is a very common occurrence, because this is what our society expects or demands. Often, deciding based on money, time or process alone is the only option available in our society.

This toxic cocktail, which abstracts us away from the real world, is slowly disrupting and distorting our decision making, eroding and disabling our common sense. It produces a world where toddlers are actively encouraged to learn to climb ladders in a local park, even though they may be wary of heights and aren't aware of the dangers, but an intelligent professional adult is not allowed to use a ladder unless they have attended a half-day training course, read a five-page document and someone has signed a piece of paper to say that they are competent ladder climber. Below are two more real examples where this toxic environment has led to decisions which contradict common sense. The first at the level of international business, whilst the second is a personal example from my workplace.

Sales of beauty products

Sometime between 2000 and 2010 there was a growing awareness and protest about the undue pressure on women from beauty product advertising. At this point, common sense would suggest reducing the pressure on women, selling fewer chemical products and reducing the environmental problem of waste plastic packaging all in one go. Unfortunately, under the financial influences and pressures of our society a different answer was produced. The decision was to produce more chemical products, increase the waste packaging problem and increase the pressure on men to buy more beauty products and look good. This may put both women and men are under similar levels of commercial advertising pressure to look good, but it doesn't resolve the original problem of too much pressure being put on women, it just increases it to include men.

Installing a new software tool

At work I recently applied to get a new tool installed on my laptop, which was simple and easy to do (and exactly how it should be). However, I had problems when attempting to log in. I later discovered that I had to make a second application for a login account to be set up. Common sense suggests that it is blindingly obvious that anyone applying for the tool to be installed on their computer would also want to login and use it – so why separate the applications? This separation may be essential and critically important for all those people that only want to install the tool and then NEVER USE IT! For everyone else it would be common sense to combine the two separate applications into one. I would like to ask the person who decided this (and at some point, someone did), "Why on earth did you do it this way?" Below is a selection of possible responses.

a) Sorry I've been an idiot, this is a mistake, I'll correct it straight away.

b) Thank you for the feedback, I'll make an improvement for the next upgrade (but this is just more modern fashionable words or 'business speak' for the first response above).

c) I wanted to, but the computer system doesn't allow them to be done together.

d) I suggested we do it as just one application, but the process said we had to separate them.

e) We get paid a fixed rate per job, so splitting one job into several small ones means we get paid more.

Whilst the first may be true, it is unlikely to be admitted openly, whereas the other four are all indicative of the problems and frustrations described earlier. This is what causes all the frustration – when simple things like this are difficult and are faced by people every single day of our supposedly hugely efficient, affluent, convenient, comfortable, considerate, intelligent modern world.

It is becoming increasingly difficult for people to make decisions that deep down they know are right, and just common sense. In todays' world, decisions are not based on what is best for people and what they need, they are based on what is affordable, what is it profitable, what processes dictate and what computers will allow. We are 'switching off', losing control and becoming slaves to what money, processes and computers will allow, instead of deciding what is good, right or convenient for people. Increasingly our decisions are made in order to feed finance and economic growth, instead of the economy and finance providing for the population.

Whilst the influences of money, profit and machines have had centuries to influence us, the much more recent advancement of computer information, feedback and continual improvement have acted to reinforce, increase and accelerate the erosion of common sense, making it even easier to make more poor decisions. In your experience, which of the following are the most dominant forms of decision making and choice of action?

- Money deciding what is affordable or profitable.
- Money deciding what is best for people.
- People making decisions based on money and profit.
- People making decisions for the benefit of other people (such as charities).
- People making decisions selfishly for their own localised benefit.
- People doing what the computer demands (or is easiest for the computer).
- Computer tools calculating decisions based on money and profit.
- Computer tools calculating what is beneficial for people.
- Computer tools constraining and controlling what people can do, change or choose.
- Processes and procedures telling people what to do, regardless of the circumstances.
- Changing something simply because it hasn't been improved recently.

Over the last few decades our common sense has had to fight a much harder battle and it will continue to get harder. Most disheartening of all is the growing acceptance, even expectation, that all of this is the best way to get things done. If you haven't yet guessed, I don't agree. This might not be an immediate catastrophic problem (with the possible exception of the environment), but it is important to recognise that these influences exist, that they steer and distort how we think, work, decide and act. As a society we are accelerating in that direction. The immensely complex systems that we call 'society' and 'economy' are driving us away from what is good for the planet, away from what is good for people, away from our natural caring side towards the more selfish, monetary side.

Eroding common sense and cracking up

If decisions were made with true common sense, neither of the two previous examples would have occurred, and a few years ago I would have been able walk into a high street bank and exchange four old pound coins within a minute by talking to one bank employee (instead of following the convoluted 45-minute process). Decisions like these are not made by people who think about, understand and have consideration for how the consequences will affect other people. We are starting to let decisions slip away from us, away from common sense and away from reality. If any of this is really happening (and is not just a figment of my cynical, grumpy, opinionated imagination), then how many of today's decisions just don't seem right, are made without allowing common sense to intervene and cause people to shake their head in sheer disbelief? How many of the following examples indicate that our use of common sense is eroding and that the cracks are starting to show in the way we make decisions?

- Asking for feedback within 3 seconds of opening a website.
- Cheaper to buy a return ticket than a one-way ticket.
- A Health and Safety process that says you must wear gloves to apply hand gel.
- Room full of educated professional people, nodding and agreeing with words that contain no real content or that don't even make sense if you think about them.
- Spending time to write a process for an intelligent, experienced, professional adult to do a task that teenage children can do at home, by buying a few items from the high street.
- Politicians breaking the rules they make.

- Trillions of pounds made available to the banks, whilst there are insufficient funds to give nurses a pay rise or to pay for more police officers.
- Making a profit from selling debts.
- Paying the head of a company responsible for 346 deaths a $62 million payoff[3] (I thought they were paid to be legally responsible, not to be heavily rewarded when things go wrong).
- The introduction of hand gestures to control the volume in your car, after the previous improvement put the button on the steering wheel, specifically so you didn't have to move your hand off the steering wheel.
- Expecting a theory that works well for machines to produce similar results for unreliable people.
- Attempting to prevent fly-tipping whilst demanding a financial cost penalty for using the preferred alternative at the local tip.
- Improving something so many times (like the organisational structure of a company) until it returns to one of its previous states.
- Paying someone more than £100,000 a week to play football, whilst people who save lives earn less in 2 years (or 100 weeks).
- Listening to a speaker read out presentation slides verbatim for 2 days qualifies you as a competent person, now responsible for judging and assessing other people.
- Parents signing a COVID-19 vaccination consent form for their 15-year-old child at school, only for the child to be refused the vaccination because their 16th birthday was a few days before the vaccination day.
- A finance company providing £16.7 billion of bonuses and benefits to employees, 12 months after accepting bailout payments in 2008.[4]
- Having to make a judgement between £50,000 debt and a university education.
- Keeping medicine from someone based on cost, whilst someone is being kept alive on life support for months against their will.
- Call centre employees never deviating from the script, even when previous answers completely invalidate the next questions.
- Earning more by serving coffee than nursing and caring for people.

- Unable to swap two appointments on the same day, at the same location.
- Destroying food harvests because starving people can't afford to buy it[5] (which happened in the 1930s and inspired the book *The Grapes of Wrath*[6]).

All of these are cases where I've thought "Something is wrong here", yet at some point our society decided that each of these were acceptable or the correct thing to do. The world is a complicated place and people have different opinions on things, but this list contains decisions that very few people would be willing or able to justify and those that do attempt to would need to resort to some of the empty, generic, standard, duplicitous language described in the WORDS chapter of Part 1 (Chapter 1). Somehow, they are just counterintuitive, nonsensical and not common sense. Yet this list can be extended and reinforced with similar examples, whenever you hear or say phrases like:

- "The world is going mad."
- "Where is the common sense in that?"
- "What on earth have they done that for?"
- "I can't believe they decided to do that."

The sheer complexity of our society and of people means that there are no perfect or easy solutions, but how many of these examples will it take to indicate that the stronger influences within our society are starting to distort our judgements and highlight cracks in our collective common sense?

The world is going mad

These days we often deride and smirk at the theories and methods of the medieval era and how detached they were from the scientific reality we know today. The days of prosecuting witches, using poisonous arsenic and lead as medicines and the more recent promotion of smoking between 1930 and 1960 are now long gone. For a few hundred years our scientific understanding of how the real world works has allowed us to utilise it for our benefit. However, is it possible that we are now in the embryonic stages of allowing the growing influences of money and computers to abstract and detach us from this reality again? There are enough clues, hints and suggestions in this book, hopefully with some degree of explanation and justification, to indicate that this is starting to happen. The popular phrase "the world is going mad" is just our own modern-day version of laughing at our detachment from reality, as we are stunned by the absurdity of some of our decisions and actions. Are these the first signs that some cracks are starting to appear, as decisions that weren't made in the best interests of the population make contact with the physical reality of the real world and get exposed for what they really are? Either that or I'm already much more of a grumpy old man than I thought.

The opinions you have read so far may appear highly controversial or totally wrong, whilst to others they may seem like facts that are so blindingly obvious they are not worth putting in a book. Either way, it is totally irrelevant whether they are valid or not and it is equally unimportant if you agree with them or not. The only thing that is important is what is real or not. We all live on a single, real, physical planet called Earth and it does not care for any of these opinions or ideas, yours or mine. It does not see or hear any of our written and spoken words (or rants) and it does not care one iota for the monetary value of anything we have, want or do. All that the real physical world does is respond to our physical actions and follow the indifferent, steadfast laws of physics and the related (but less formal) 'law of diminishing returns' by telling us the physical consequence of those actions, like a cup of tea going cold, buildings collapsing if they were made with poor materials or warming up the planet when we release too much carbon dioxide into the atmosphere. The real physical world tends to keep simple things simple, complicated things complicated, difficult things difficult and people as unreliable and imperfect as they have ever been, so continually attempting to squeeze lumpy, round human pegs through increasing tighter small square holes won't change any of that either.

Despite all these moans and groans, over many centuries and huge amounts of effort, endurance, ingenuity, common sense and technological advances, the world is getting better and more comfortable, albeit with some consequences. The real physical world does not provide 'something for nothing' and all this comfort is at the expense of generations of slaves and workhouses, pollution, diminishing natural reserves, a reduction in forests and wildlife, increases in carbon dioxide emissions and the poor treatment of many working people worldwide. Naturally this version of our very comfortable Western society can continue, with the same benefits and the same consequences, until the real physical world responds and shows us what is wrong, such as running out of some essential rare metals, losing another species of animal or passing one of the environmental tipping points. The financial world won't mind any of this, providing an alternative supply of profit can be found elsewhere. It will continue because it can't stop without allowing the 'financial inverted mountain' to wobble and fall yet again. Again, there will be politicians, financiers, corporate leaders, optimists and wordsmiths that will dismiss all this with yet more bland, empty sets of words like "With the right incentives we can improve and together we can solve these issues to make the world a better place for everyone". Apart from the fact that this rather vague collection of words does not actually say anything whatsoever, what exactly do they think these 'right incentives' are and when do they think the incentives will change? For centuries, the incentives have been money and profit, and their influences are increasing not reducing. Some possible candidates for the 'right incentive' over the last 50 years include partial nuclear disarmament, world famine, growing population numbers, pollution and climate change, but these have not shifted the incentive away from money and profit. Perhaps these five alternative incentives were too trivial and not significant enough. Perhaps what is needed is a global financial meltdown or a global pandemic. Oh, of course, we have had both these in the last 20 years. So, what exactly are the 'right incentives' and when are they going to replace the current incentives of money and profit? Because until then the influences shown in the earlier flow diagram, from our financially driven society, will continue to grow and the direction will not change. We will continue to allow monetary value, processes, computer information and the market (which is supposedly always right yet doesn't have a clue about human values) to provide all the good answers and all the right decisions. Increasingly they will decide what is good for people, they will continue to nudge and abstract us away from both reality and human values, whilst we accept having a bit less understanding of the consequences of those decisions. This kind of erosion of common sense is one of the most dangerous things possible, as it essentially means we are starting to ignore or lose a grip on reality, so perhaps the world really is going a bit mad.

A long hard look

It can be very difficult to see the things that we have known and experienced since birth in a different way. This chapter has attempted to step a long way back from all the familiarity and detail that we are immersed in every day, to see society from a very different, analytical, almost alien viewpoint, so that some of the different, less popular, unconventional, controversial and under-publicised aspects of our society become more visible.

In this respect, the work, thoughts and ideas that produced this book can be considered to be a 'long hard look' at society, albeit from the perspective of only one frustrated, grumpy, middle-aged, analytical mind (which means it might be nothing more than a collection of totally incorrect, invalid assumptions, opinions and conclusions). However, this type of occasional long hard look at things is necessary to see what is really happening, to not just sit back and accept or be blinded by the detail or normality of it all. It is always important to see, to think and to understand things, if you are going to make good decisions. Making decisions based on finance will only lead you in the direction that finance wants you to go. Making decisions based on what you want yourself will only benefit you and probably have a detrimental effect on others (like not indicating when driving). In whatever you do, stand back, look and think before you decide and act. In recent history, there have been several significant occasions when humanity has had the opportunity to do exactly this – take a big step back and have a long hard look at what is happening and how our society operates and works. Some of these were:

- 1918: End of the First World War
- 1929: Great financial crash
- 1945: Use of nuclear weapons
- 1945: End of the Second World War
- 1948: Declaration of Human Rights
- 1969: Moon landings
- 1972: Apollo 17 blue marble picture of Earth

- 1980s: Use of computers and the internet
- 1991: End of the Cold War
- 1995 onwards: Growing awareness of global warning and pollution
- 2001: dotcom bubble financial crash
- 2008: Global (and yet another) financial crash
- 2016: Awareness of environmental tipping points around the globe
- 2020: COVID-19 global pandemic

How many times have these significant points in history made any fundamental change to the way that our society operates? The answer is **ZERO!** Despite horrible catastrophes of war, the repeated shattering failures of the financial system, natural disasters and many inspirational life-changing human achievements, the total effect on the underlying structure of society and the way it operates is **NOTHING!** How many times has the answer to the question "Are we heading in the right direction?" changed the underlying structure of society – take a guess, **NONE!** The fundamental operation and characteristics of modern Western society are exactly the same as they were at the start of the list above and centuries before that. Naturally there have been some good points as well, new laws, increasing levels of equality, some attempts to make environmental changes and the introduction of some shiny new 'carbon dioxide tokens' that can be traded just like cash, debt and shares, but all of these have been done within the same underlying profit-driven, capitalist financial framework and in this respect nothing has changed. So, after all these significant historical events, more financial difficulties from the recent COVID-19 pandemic and rising energy prices and the possibility of several imminent environmental tipping points, is there any reasonable chance for change soon? **NO!** Everything will remain the same comfortable and accepted normality, exactly how it has been for centuries, and nothing will change.

Therefore, the next chapter assumes that there is no change or alternative to the direction our society is heading, that the influences on our decisions and the self-feeding loops will continue unrestrained by any financial limits. It attempts to predict where this will lead in the future. For those in some desperate need of a bit more optimism, the chapter after that awaits and attempts to find an alternative version of society which overcomes many of these problems and explains how things could be very different from today.

"Why is common sense less common than it used to be?"

15

WHEN IS ENOUGH?

"Capitalism is the astounding belief that the
most wickedest of men will do the most wickedest
of things for the greatest good of all."
(John Maynard Keynes, 1883–1946, economist)

Predicting the future is an interesting subject or game that many people, including writers, filmmakers, politicians and schoolchildren, attempt, but it is difficult to do and even more difficult to justify. Therefore, this chapter moves away from the relatively firm ground of real-world examples and crudely explained but hopefully reasonably justified opinions, onto the less certain terrain of thin ice. Predicting the future is always based on a collection of assumptions, predictions and more questionable ideas. One way to generate a believable or sensible vision of the future is to start from something that already exists and then extend, exaggerate or extrapolate it into the future and try to assess the consequences. This is the approach taken in my attempt below, but first here are four independent examples, which are all based on Earth, without any alien intervention and so represent a range of possible evolutions of an isolated human society on Earth.

The Hunger Games[1]

The Hunger Games, written by Suzanne Collins, has a society dominated by a strong authoritarian government, which concentrates wealth in an opulent capital city. There is a definite split between the haves and have nots, with many outside the capital city living in poverty, whilst rebellion is suppressed by strong police and military forces. This is therefore a politically led dystopia, where power and control are held by the government.

Idiocracy[2]

This film, released in 2006 by 20th Century Fox, is set 500 years in the future where common sense has been eroded and, as the title suggests, society is run by idiots. Here politicians are elected on little more than popularity alone and decisions are made on the (profitable) suggestions of rich businesses which hold the real power and control. Poor decision making leads to extreme situations, such as poor food production, as the film comically highlights the effects of disabling or removing common sense from decision making. Incidentally, the first 5 minutes of this film show how humanity arrived in this unfortunate state and this provides a poignant social-political statement in itself. It demonstrates how shockingly simple and easy it would be to slide in this direction and, based on a few surprising election results since 2015, a few people have claimed that it has already started to happen.

Science fiction anthology extract

About 20 years ago I was lent a science fiction anthology book, containing about a dozen extracts from classical or ground-breaking science fiction books (I tried to find the book title to reference here, but unfortunately failed). One of the extracts described a world where business corporations had become the dominant power. In fact, each corporation was an entire walled city where all the inhabitants were employees who never left the city enclosure. All the amenities such as restaurants, cinemas, sport facilities, hospitals, schools etc. were provided within the walls by the corporation. The city was defended by the corporation's own army and all deliveries in and out were made by armoured vehicles, because outside of the city walls was a lawless society where groups of people lived by scavenging what they could, an extreme example of haves and have nots. This was a society dominated entirely by huge, powerful business corporations. Life inside the city walls seemed good, but for an inquisitive mind, it does raise questions about the level of control the corporation would have over its employees and inhabitants, including education of children, and how easily this level of control could be exploited.

The Matrix[3]

No list of predictions about our future would be complete without mentioning the 1999 Warner Bros film *The Matrix*, in which machines have overtaken human capability and intellect and have control of the Earth, except for a few pockets of hidden human resistance. In this world it is computers and machines that hold the power and control. This version of the future pivots about a point in time when computer AI becomes self-sufficient and able to generate the instructions for other computers. Some AI experts predict that if or when this pivotal self-sufficient point happens, the acceleration will be phenomenally fast and uncontrollable, making computers and machines truly dominant. To reiterate, whenever a system is uncontrolled and self-feeding, the result will always be unstable or extreme.

These four dystopian futures all differ in which aspect of society has become dominant, exaggerated or extreme, be that a dominating government, a loss of common sense, all powerful self-governing industries or the dominance of machines over humans. My prediction of the future extrapolates the influences, the direction and the cracks from the previous chapter into the future. The collection of small sections below each looks at a separate trend or loop within our society and considers where it might lead, whilst taking the opportunity to compare and contrast my pessimistic (or realistic) dystopian opinions with some of the more optimistic utopian views that are more commonly promoted. However, you should be warned (and probably expect by now) that these more optimistic, utopian style views are not quite what they seem.

Financial influence and commoditisation

Under the influence of finance and money, more and more things become commoditised (given a monetary value), making it easier to buy, sell and trade. In a rough (but not accurate) chronological order, the following have all been commoditised over the centuries: precious metals and gemstones, weapons, simple machines, time (labour markets), land (real estate market), coal, energy, risk of accidents (insurance), occupying a space (such as car parks), clean water (which was a public service in the UK until 1989) and debt (yes banks can and do sell debt for profit). More recently, this has extended to giving value to a left arm, a thumb, a right foot or loss of sight (via incapacity compensation), charging for information (cloud storage and download quotas), renting a womb for 9 months (surrogate mother) and even reports of people illegally selling healthy organs for transplant on the black market.[4] More strangely, things that don't even exist are given monetary value, such as virtual pets, clothes, weapons and extra powers in computer games. You can even spend real money to buy virtual money in a game. One of the latest things to be commoditised is carbon dioxide emissions, as nations attempt to reduce them and stop the economy and financial world from just ignoring them.

Therefore, the question for the future is not "Will this continue?", but only "What will be commoditised next?" Things that do not yet have a monetary value are the weather, large parts of the sea, wildlife, orbital paths around Earth, the moon, our health, the polar ice caps, the countryside, animal species, movement of people, blood and oxygen. The nightmare of having to pay for oxygen was used in a BBC *Dr Who* episode called "Oxygen" (Series 10, Episode 5),[5] a repulsive concept that would make aerobic sports a costly exercise. Interestingly, countries that provide token payments for blood donations get fewer donations than those that don't, presumably because this removes the altruistic nature of the donation – so there really is more to life than just money. It is the totally abstract nature of money that allows it to be used to apply a value to anything and everything. There are no natural or physical limits for its use, so it can and will be applied to anything and everything. As this happens, more decisions will be based on or biased towards this abstract monetary market value and so abstract us further away from reality and human values, diminishing our common sense just a little more. My problem is that I don't think that all things are suitable for being commoditised, being bought and sold, or measured by monetary value, including water, prison places, care of people, medicines, education, nature, the atmosphere and blood – or is that just a bit too old fashioned?

Funding public services

The previous chapter explained the politically polarising topic of public or private funded services and how the 'lazy river' undercurrent loop drifts us towards private companies. Popular consensus says that this provides 'value for money' services, which, as I'm not inclined to contradict my earlier claims that the government is inefficient and ineffectual, is likely to be true. However, this value for money introduces a shift of emphasis and, just like most other things, it has some consequences. Consider a fortnightly rubbish collection, where some people request a weekly collection following hygiene concerns about rats and foxes. If your incentive was to benefit the public and provide a public service, the answer would be "yes of course, no problem" and doing it might even win you some appreciation, acclaim or votes. However, if your incentive was for profit and keeping costs down the response would be closer to "get lost, you must be joking" or "pay up-front first". Generally, businesses can and do provide the main essential service reasonably well and efficiently, but equally they are unlikely to provide more than the absolute minimum needed, due to the adverse effects on profit. Businesses are really interested in those areas where a profit can be made and so it is no coincidence that water, national grid, energy, postal system, transport services etc. are now all run as private businesses. If it can generate a profit, then businesses want to own it. Conversely, if it can't generate profit then they are not interested.

Therefore, it is not surprising that the government is left holding only those public services that are costly and not profitable, the time-consuming services that must be provided rather than sold. These remaining (costly) services then attract headlines highlighting how the NHS, police, education, councils etc. are underfunded. As tax revenues and expensive government (or national) borrowing struggle to keep pace with the continual rising 'cost of time' and wages, it will become increasingly difficult to provide these time-consuming public services. In future there will be more and more private dentists, hospitals and care homes instead of NHS ones, more and more private schools instead of government funded ones. Although politicians in government try hard to convince us, with their statistical BINFORMATION and vague 'politician speak', that public services are well funded, the real world suggests the opposite. If education is well funded, why do you need to get a £50,000 student loan and pay interest on it for 10–15 years? If care homes are well funded, why do you need to sell your home and hand over the cash to a private, profit-seeking company? If the NHS is well funded then why aren't there enough doctors, nurses and dentists? And why does full-time childcare cost about the same as a mortgage? Do you believe what happens in the real world or the words of politicians? Despite what politicians say, and regardless of your views or how you vote, this gradual replacement of public services by businesses has happened, is happening and will continue to happen. Less will be provided (funded by taxation) and more will be sold (by private businesses), as that is simply an unavoidable consequence of the 'lazy river' undercurrents within our society.

This decline in public services is already being filled by businesses in another more subtle way. To encourage current employees to stay and to attract new employees, businesses can provide incentives that are either expensive or difficult to obtain. These incentives started small, with things like onsite restaurants, company cars and access to sports facilities etc. but are now extending into areas where public service is decreasing, such as childcare and private medical care (as an alternative to the over-stretched NHS). If house prices continue to rise and become more unaffordable, it is not unreasonable to think of businesses starting to offer accommodation for employees as an incentive (if this is not done already). A small step from this could be for businesses to employ security patrols for their employees' accommodation, especially if police patrols in that area are not possible due to underfunding. From here it is foreseeable to see people working and living on a business-owned protected site. Eventually, step by step, we reach a small-town version of the fully protected armoured 'corporate city' described in the anthology extract above.

Large corporations

We already live in a world of powerful business and financial corporations that regularly buy whole businesses to grow their production capability, extend their distribution network, expand into future markets or obtain the intellectual rights that they want or need. These corporations can adequately be described as huge profit-making machines. They already have a large amount of power and control and there is no reason to believe this will stop. These powerful corporations will continue to expand, producing even bigger, more powerful corporations, perhaps eventually becoming rich and powerful enough to establish a 'corporate city' – at least, things seem to be heading in that direction.

Battle of the giants

The previous sections suggest that the power and influence of the large 'Demanding' businesses and the 'Detached' world of finance will continue to grow. Conversely, the 'Deceitful' government demonstrates signs of weakness in this three-way power struggle. Whilst it struggles to raise enough income through taxation to maintain the level of public services, it had to bail out the financial industry following the catastrophic financial crash in 2008. When the irresponsible financial institutions cheekily asked the government for a rescue package, in the manner of a teenager reporting to parents "I just crashed the uninsured car, can I have a new one?" the government dutifully paid up with some guidance along the lines of "Yes of course, but please be a bit more careful with it this time". This is yet another great unexplainable contradiction – the market forces and freedoms that the financial industry so vigorously promote and endorse count for nothing when they themselves need a bit of government help, support and backing.

Similarly, the government's inability to get all, enough or even any tax from those large corporations that control a significant portion of the employment and trade deals also suggests a weakness, an inability to penalise or control. Incidentally, this partially contradicts the more popular consensus view that stronger businesses provide more tax income to provide more public-funded services. It would therefore appear that the government is the weakest of these three giants, as it is more reliant on the large financial and business institutions to provide economic growth than they are reliant on it (there is a lot more of this in the two financial books described in the FINANCIAL PLAYGROUND chapter, Chapter 9).

I'm no expert, but between the remaining two giants my instinct is that business corporations are the stronger, because without any businesses the financial markets would have little to work with (company shares, investments etc.). However, this might be a little unjust, because the financial world does seem very apt at inventing and generating something out of nothing (or at least fresh air). In fact, some might claim it is their fundamental (perhaps only) role in society. Conversely, without the financial institutions, businesses could probably continue quite happily; they could still make and sell things, still make a profit just as businesses did hundreds of years ago, long before the financial markets started casting their magic spells.

Anyone can become rich

Here, the common consensus view is that our society is good and fair because "anyone can become rich" and this is factually correct and a good thing. However, it is another example of false logic to then interpret this as "everyone can become rich". Whilst it is factually correct that any single person or a few individuals can become rich, it is both false and impossible for everyone to become rich. This is very similar to the false logic where, although one process can solve "one" problem, it is incorrect to assume processes solve "all" problems. To make some people rich, many other people must pay a bit more for things and so remain a bit poorer. You can't have everyone making money from everyone as it will all cancel out and everyone will remain the same. You can try this at home with a group of people all with some money and you can even borrow from a pretend bank with 0% interest: if some get richer overall, then some get poorer (once all debts have been paid off). There is simply not enough money to go round and so those getting rich are entirely reliant on others being a bit poorer (or in debt). By its very nature being rich is at the expense of others being a bit poorer. This is true today and in future.

Therefore, there will always be a 'few rich' and 'many poor'. Despite all the claims and words from financial leaders, business leaders, politicians, workers' unions, campaigners and the general public wanting and trying to close the widening gap between the 'haves' and 'have nots', the previous chapter explained that this is simply not possible in any society where money can make more money, such as the capitalist approach of syphoning money towards shareholders. This does not make it inherently wrong, but it does make it impossible to close the gap (at least in raw monetary terms). Although it is slightly uncomfortable to admit this today, if this continually widening gap coincides with a future reduction or decline in the 'free' public services available, then ultimately more and more people will simply fall off the bottom of the care system. More of the 'have nots' will become scavengers.

Litigation loop

The popular consensus view on litigation is that it ensures a safer environment for everyone. One hundred years ago the concept of suing a business following the death of an employee was incomprehensible. The best that could be hoped is that a kind business leader would voluntarily make a one-off payment to the bereaved spouse. Since then, via regulation, employees gained more rights and eventually claims could be made against the business for injuries or death, protecting employees against unscrupulous employers. In many ways, this was both common sense and successful, until that unfortunate tipping point described in the SEWER SYSTEM chapter (Chapter 12) was reached. In theory, the small step of allowing lawyers to take a share of any financial gains was of little consequence at the time, but it added an extra interaction (or arrow) into the 'society jigsaw' and produced a self-feeding loop. This self-perpetuating loop quickly gained momentum, so that every lawyer could gain financially by encouraging anyone to claim against their employer, hospital or school, which in turn led to the explosion of documented evidence, processes and procedures that we are trapped in today, just to prove your innocence when assumed to be guilty.

Currently this litigation culture seems limited to 'employees vs business', 'patient vs hospital', 'student vs school' or 'public vs council' but it has recently spread to police using body cams and drivers using dash cams, for the sole purpose of collecting evidence that they have not done anything incorrectly. This is all a gentle slide towards the "guilty until you can prove your innocence". Taken to its extreme in the world of business, this type of litigation is effectively "you are guilty of negligence, until you can prove yourself innocent of it". Reading this is counterintuitive, it is against common sense, it is the reversal of everything we are taught about Western justice where you are "innocent until proven guilty". However, it is also the path we are on and the direction in which we are heading. Businesses must already deal with this for Health and Safety reasons, generating copious amounts of information, records and processes just to try and prove they are not negligent. No wonder Health and Safety has the ability to squeeze out every ounce of pragmatism and practical common sense from people, with this guilty until proven innocent burden hanging over you.

It would be a very unpleasant world to have to do the same at home. If you are already dismissing this prediction as preposterous, remember that litigation is a self-feeding loop, where the financial benefits encourage more people to become lawyers, who then need more litigation cases to work on, tempting future lawyers to extend the scope of litigation a little further. The number of practising solicitors tripled between 1980 and 2011 to around 118,000.[6] Assuming a similar rate of increase (of around 2,500 per year) would mean around 143,000 in 2022, which is lower than several online estimates. Do you think these increases might indicate something? With that in mind, now follow these few incremental steps into the future. Today it is possible to sue the owner of a building you are renting, say a group of friends using a local hall for band practice. If someone was injured by electrocution or something was to fall from the ceiling, it would be possible to sue the owners of the local hall. Perhaps a few years later a judge is convinced that there is very little difference between this situation and the band practising in someone's garage and so allows that claim to succeed as well. It is then only a small step to apply the same judgement to friends in your garden and then of course to people in your home, allowing homeowners to be sued for the poor condition of our gardens and houses. I believe there are already cases where burglars have tried to sue homeowners because they have injured themselves whilst committing burglary, but thankfully I believe common sense has prevailed so far and none of these ridiculous types of claims have won (yet?).[7]

At some time in the future, will everyone need to document or provide evidence of everything we do, just in case someone else thinks our action or lack of action has resulted in their injury? That is a frightening thought, but, to add insult to injury, in future there will be ever-increasing numbers of (blame and claim) lawyers, all encouraging more and more people to point the finger and say, "it was their garage", "it was their garden", "it was their house" and "it was their fault".

Technology advancement

It is true that our capitalist market society drives and incentivises the advancement of technology, which then provides so many benefits to so many people. This more optimistic fact and outlook will also continue into the future. However, a lot of this new technology will be expensive and so, just as today some dental treatments are only available privately and not on the NHS, the 'lazy river' effect will make it increasingly difficult for any (underfunded) government-provided services to use this new technology. Whether it is better dental fillings, targeted cancer treatments, new medicines or robotic surgery, many of these new technologies will be limited to or biased towards private hospitals, giving them a further market advantage for more customers (or patients who are willing and able to pay). Although our capitalist market society undoubtedly drives technology advancement, there is another common misinterpretation here. It is based around another case of false logic, where the negated version of a true statement is also believed to be true.

Capitalist market society drives technology advancement.
...incorrectly negates to...
Without capitalist market society there would
be no technology advancement.

Humans are naturally inquisitive and innovative, and were so long before there was any concept of profit, finance or market value. Stone-Age humans were using sticks and stones to make tools, children are inventive and inquisitive long before they learn about money and profit and most early science was done solely for understanding and genuine interest and not for profit. Newton's visible light spectrum experiments using prisms were done at his home in Lincolnshire whilst isolating from the plague around London and not at Cambridge University. Scientists are just people who have kept their childhood inquisitiveness, and many would be willing to do research at home or as a hobby, if it were possible.

Therefore, the premise or suggestion that only market economies, capitalism and profit can drive technology advancement is wrong and the idea that scientists would not do research without knowing it was profitable is simply absurd. Today the role of capitalist markets and profit is to provide enough money for expensive research equipment and to pay the salaries of scientists, in the hope that any new discoveries will then produce more profit in the future. They are therefore 'an' incentive, but not the 'only' incentive. Science and technology advancement can and will continue whenever and wherever scientists can be given access to experimental equipment and are paid enough to live comfortably.

Unlimited economic growth – when is enough?

Our society's self-inflicted addiction and dependence on unlimited economic growth was raised in Part 3. Unlimited economic growth means there is always a need to sell more – today, in the future and then after that. As more needs to be sold, more needs to be manufactured and we will need more materials and more energy. The big food and drink manufactures will see potential growth opportunities until everyone is eating their product every day. When eventually everyone is consuming one chocolate bar, one can of drink or one bag of crips a day, the manufacturers will need to aim for two a day, because they must grow more and sell more.

This growth all needs raw materials and energy. Recently, the limited and reducing levels of material resources means that recycling is now heavily promoted as part of the solution and it is essential to fuel further growth (we can't just keep digging copper and other metals and minerals out of the ground – they run out). Today recycling and reusing 100% of materials is considered the ultimate aim. To achieve it would be considered a utopian dream, pure perfection. However, assuming we can reach this utopia and the economy grows to the point at which we are using and recycling 100% of materials, how would economic growth and more sales be maintained? In this situation, further growth and sales can only be achieved by buying, using and recycling the materials more frequently. Instead of having a t-shirt or phone for 1 or 2 years, we will be encouraged and pressured into buying a new one every 6 months. Then perhaps every few months, few weeks or after only a single use. Eventually, you will need to replace your brand-new phone within minutes of getting it set up and wear clothes only once before they have to go for recycling to be sold again. We must have growth and more sales. Meanwhile, all this increasingly frequent recycling will take more and more energy. A possible alternative to this is a future where new growth is generated from the sale of non-material products, like online experiences, therapies and words, but presumably we will still need physical products like clothes, furniture, phones, gadgets and machines etc. If these industries can't sell more products, then how are their profits going to increase and what will then happen to the share price of these stagnating businesses?

Our current capitalist economy won't stop trying to grow, it can't stop trying to grow, so when does it end? When do we stop wanting more growth, more money and more things? Is it possible that our economy will ever allow us to say "£5 million profit is enough, we don't need more than that" or "five blades is more than enough to shave with"? Will it ever allow us to accept that our current phones work well for 3–5 years or more and that we don't really need a new one every year or two. Will it ever say that you have enough beauty products and clothes and now look good enough?

Even when all our products become totally environmentally friendly, there will still be the pressure to sell more and more and more, as our profit-driven capitalist market economy demands more growth. However, I'm fairly certain that neither Planet Earth nor Mother Nature need this growth. They both did perfectly well before the idea of economic growth was dreamt up. The laws of physics do not need this growth, the raw materials, plants and animals we utilise do not need this growth and individual people and our time spent on Earth do not need this growth either. What I'm suggesting here is that only the economy itself needs this growth, which is just a circular argument: "We need to grow the economy, because this type of economy needs to grow". This may be pedantic, but you would laugh at anyone who claimed, "I have to eat chocolate, because chocolate is what I choose to buy". For many centuries, this is the only economic system the Western world has known. Hence it is natural to assume that it is the only one we need or the only one available but, presumably, if we had a different type of economic system, then we may not need to be pressured by the influences of this type of unlimited growth. This is an important point to remember for the next chapter, which attempts to see if an alternative to today's economy is possible.

Knock-on effects and influences

As all these efforts to maintain economic growth, to sell more and more, continue, then so will all the influences, effects and consequences of it. All those self-feeding loops will continue to grow in strength and influence. Technology advancement, machines doing work and the cost of human time will all continue to increase, as will our use of computing, AI, (efficient?) processes and the abstractions they introduce. As our use, trust and reliance on this collection of abstractions continues to grow, more of the understanding, reasoning, context, relevance or even the truth of our information, decisions and judgements will be lost. Our common sense will erode and gradually be defeated, creating a population of idiots and a path leading towards a future of Idiocracy. Perhaps this type of losing touch with the real world will not matter, provided we can satiate ourselves by living alternative virtual lives in an abstracted online virtual world? We would only need sustenance, because our contentment and stimulation will come from being plugged into or connected to the virtual world, in something approaching the future depicted in the Matrix films.

In the future, to make things even better than they are today, there will also be even more of those helpful and efficient processes, administration, insurance, monitoring, Health and Safety checks, controls and record keeping. We are heading into a future where procedures will hinder, prevent, dictate, constrain and control everything we do. I'm fearing the day we have record and document when we blow our nose or wipe our arse, simply because it will be possible to do and might help to monitor the health of the nation. Just because technology makes it is possible, doesn't make it good, better or an improvement. These checks and processes, which previously made it difficult to offer some leftover balloons to a school and impossible to pass on and reuse a nearly new metal cabinet, will increase. They will continue to make all those simple, helpful things more difficult (perhaps even impossible), turning any attempt to help someone into an arduous, time-consuming quagmire that removes any pleasure, enjoyment and incentive to do it. More of those people who would really like to help, if only it wasn't so turgid and burdensome, will be further discouraged by the ever-growing risk of being blamed or sued for not doing it quite right (according to process), missing something or not having the right insurance. Putting all these hurdles and obstacles in front of the altruistic part of human nature might not be the same as increasing selfishness, but the practical real-world consequences of it are the same. There will be less help available to those who need or benefit from it. As bad and unintuitive as this sounds, in this future the inherent good part of human nature, the ability to help people and the option to do the right thing, will continue to be slowly squeezed and eroded.

Open your eyes

It is not until our society starts rewarding a more altruistic approach and stops financially rewarding more selfish behaviours, that people will change their attitude. When will the emphasis change to thinking about the wider society, to providing what other people need, to thinking and caring for others, instead of making changes that only benefit us locally or our abstracted economy? This idea of change always seems one more step away, one more month, one more pay rise, one more promotion, one more year, one more holiday, one more house move, one more election etc., but even then, the pressures, the influences and the decisions of our society always remain the same and it ultimately becomes just one more generation away. Within any society, people naturally follow the behaviours and expectations of that society; they do so to survive, fit in and be comfortable. This then promotes these same behaviours in others and the next generations. Nothing changes and even after major global events it all remains the same, under the same strong driving economic forces and influences.

Despite all this negativity and pessimism (or realism, as I would prefer to call it), the premise of this book is not to claim that Western society is broken or that everything is in a terrible state. In fact, many chapters have stated that the standard of life in the Western world is very good. The aim of this book is only to provide an alternative look at society, to view our society from a different perspective and to highlight some of the less well promoted aspects of it. The intention is to compare the "Why on Earth have they done that?" side of life, against the "Your feedback is important and with the right incentives we can continue to make improvements" side of it. My opinions are different, more questioning, more cynical, more analytical, more concerned with trying to understand what is real.

Some people may be shocked that the ideas of feedback, continual improvement, Health and Safety, money, profit, democracy etc. can be questioned, scrutinised or blasphemed in the way I have attempted to do. However, they are only my opinions, often justified with nothing more than a few exaggerated flippant explanations and a couple of real-life examples. They may be grumpy, cynical, entirely wrong, unjust, invalid or simply not what you believe or agree with. This does not matter, because the aim is not to persuade you to change your mind. The intention is only to emphasise how critically important it is to open your eyes, to understand and question what really happens, not to be blinded by the normality of it all. Equally not to passively accept all those vague, empty, almost meaningless collections of words that pass as a justification for the way our society operates. Hopefully this book has opened some eyes a little wider, provided some food for thought and raised some important questions to consider, but those are for you to decide.

In my experience, homes, pubs and offices are filled with far too many moans, groans and the claims that "The world is going mad" or "This isn't right or fair" to simply ignore or dismiss them with a few vague words like "By making improvements in the way we work, we can make a fairer society for all and look after the planet". If the content of this chapter is correct, then this last vague statement is simply false. Analytically I can't see an escape from these unlimited loops and this dystopian future, whilst the influences and knock-on effects of economic growth and higher finance continue to be the driving force behind most of our decisions and activity. We are heading towards a future where everything will be decided by money and the most valuable thing available will be human time, our hourly rate or minimum wage. Our time is something that is intrinsically available and free to every single person, yet it will become abstracted and distorted into the most financially expensive and important aspect of almost everything we do. That just seems to be inherently wrong.

Fundamental change

This book has attempted to explain how money and profit, along with several other contributions and influences, are abstracting our decisions away from reality. In stark contrast to this, I think the best way to benefit people and the planet is to make our decisions and actions more connected and consistent with the real world. If your common sense and instincts say it is a bad idea to close a hospital, then it probably is a bad idea to close a hospital, regardless of what the budgets say. If decision making was firmly based around people's needs and the real world, there would be much less need to disguise them behind vague, ambiguous words that attempt to justify them as the right choice.

This need to change our current approach was emphasised in a statement made by Sir David Attenborough on Easter Island, where he states that real success relies on changing our society, economy and politics.[8] However, this is far from easy. Apart from the sheer scale and complexity of the changes needed, there are also plenty of people in powerful and influential positions, with lots of self-interest in maintaining the current system. It is an endlessly growing, profit-making system that generously syphons money out of those financial pipes, towards personal portfolios and bank balances that already contain more cash than needed. Meanwhile, much further down the financial pipework, this is all to the detriment of those who have had to pay a bit more or have been paid a bit less.

I therefore struggle to see how such a dramatic social change could be achieved, even with the help of those in the powerful positions. However, for those younger people who agree with Sir David Attenborough or, more strangely, with this collection of frustrated opinions and viewpoints, it is necessary to take hope and inspiration from the idea that in 30 years, the beliefs and opinions of today's students will become the policies of government. Their views and beliefs are only valid if our society, economy and politics do not mould their behaviours, decisions and actions towards the current accepted norms, before they get a chance to change society itself. As the dominant species on Earth, it is only people who can choose to change society. Some may argue that insects, bacteria or viruses are the more dominant species, as they have existed on Earth for over 250 million years, which is 100 times longer than humans (about 2.5 million years), but I won't be waiting for cockroaches or worms to change our society, even if they do sometimes seem more competent and capable of enacting significant change than most politicians and business leaders. Furthermore, the COVID-19 virus has arguably provided more benefits for climate change than over two decades of collective attempts by world business and government leaders.

Perhaps change will only be considered after the next financial crash (and there will be one), another large scale war, environmental collapse, an asteroid strike or some other weird global event, like some kind of collective epiphany where world and business leaders, instead of just trying to add another zero to the end of some balance sheet, suddenly realise that money doesn't have to rule everything and that it might be good to help people for a change. Either that or wait until there is a generation that is willing and able to escape the addictive, never-ending, unlimited financial loops that we are currently caught in. If there is ever going to be any significant change in the way society operates, what could that alternative society look like and how would it operate? Although any such change would be immensely difficult in practice, thankfully this is only a book full of words, so it becomes just another tempting and intriguing puzzle to solve on paper. Therefore, the next chapter is my attempt to produce an alternative, more optimistic, utopian solution to this highly complex puzzle of society. For those who have struggled through this quagmire of pessimism and realism to get this far, it will hopefully also provide some well-earned relief and optimism.

---

*"Every decision made in consensus with current
views is a further step in the same direction."*

16

ALTERNATIVE SOCIETY

"We are made wise not by the recollection of our
past, but by our responsibility to the future."
(George Bernard Shaw, 1856–1950, winner of Nobel Prize for Literature)

The last two chapters have suggested that our decision making is being disturbed and abstracted away from reality, diverted away from the needs of people and planet towards the needs of profit, economics, finance and what computers or processes mandate. Those claims were first based on the relatively firm ground of some partially justified opinions backed up by a few real-world examples, before then venturing out onto the thinner ice of prediction and extrapolation into the future. This chapter now ventures even further out into the etheric void of 'thought experiments'. Whenever real experimentation has not been possible, thought experiments like "Chinese Box" (for AI) or "Schrödinger's Cat" (for quantum mechanics) are good analytical tools for testing ideas, theories or concepts. This is a world that philosophers and theoretical physicists use all the time to tackle some of the biggest unanswerable questions, using different hypothetical situations to see what the expected behaviour might be and whether the results would be sensible and consistent with other knowledge and experiences.

Therefore, the first half of this chapter creates an idea or concept of a hypothetical alternative social system, which aims to remove many of the problems and frustrations that I associate with today's modern society. The concept described below is not simply the first idea or concept that popped into my head, it is the result of repeatedly trying many different ideas and combinations over a couple of years (I just like doing complicated puzzles). Most ideas collapsed under the weight of inconsistency or just re-introduced the same problems that exist today. Eventually, there were enough different failed ideas and options to start mixing partial successes from one idea with partial solutions from another. As with previous chapters, only the main underlying driving mechanisms of society are considered, as again it is impossible to cover every aspect of human life. Hopefully this is sufficient to assess how people might react and behave to different situations and circumstances within this new society, such as how much people are paid, which jobs would be most attractive, how farming or big projects would be done, how social issues such as the need for prisons or schools would be tackled etc.

This particular thought experiment started from a completely blank sheet of paper as, in theory, this alternative society could be anything. So, if you are expecting just a few minor alterations, tweaks or improvements to today's society, you will be either disappointed or surprised. Also, if you are going to judge any new concept fairly, you must also remove any preconceived ideas of what the solution is or how it should relate to the existing system. It will be necessary to clear your mind, to be open to new concepts, and to loosen and break some of the mental constraints. Just as we don't judge cars as being wrong because they don't contain swimming pools, then it would be incorrect to say a concept is wrong because it does not contain a bank, especially if that concept can exist and operate well without the existence of banks.

A blank sheet of paper

Although the starting point was a blank piece of paper, there were a few essential starting principles to help define which options and solutions should be considered valid or not. These were intended to ensure the very best parts of the current system are kept and the very worst parts (according to my opinion) of the current system are not repeated. These self-imposed starting constraints are described below and should now be recognisable.

Human needs

A civilised human society needs to provide the three essential things that people need: 'sustenance' in the form of food and shelter, 'safety' in the form of an environment they feel safe in and 'stimulation' in the form of education, entertainment, hobbies, work etc. These must all be provided, and our current standard of living needs to be maintained. There is no intention to knit socks or grow your own potatoes.

Contribution and fairness

The current system rewards the contribution of a person in the form of wages/salary/money, so that those who contribute the most are rewarded the most (although today our notion of contribution is somewhat distorted or corrupted by endless profit making, with those who can kick a ball or sing earning far more than those who save lives). The underlying concept that people should be rewarded for their contribution must be maintained, by providing an equal and fair incentive for everyone to contribute and an associated disincentive or punishment for those who do not contribute to society.

Technology advancement

As technology advancement produces many of the true improvements that benefit the majority of the population, the drive for technology advancement must be maintained by some method, as without it, progress would probably stagnate.

Stability

The society must be stable. In my own clumsy way, I have already attempted to explain why the current financial system is an unstable, uncontrollable loop which can feed itself endlessly. I've also referenced much more qualified people who think the same and can explain it far better. Therefore, this alternative society should not contain any loops that allow constantly increasing benefits, without a means of constraint, limit or control.

Money

The original concept of money to ease (or lubricate) transactions is an essential part of our society and this fundamental role should be maintained (I don't fancy having to keep chickens, just so I can use them to buy clothes). The problem today is that cost is just an abstract value of 'what people are able or willing to pay' and so in this alternative the concept of money is retained, but the 'cost' is something is very different.

Planet Earth

Everything people do is limited by the resources available to us on Earth and the laws of physics. There should be some link, connection or method to ensure that our decisions do not become detached from the realities of the real physical world.

Other than these few self-imposed constraints, anything goes.

For those of you who like solving puzzles (and this is a really big one), you could now put this book down for a day, a week, a month or longer, pick up an empty pad of A4 paper, start scribbling and see what ideas you generate. You can choose to use the constraints above or use different ones. Either way, there is no puzzle more complicated than human behaviour and our society. Developing a thought experiment makes you think deeply about how people will react and use different types of rewards, rules, constraints etc. By starting from a blank sheet of paper you have the benefit of freeing yourself from any existing rules, rewards, restrictions, constraints or methods and you can invent your own new ones. Naturally this can only be done at a very simplistic top level, as it would take far too long to do in any level of detail. To emphasise this point, it is reasonable to suggest that even our current social system is still inconsistent and incomplete, with the combined effort from millions of people over several millennia. Therefore, the concept of this 'alternative society' is only done to the same basic level as the earlier 'society jigsaw'. It is now time to clear your mind and start to explore at least one concept for an alternative society.

Where to start?

It is incredibly difficult to break away from the grip that money and finance have over us. Questions similar to those below are difficult to answer with anything but "yes".

> Should we provide care for people in need?
> Should education be free?
> Should we have enough police, doctors, nurses and prison spaces?

Equally asking questions like the following also produce the answer "yes".

> Do we have enough people willing and able to be teachers, nurses, police etc.?
> Do we have the ability (materials, people and skills) to build schools, hospitals and prisons?

Nevertheless, our current society struggles to provide them, because if you follow the trail far enough back to the root cause, you eventually reach the point of "we can't afford to". Yet money, profit and affordability are all totally abstract concepts that we have forced on ourselves through the evolution of our society; they are not real physical constraints. The real physical world does not care about how we choose to measure and judge what is possible or not. It will only tell us the result of our actions and decisions, like overcrowded prisons or old people without care. The 'alternative society' concept below attempts to break out of this financial grip and switch the emphasis towards benefiting people and the planet and find a way to guarantee (and I do mean guarantee) that the things above are always possible and done, because in theory, in desire and in reality, they should be possible. It also attempts to remain a completely stable system which cannot collapse (like in 2008). It contains some limits to constrain any endless push in the same direction, which are in keeping with the natural 'law of diminishing returns'. These limits are intended to let people know when "enough is enough".

By way of introduction and acclimatisation to this alternative society, and before explaining some of the more specific aspects, it is probably beneficial to break down a few mental barriers and disperse some preconceptions in preparation for what is about to come. This is just the mental equivalent of dipping your foot into the water to prevent being stunned by the shock of jumping into a cold lake. The list below provides some idea about what you should start to mentally let go of; don't get unnerved by their absence and don't waste time grasping for equivalents. This alternate society has:

- No tax.
- No inflation.
- No stock and shares.
- No profit.
- No banks.
- No interest rates.
- No insurance.

Similarly, you should get used to the idea that in the real physical world both time and raw materials are freely available to us and so to be consistent with this, neither of them carries any intrinsic monetary value of their own. Essentially, both time and raw materials remain free, but it is not quite that simple. For now, just contemplate the idea that the cost of an employee's time is free, so that businesses or employers do not pay any wages. You should also be prepared to accept that being sacked (or 'culled') from your job is acceptable and common (which is explained later but sounds a lot worse than it is). There is also a much-reduced role for government and a very different voting system, in which you don't vote for politicians, parties or people, but for government departments. Hopefully that is sufficient to loosen some of those 'mental chains' and at least get over some of the initial shock, in preparation to see something very different from our current version of society.

A bit more democracy

The DEMOCRACY and JIGSAW chapters (Chapters 13 and 14) outlined my view that, in practice, our version of democracy is not actually that democratic at all, with most decisions and budgets set by a small group of like-minded people. In our current society, the need for a new hospital in Yorkshire or a train link in Cornwall requires a huge amount of discussion, time and inefficiency, which can also be extremely expensive, as all that discussion time has to be paid for (I once heard that

£50 million was spent on the new Wembley Stadium before a single brick was moved; I don't know if this is true or not, but even £5–10 million is a huge amount of expensive talking). Equally, a new sports centre in the Midlands or a new cinema in Newcastle can't be provided or even started until a commercial company judges it to be a profitable venture. Our current society is one where a lot of people don't get what they want or need and, on the few occasions they do get what they asked for, it often comes a lot later than they originally needed it.

To overcome this, the alternative voting system allows each voter the same fixed allocation of 'voting funds', which they can spread across the different government departments (education, sport and leisure, health, law and order, transport, industry, defence etc.). These voting funds will remain within the voters' local area (or 'constituency' in today's language), meaning more funds will be available in large cities with lots of people and less in rural areas with fewer people. In this way, areas that want to build new schools can provide their own budget by voting a large proportion of their voting fund to education. Similarly, an area with a lot of crime can vote a significant proportion of their funds to law and order. A list of what the local public want to be provided will be kept in local registers or petitions, then when there are enough signatures (say 10–20% of the local population) and enough voters' funds provided, the work will automatically start. No debate, no financial assessment, no decision making, no backing out, no talk, just action. Here, what the people ask for in the local registers and pay for with their voting funds, they get in their local area. In this way a medium-sized town near a lake could get the water sports centre they wanted, a town can get a bridge over a busy road, a quiet country village could get a small municipal swimming pool, or a large seaside town could get a new water park or roller coaster to attract more visitors to the area.

It also means that initially there will be some frivolous public vote moments (remember Boaty McBoatface[1]) and some embarrassing, humorous or inappropriate statues erected in a few town squares. However, this playful experimentation with a newfound control and responsibility won't last long. People may be unreliable and lazy, but they are not stupid and can be quite selfish, especially when trying to obtain what they really want. As soon as they realise this is the only way to get a community hub for their children to go to on Wednesday evenings, or a bypass to remove the 30-minute traffic jam on their daily commute, then they will very quickly start to use it sensibly. This is a far more democratic and efficient way of providing what people want and need locally. It removes the problems of inefficient decision making and insufficient tax revenues and means that people's votes become much more 'strongly coupled' or linked to local needs. In stark contrast to today, people will have far more democratic control over changes in their area.

Importantly, these voting funds are not available for individual people to spend themselves; there is no 'opting out' of the system and pocketing the funds yourself. To spend them you must vote, which would also probably solve the decline in voting numbers we see today. To make this type of system work in practice, people would probably allocate their voting funds annually, as 4 years is still a long time to wait for something you need soon or have a problem with today.

A different type of business

Once the voting system has made funds available within the various government departments, they are then used as taxes are today, to pay businesses to provide various work, products and services, such as a new school, more police, a sports club, a bus link or new footbridge etc. However, as businesses do not have to pay any employee wages, the funds are only needed to purchase materials, products, machines and fuel etc. This means that all business costs and budgets are limited to 'purchases only' and are not affected by either wages or time delays. It is hoped that this approach will remove the need for those endless re-planning and re-costing exercises that sap even more time and effort away from delivering the product itself, an irony that some readers will recognise directly from their work or from the Dilbert cartoons.[2] Despite the earlier attempt at a brief acclimatisation, you are likely to be still very much in the mindset of today's business, so you will now be asking "If time delays don't have any cost, then where is the incentive?" The explanation of 'incentive' will come later, but to partially allay any doubts immediately, any delays that reduce sales will directly affect each and every employee directly in their pay, so you now have the incentive back and it is arguably a much stronger incentive.

This novel approach now raises many more questions, so in the true style of FAQ (frequently asked questions) website pages, here are some more things I want to tell you about, without actually answering the specific questions you have.

1. **What happens to funds that the business does not spend and are left over?**
   Any unspent funds remain available to the government department to spend on other local projects that people have specifically asked for in the petitions or are otherwise considered to be of wide local benefit. All the funds in and out of the business are recorded (just like today), but as there is no concept of profit a business cannot benefit from the unspent funds. It could choose to spend any leftover funds buying shiny new equipment, but there are other incentives or deterrents to prevent this from happening.

2. **If all labour is free to the business, who pays the wages?**
   All wages are paid from a single Central Administration, similar to the civil service today, which carries out two roles. Firstly, it monitors the performance of each business and secondly it pays wages to employees based directly on that performance (this provides the 'incentive' not to spend or waste leftover funds). As you now probably expect, business performance is not a measure of profit, but is more related to the real physical world, in the form of waste and customers.

3. **This sounds like everything is state-funded work and so is likely to be inefficient?**
   In this alternative society, funds are provided by government departments to businesses, but the work is not necessarily controlled by the government or even for the government. The government simply provides sufficient funds for the business to purchase everything they need for a particular job or project. The drive and incentive for efficiency, delivery and sales will come directly from the business employees themselves, as their take home pay is directly related to the business performance, as you will see later.

4. What happens if the business needs more funds to complete the work?

They can simply spend more to complete the work. The work is needed and is already part way through, so why delay or stop it with wranglings and debate? However, any large overspend will affect the business performance and employee take home pay.

5. If this method is used to fund local amenities, roads, schools, skate parks, cinemas etc. then how is the manufacture of other products such as TVs, phones, toys, small electrical products, carpets, magazines, machines, tools etc. funded?

This is not covered above. The consumer-driven industries that provide everyday items and services will operate in the same way as those businesses already described, with only one small difference. Instead of receiving funds from a government department, they receive funds from the Administration that monitors and measures their performance. These businesses recover the spend back from sales to customers, much as they do today. The difference here is that no profit is possible, so a perfect business will continually operate with a balance of zero, where sales exactly match purchases. The operation of businesses is explained in more detail later.

6. What happens if people don't vote for essential national items, such as inoculation programmes, defence, refuse collection, rules and national standards etc.? How are these funded?

The truly national decisions of this type will be carried out by a 'slimline government', using a very similar method of funding. However, this part is not controlled or chosen by the voting public and is explained next.

A slimline government

Not all the voting funds are spread across the government departments. Some fixed percentage is provided directly to a reduced, slimmed-down government. The role of this slimline government is not to set budgets, set tax levels or make decisions on sports stadiums. This removes the need for a lot of inefficient time wasting, delays and compromised, watered-down decisions. Here the role of the slimline government is only to decide on truly national decisions such as national laws, defence, education, inoculation programmes etc. These fixed funds, over which the public has no direct influence, would be used to fund businesses in providing the national products and services needed, in a very similar way that our taxes are spent today. The diagram below suggests that only 30% of these voting funds go to this slimline government, leaving 70% for the public to spend on local projects. If this seems like giving too much responsibility to the 'unreliable' public, then reversing it and giving only 30% for voting public control would still provide far more true democratic control to voters than the current (fully?) democratic general election voting system.

This initial outline and brief introduction are sufficient to show this alternative society in a diagram at the same level of detail as the earlier jigsaw diagram. This alternative is intuitively and visually simpler, with two fundamental points. Firstly, the (unreal) finance world has disappeared, taking the contradiction layer with it. Secondly, the fresh air source of money is now feeding directly into businesses (as business funds) and to the public in the form of their take home pay and voting funds.

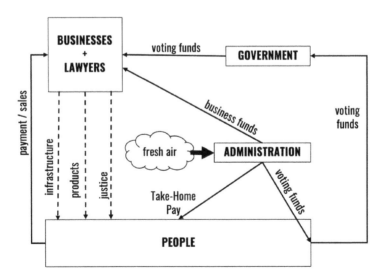

The next diagram adds some extra detail (not shown in the original jigsaw diagram of our current society) by separating the government box into the slimline government and the separate departments and also adding links to represent the monitoring of business performance by the administration, as this detail will be useful later.

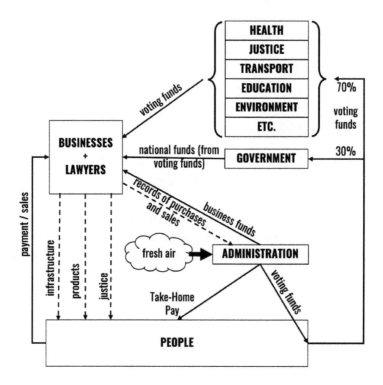

So far, all this has skirted around the topic of what these funds and wages actually are, and admittedly it is still far from clear what this new 'incentive' looks like. Hopefully this initial outline and context will now allow both the funds and incentive to be explained more clearly.

Funds, money and allowance

At best our current version of money is a very loose, open, changeable, almost arbitrary measure of what someone is willing to pay based on supply and demand, such as £50–100 for a white t-shirt with one logo or pattern, but only £5–10 for a very similar t-shirt with a different logo or pattern. At worst, it is a measurement system entirely detached from reality and totally unsuitable for measuring the value of education, care, conservation or the level of carbon dioxide (CO_2) in the atmosphere, in just the same way that a thermometer is unsuitable for measuring weight or a ruler is unsuitable for measuring nutritional value. I have argued that things are a lot clearer and easier to understand if they are not abstracted but instead represent something real, and so in this alternative society money is fundamentally a measure of waste. Mother Nature provides raw materials for free. We can grow trees and food; limited oil and metal ore exist in the ground, and everyone has time available to use freely (literally all the time). As indicated during the earlier acclimatisation, these all remain free. It is only our use of these materials – cutting wood, refining oil, producing steel, preparing and packaging food and the manufacture of other products – that takes energy and creates some kind of waste. Consider the rather convoluted process of converting oil into a plastic toy (many plastics are derived from a by-product of oil).

Starting with the raw material, the oil is provided free by Mother Nature, but it requires a lot of machines and fuel to get it out of the ground. The fuel used can never be returned, reused or recycled, as it all turns into waste energy predominantly in the form of heat and noise, so adding to the ever-increasing levels of entropy (as defined in the second law of thermodynamics). The machines themselves must also be made, generating their own level of waste and cost. As is already done today, the cost of each machine is spread across all the oil it can produce. Therefore, the sale price of the raw oil is only the price of the machines and fuel used to obtain it.

Once you have the oil out of the ground, it then needs to be distilled into several factions from thick bitumen, through ever lighter factions of diesel, naptha, petroleum and gas, amongst others. This distillation will require heat (which is again lost), pipes and containers, so the sale price of the distilled products will then be the 'waste cost of raw oil' plus the 'waste cost of oil distillation' and so the chain continues.

The naptha and gas products, along with some additional chemical ingredients, produce a wide range of products including glues, rubbers and plastics. This hydro-carbon chemistry needs more fuel and chemicals, which are used or lost during the production of the plastic. So, the price of the plastic sheeting will be the cost of 'waste from raw oil' plus the cost of 'waste from oil distillation' plus the 'purchase cost of other chemicals' plus the 'waste from the chemistry used to produce the plastic'.

Finally, the plastic sheets need to be cut, heated and moulded into shape, requiring more fuel, heat, cutting and moulding machines and some more waste products. The moulded plastic will then be assembled with some other non-plastic parts to make the whole toy. In this way the sale price or 'waste cost' of the toy will represent only the real waste generated in its production.

- Waste from raw oil.
- Waste from oil distillation.
- Purchase cost or waste cost of other chemicals.
- Waste from the chemistry to produce plastic.
- Waste from the plastic moulding and cutting.
- Purchase cost or waste cost of the non-plastic parts.

In this way the cost of every single product, be it a plastic toy or the oil drilling machine, is nothing more than the accumulative cost of the energy and waste required to produce it. To clarify and avoid misinterpretation, at each stage the 'waste cost' is always spread evenly across the quantities produced, so the cost of a machine capable of producing 1,000,000 gallons of oil is divided by 1,000,000 to contribute the waste cost of 1 gallon of oil, just as is done today. The same is done at each step. Interestingly, because no profit can be made, if the oil drilling machine was reliable and went on to produce 2,000,000 gallons of oil, then all the additional oil would be sold more cheaply, because the waste cost of the machine has already been accounted for in the oil already sold. The lower cost of oil would benefit the customers directly and not the finances of the company.

To summarise, the cost of any item is simply a direct measure of all the waste generated while making it (all the things which are not resold, reused or recycled). So, what is the money in our pockets? Money is essentially an allowance system, where this allowance represents the amount of 'waste' you are entitled to use. For example, a well-paid job will give you a large allowance, allowing you to purchase lots of products that have generated a reasonable amount of waste. At this point, astute readers who have been able to release themselves from the mould of our current system will now be starting to realise two important things about this approach, both entirely consistent with the real world. Firstly, the most environmentally friendly products will now automatically be the cheapest and so be the most desirable to buy (there is some common sense at work here). Secondly, the better a company becomes at managing waste, reusing it, selling by-products to other industries etc., the less waste it will have and the cheaper its products will become. Here the overriding incentive of the business switches from maximising profit, to just reducing waste. Again, that seems more like common sense to me. Admittedly, reducing waste is already part of today's profit-driven businesses, but unfortunately the high and increasing cost of people's time means that, financially speaking, reducing time is far more important than reducing waste. This alternative approach would mean that the average personal wealth, how much we can have, is now related to how efficiently we can extract energy from our environment and reduce waste in production. That is much more closely related to reality than becoming increasingly dependent on constantly chasing further economic growth.

Extrapolating this new approach to its ultimate theoretical extent means that any business that can produce products for zero waste can offer products for free. If all businesses did that, then all products would be free to all. Unfortunately, this 'pure utopia' is not possible in practice because of physics and that unavoidable second law of thermodynamics (which states that no energy transformation can be truly 100% efficient and some energy is always wasted). However, those industries with a good renewable source of both energy and materials could produce products with a very low 'waste cost' sale price. This approach means that prices are continually being driven down, tending towards zero with ever more waste-efficient production, meaning that more people can have more things that are more environmentally produced. Isn't that one vision of a real utopia and doesn't it indicate that the direction of this alternative approach is at least correct? It is also in stark contrast with today, where the constant demand for more means that prices are caught in a never-ending cyclic loop of economic growth and profit. Despite today's claims that production is more efficient and waste is being reduced, prices must still increase, which seems strange and contradictory when put that way.

Basic allowance and Take-Home Pay

Now that it is understood that funds and money represent 'waste' and wages are a form of a 'waste allowance' that can be traded for items that have a waste cost, the next most important question, at least for that selfish part of you, is "HOW MUCH DO I GET?" This depends on what you do, how much you do and how well you do it, very much like today's monetary reward system. In this alternative version of society, the 'Take-Home Pay' is based around a fixed 'Basic Allowance' and two ratings, a 'Job Rating' defining the type of work you do, and a 'Business Rating' based on how well it is done and how many people benefit, as in the calculation below.

Take-Home Pay = Basic Allowance + (Basic Allowance × Job Rating × Business Rating)

Both the Job Rating and Business Rating are described in more detail below, but to provide a very quick initial illustration, a business with zero customers and zero sales will not benefit anyone and will have a Business Rating of zero, so every employee of that business will be paid only the Basic Allowance regardless of their job or role. As the same Basic Allowance is also paid to anyone with zero customers and zero sales, including unemployed and retired people, it acts directly as both 'unemployment benefit' and a 'basic state pension', without any complicated application processes, assessments, delays, backdating, personal circumstances, personal savings or form filling. This is not a happy coincidence: the calculation was intentionally designed to work this way, so that if someone leaves employment, their Business Rating is zero and they automatically receive the Basic Allowance without any bureaucracy.

Although I was not aware of it when creating this calculation, the idea of a basic income payment is not a new idea and is commonly known as either the Universal or Basic Income Guarantee (UIG/BIG).[3] The main problem with these proposals today is that it would be extortionately expensive, and someone must pay for it, presumably via taxation of some sort. Conversely, here the Basic Allowance comes directly from fresh air, so the whole population get a little bit of the benefit and convenience that only the finance industry has today. The aim of all these concepts (UIG, BIG or this Basic Allowance) is to provide sufficient funds to support a minimum standard of living, including food and cheap housing etc. Remember that in this alternative society, cheap only means 'very little waste' and is therefore not necessarily directly associated with unpleasant, although that may also be the case. Like today, this minimum Basic Allowance is not the full pension. The full pension is calculated on contributions made over your full working career and explained in more detail later. For now, both the Job Rating and Business Rating that define your Take-Home Pay need explaining.

Job rating

Today the highest paid jobs tend to be those that generate the most profit – market traders, bankers, business leaders and lawyers etc. – whilst those doing the essential jobs we rely on like nurses, paramedics, teachers, farmers, delivery drivers, firefighters etc. tend to get very little in comparison. As you have probably guessed, this alternative society changes all that. Here the biggest wages (or allowance) go to those who provide the most benefit to other people, based on three ratings.

- Job Role Rating, scored from 1–3, is a measure of how essential a job is to society. Health, hygiene and basic food would all score 3, whilst producing plastic flags and fingernails would be the lowest score of 1 because we could all live without them if we had to.
- Job Skill Rating, scored from 1–3, is a measure of how much education and training is required, so doctors, vets, pilots and lawyers would all get a score of 3, whilst a shop assistant or parcel delivery may only score 1, with a bus, train or articulated lorry driver somewhere between.
- Job Experience Rating, scored from 1–2, is a measure of how long you have been doing this work or how good you are at it.

$$Job\ Rating = Role\ Rating \times Skill\ Rating \times Experience\ Rating$$

This means that the lowest paid job would have a Job Rating of 1 (from 1 x 1 x 1), whilst the highest paid job could have a Job Rating of 18 (from 3 x 3 x 2). The highest paid person who provides the biggest benefits to people in society would earn 18 times more than a person providing the least amount of benefit to society. This factor of 18:1 would go a long way to dramatically reduce the gap between the haves and have nots, as it is much smaller than the difference today. To put this into some kind of context, today many charities tend to work on a ratio of 15:1 between their highest and lowest paid employees, whilst in normal businesses the average ratio is around 70:1, with ratios of 100:1 being common. Some companies operate with ratios up to around 300:1 before reaching the rare anomalous businesses that think a ratio of up to 1000:1 is acceptable.

To provide some idea how this would work, the table below contains some suggested numbers for both the role and skill ratings, whilst using an experience rating of 1.0 in all cases. The jobs have been ordered from highest score to lowest, to clearly show how those helping society the most get rewarded the most.

JOB	ROLE RATING	SKILL RATING	JOB RATING	COMMENT/REASONING
Surgeons/ Doctors	3.0	3.0	9.0	Essential and highly skilled
Teacher	3.0	2.5	7.5	Essential but not as skilled as surgeons
Emergency services	3.0	2.5	7.5	Includes police, fire and ambulance
Pilot	2.5	3.0	7.5	Highly skilled, but not as essential as saving lives or teaching
Farmer	3.0	2.0	6.0	Essential and skilled
Nurse/Caring	3.0	2.0	6.0	Essential and skilled
Lawyer	2.0	3.0	6.0	Highly skilled, but not as important as saving lives or food
Engineer/ Research	2.0	2.5	5.0	Skilled and required to provide essential infrastructure
Vet	1.5	3.0	4.5	Highly skilled, but for the benefit of animals, not for people directly
Athlete/Sports	2.0	2.0	4.0	Skilled and dedicated, important for entertainment
Performer/ Artist	2.0	2.0	4.0	Skilled and dedicated, important for entertainment
Driver	2.5	1.5	3.75	Important and partially skilled

JOB	ROLE RATING	SKILL RATING	JOB RATING	COMMENT/REASONING
Hygiene worker	3.0	1.0	3.0	Essential, but not very skilled
Administrator	1.5	1.5	2.25	Requires some skill and is needed (but computers do a lot of the work)
Accountant	1.5	1.5	2.25	Accounting is far easier without tax, investments, inflation etc.
Shop assistant	2.0	1.0	2.0	Useful and helpful but not very skilled

If you find yourself nudging some numbers up and down a bit or even increasing and decreasing the range of scores to match your own opinions and preferences, then this is all perfectly valid and acceptable; these numbers are only indicative of how it could work. However, an inclination to alter a few numbers could be interpreted as a subconscious acceptance of the basic underlying principle, in contrast to the dismissive disgust at an outrageously silly idea. Although this is not a complete reversal of what we have today, it does come quite close, especially if you compare accountants with teachers and nurses, for example.

As with any new idea, this raises lots of questions and contention. Specifically, animal lovers might disagree and campaign for the Role Rating of vets to be increased, whilst others will raise the point that sportspeople have short careers and need to earn enough money to see them through 30 years of not working. To my mind this is just another case of false logic, as shown below.

1) A profession football career lasts 20 years.
2) After a 20-year career a player can no longer play professional football.
3) After a 20-year career a player can no longer earn money.
4) Therefore the 20-year career has to fund the whole working life.

Can you spot the break in the logic? It's at step 3. A professional footballer can continue to earn money, just not playing professional football. There are plenty of other jobs they could do that would continue to benefit others (and, to be fair, many do). This alternative society is not one to encourage earning huge amounts of money over a few years, it is designed to encourage all people to continue benefiting other people and to be a bit less concerned with self-interest. The intention here is to allow people to work in a job they enjoy doing or want to do, rather than jobs that just pay more. Equally, the essential but the less enjoyable jobs are made more attractive by having much better rewards than today.

The Experience Rating, which was not included in the table, would gradually increase from 1 to 2 for those who stayed in similar roles throughout their career, acting like promotions do today. This represents the fact that people with lots of experience tend to provide some additional benefit. They are able to do things a bit quicker, are more able to teach or coach new people and can help resolve other people's problems. Conversely, a significant career change might render previous experience useless, prompting the Experience Rating to be reduced closer to 1.0 again. For example, a pilot aged 50 with an Experience Rating of 1.75 may choose to spend the last 10 years of their career realising their dream of performing on stage. There is nothing stopping this type of career change, but it would be wrong to transfer the Experience Rating of 1.75 that applies to flying passenger planes to the new role of performing on stage. In this case, their new stage career would start with an Experience Rating of 1.0 for a novice performer and slowly start to climb back up with experience.

Although this collective Job Rating provides a rating for each job or role, it would be unfair to pay a pilot who flies thousands of people every month the same as a second pilot who only flies a few people or even none. Therefore, the Take-Home Pay also requires a Business Rating which relates to how much work is actually done and how many people benefit.

Business rating

Measuring business performance was initially a difficult thing to comprehend, especially without using the concept of financial profit that we are so used to. A significant part of this problem is the vast variety of businesses, organisations, types of work and number of customers, as indicated in the diagram below. Shops can have thousands of customers and only a few staff, whilst a large civil engineering project such as building a bridge or office block will have many employees working for only one main customer. Some industries like manufacturing can operate on different scales, being small and local or large and nationwide. Furthermore, other types of work such as law, art or architecture are almost individual in scale, where one person does a job for only one customer. The diagram below uses ellipsoids to try and illustrate both the range of industries and their differences.

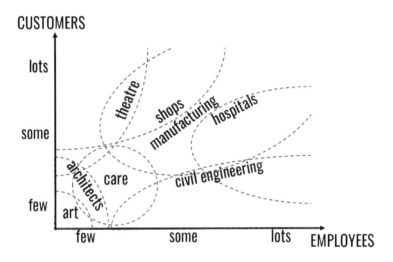

These wide differences are exacerbated further when the purchase and use of materials is included. Supermarkets, hospitals and steel production spend large amounts on products and energy, whilst architects, lawyers, musicians, teachers and artists can work with very little. Beyond these significant differences, there is also a need to include some self-limitation to provide a sense of 'this is enough' or 'this is stable', so that businesses are not forced to continually chase additional customers with incessant advertising that claims everything will be better if you spend your money. This is all starting to sound a lot like one of those contradictory wordy statements that were strongly criticised in the WORDS chapter (Chapter 1), and some may now claim that this is precisely why using the abstract measure of monetary value is such a good solution today. Below is one attempt at an alternative solution to overcome this difficult problem.

When attempting to measure how a business or organisation is performing, there are some numbers that are readily available or easy to measure:

- Amount of funds spent (money out).
- Amount sold (money in).
- Number of customers.
- Number of employees.

Intuitively, high ratios of 'customer to employees' and 'sales to purchases' should be rewarded. Importantly, however, hospitals and education etc. need to be provided to the public for free, so these kinds of essential services cannot have any sales (or money in). The problem is now how to combine these measures into something that could be used across all types of industry. By way of warning, the explanations in the rest of this Business Rating section become a bit more mathematical, so anyone wishing to skip the maths should now jump forward several pages and restart at the 'Self-employed' section.

The solution is based around the calculation below, where C is a fixed constant value and x can be different values. The first part of the calculation dominates when x is very small (approximating to $C/C = 1$) but allows the second part to dominate when x is very large (approximating to $x/x = 1$).

$$\frac{C}{(C + x)} + \frac{x}{(C + x)} = 1$$

The variable number x is chosen to be the total waste cost of all materials and energy etc., which is just a total of all the purchases (P) a business makes. The value of C is chosen to be some acceptable low level of waste (Cw) that does not require undue effort or concern to reduce it further (physics and the second law of thermodynamics means there can never be zero waste). The new version of the calculation is shown below. When the total purchases of a business (P) are lower than the acceptable level of waste (Cw), the first half of the calculation is dominant. Here the low level of waste is not important, so the number of customers and employees will dominate performance. Conversely, whenever the purchases of a business (total waste) are high, the second half becomes dominant, so it is important that all this waste is useful and purchased by customers in the form of sales.

$$\frac{Cw}{(Cw + P)} + \frac{P}{(Cw + P)} = 1$$

The next step is to introduce two more numbers or factors (both of which should always between 0 and 1 for mathematical reasons): Fn to represent the 'relative number of customers to employees' and Fs to represent the 'ratio of sales to purchases', both of which will increasingly reward employees the closer they get to a value of 1. The calculation now becomes a value which is always less than or equal to 1 (because both Fn and Fs cannot be greater than 1).

$$\frac{Fn * Cw}{(Cw + P)} + \frac{Fs * P}{(Cw + P)} < 1$$

The penultimate step is to define Fn and Fs. Fs is just the ratio of sales to purchases and so $Fs = S/P$, as without profit the total sales can never be more than the total purchases. The definition of Fn is more complicated because some businesses can have more employees than customers and vice versa. This means that the calculation of Fn has to be designed to have the correct characteristics. For example, to create a strong deterrent to just employing more people without increasing customers or sales, it is necessary to make Ne (the number of employees) more dominant than the number of customers (Nc), hence the use of $5Ne$ below.

$$Fn = \frac{Nc}{(Nc + 5Ne)}$$

These two additional factors produce the following calculation for Business Rating.

$$Business\ Rating = \frac{Nc * Cw}{(Nc + 5Ne) * (Cw + P)} + \frac{S}{(Cw + P)}$$

However, when purchases and sales are very high (many times the value of Cw) they dominate the calculation and so there is still not enough deterrent to overemployment. To prevent this a final extra factor is included in the form of a multiplying factor applied to Cw, in the right part of the calculation. This produces the final business performance calculation below.

$$\text{Business Rating} = \frac{Nc * Cw}{(Nc + 5Ne) * (Cw + P)} + \frac{S}{\left(\left(1 + \frac{3}{Nc}\right) * \sqrt{Ne} * Cw\right) + P}$$

This calculation always produces a Business Rating value between 0 and 1, depending on the number of customers (Nc), employees (Ne), purchases (P) and sales (S). The table below shows the example for a business with purchases that are equal to the acceptable waste level (Cw) and with 100% sales (so S = P).

CUSTOMERS

	1	2	5	10	25	50	100	250	500	1000
10000	1.000	0.914	0.808	0.738	0.660	0.612	0.567	0.504	0.443	0.364
5000	0.999	0.913	0.806	0.735	0.654	0.600	0.545	0.459	0.376	0.281
2000	0.998	0.911	0.803	0.728	0.637	0.568	0.491	0.367	0.265	0.173
1000	0.997	0.909	0.796	0.716	0.611	0.524	0.424	0.282	0.186	0.114
500	0.994	0.903	0.784	0.694	0.566	0.457	0.340	0.202	0.126	0.076
250	0.987	0.892	0.761	0.655	0.498	0.373	0.257	0.142	0.088	0.054
100	0.969	0.862	0.703	0.568	0.385	0.264	0.172	0.095	0.061	0.040
50	0.940	0.817	0.630	0.480	0.302	0.201	0.132	0.076	0.050	0.034
25	0.888	0.744	0.535	0.387	0.235	0.158	0.106	0.063	0.043	0.030
10	0.768	0.602	0.399	0.279	0.170	0.117	0.081	0.050	0.035	0.025
5	0.635	0.473	0.302	0.210	0.130	0.091	0.064	0.040	0.028	0.020
2	0.429	0.304	0.189	0.132	0.082	0.058	0.040	0.025	0.018	0.013
1	0.283	0.196	0.120	0.083	0.052	0.036	0.025	0.016	0.011	0.008
	1	2	5	10	25	50	100	250	500	1000

Higher pay when more customers

EMPLOYEES

Higher pay when fewer employees do the work

Below are some smaller pairs of tables, showing how this Business Rating value changes when sales drop from 100% (left table) to 50% (right table), for businesses with different levels of purchases.

The first pair of tables assume the business has very low purchases and waste (only 10% of the acceptable Cw level of waste). Here the very small amount of waste is not significant, so only the number of customers affects the Business Rating and halving sales (of the small amount of waste) has little effect on performance.

CUSTOMERS				100% sales	EMPLOYEES
1000	0.995	0.896	0.741	0.410	
100	0.954	0.636	0.273	0.073	
10	0.677	0.175	0.046	0.012	
1	0.176	0.026	0.007	0.002	
	1	10	50	250	

CUSTOMERS				50% sales	EMPLOYEES
1000	0.950	0.881	0.734	0.407	
100	0.910	0.621	0.267	0.070	
10	0.642	0.163	0.040	0.010	
1	0.164	0.022	0.005	0.002	
	1	10	50	250	

The next pair of tables are for a business with a low level of purchases (equal to the acceptable Cw level of waste, as in the initial large table). Here waste is more significant and so the reduction in sales does affect the Business Rating, but Business Ratings stay reasonably high provided there are lots of customers.

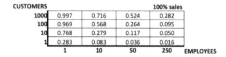

CUSTOMERS				100% sales	EMPLOYEES
1000	0.997	0.716	0.524	0.282	
100	0.969	0.568	0.264	0.095	
10	0.768	0.279	0.117	0.050	
1	0.283	0.083	0.036	0.016	
	1	10	50	250	

CUSTOMERS				50% sales	EMPLOYEES
1000	0.747	0.596	0.462	0.252	
100	0.722	0.451	0.203	0.066	
10	0.551	0.181	0.068	0.027	
1	0.183	0.046	0.019	0.008	
	1	10	50	250	

The next pair of tables are for a business with a high level of purchases (10 times the acceptable level of waste Cw). Here the high level of waste is significant, so the reduction in sales from 100% (on the left) to only 50% (on the right) almost halves the Business Rating. Now good performance is achieved by sales, but the number of customers still has some lower level of influence.

CUSTOMERS				100% sales	EMPLOYEES
1000	0.999	0.846	0.658	0.427	
100	0.993	0.815	0.605	0.387	
10	0.946	0.724	0.525	0.328	
1	0.729	0.443	0.262	0.137	
	1	10	50	250	

CUSTOMERS				50% sales	EMPLOYEES
1000	0.545	0.466	0.365	0.234	
100	0.540	0.438	0.315	0.197	
10	0.503	0.369	0.264	0.164	
1	0.372	0.223	0.131	0.068	
	1	10	50	250	

Finally, the last pair tables is for a business with a huge level of purchases (100 times the acceptable level of waste Cw). Performance is completely dominated by this high level of waste – the purchases needed to build a new office block, for example. Now good performance is only achievable by selling all this (wasteful) product, even if that is to only one customer.

CUSTOMERS				100% sales		CUSTOMERS				50% sales
1000	1.000	0.979	0.942	0.868		1000	0.505	0.494	0.475	0.436
100	0.999	0.975	0.935	0.861		100	0.504	0.491	0.469	0.431
10	0.994	0.962	0.916	0.830		10	0.500	0.482	0.458	0.415
1	0.963	0.888	0.780	0.613		1	0.482	0.444	0.390	0.306
	1	10	50	250	EMPLOYEES		1	10	50	250 EMPLOYEES

Importantly, in all cases the Business Rating and Take-Home Pay increase with more customers, fewer employees and increased sales, just as intended. This creates a constant deterrent against employing more people than necessary or losing customers and sales, which is subtly different from needing to constantly attract more customers through coercive advertising.

In this calculation, sales should never be able to exceed the purchases, but some industries could cause it to happen (such as the software industry, which is discussed later). To solve this problem and deter this from happening, any excess sales above the total amount of purchases could be treated in exactly the same way as lower sales, meaning that 110% sales would create the same reduction in Business Rating as only 90% sales would. However, this is still not the complete picture and there are several other problems with this solution so far.

Service Level
Despite providing a suitable answer for many industries, the table above would not be fair for those industries providing a free service without sales, such a hospitals, police and firefighters etc. (just like today, there is no intention here of asking for payment details during 999 emergency calls). The purchase of equipment, such as fire engines, MRI scanners, life-support machines, police vehicles and consumable products such as gloves and testing kits, would dominate the calculation even if there were lots of customers. It is therefore necessary to introduce an additional 'Service Level' (SL) factor, again with a value between 0 and 1, so that these free and essential services do not need to generate sales.

Research Level
Research scientists would suffer in a similar way, by purchasing research equipment without any direct customers, sales or even a guarantee of discovering something useful. However, scientific research and

technology advancement are critically important and so a solution is needed to make employment in scientific research attractive. The answer is another additional factor 'Research Level' (RL), again with a value between 0 and 1, which is based on the amount of research being done and the success of that research over time.

For example, a medical research centre could have a Research Level of 0.7, meaning that all employees get a minimum Business Rating of 0.7, which provides a reasonable Take-Home Pay. This Research Level would then increase with significant discoveries. A significant contribution to curing cancer could increase it to 0.9, as the results get confirmed and more people receive the benefit. Conversely, 4 years of fruitless research may see it reduce by 0.1 per annum from 0.7 to 0.3. This provides both an incentive to produce beneficial results and a deterrent for spending too long on unpromising fruitless work. However, to reiterate the point made in the previous chapter about the nature of some scientists and not needing profit for research, some scientists may be so interested in their research, they may consider continuing with nothing more than the Basic Allowance (to them, money isn't everything). Importantly, scientific research has access to the same extra funds as businesses, so neither scientific research nor more general business work will need to stop due to budget constraints (does that still sound strange, or have you acclimatised yet?). Here it is people and scientists (not finance) who decide if research work should continue, based on the importance and the progress being made.

This same Research Level could then be used more wildly across other technology businesses to supplement their Business Rating, to acknowledge, reward and encourage internal research. For example, the Business Rating and the Take-Home Pay for a car manufacturing business would normally be dominated by purchases, production, sales and customers. However, if they also develop ways to reduce road accidents via driverless car technology or develop a revolutionary change in power efficiency, then they could be awarded a 'Research Level' increase of 0.1, which would increase the Take-Home Pay of all the employees by about 10%. This reward and encouragement for research applies across a wide range of industries. The balance and consequences of needing extra purchases and employees for research is considered later, when this thought experiment is tested in the section named 'How would all this affect people and businesses?'

These two simple additions now provide the full calculation of Business Rating below,

$$Business\ Rating = RL + SL + \frac{Nc * Cw}{(Nc + 5Ne) * (Cw + P)} + \frac{S}{\left(\left(1 + \frac{3}{Nc}\right) * \sqrt{Ne} * Cw\right) + P}$$

where:
RL is the Research Level.
SL is the Service Level.
Nc is the number of customers.
Ne is the number of employees.
S is the total Sales.
P is the total Purchases.
Cw is a fixed value representing an acceptable low level of waste.

As each number in this calculation is easy to monitor, measure, set or know, it provides a relatively easy way to measure the overall performance of a very wide range of businesses and other organisations. However, it is not suitable for the self-employed, who are considered soon.

The self-limiting nature designed into this calculation has several important and intentional consequences. Firstly, when a business reaches a reasonable balance of customers, employees and sales, it provides a sense of 'this is enough' by limiting the benefits of further growth, without preventing it. This means that businesses do not need to use aggressive advertising to generate more sales. Equally, they do not need to continually chase those tiny (non-existent) improvements, so removing some of that endless unnecessary tinkering and continual change. Secondly, it means there is less benefit and incentive to create larger and larger businesses via mergers, unless it would provide a significant reduction in their collective purchases (or overall waste). In these cases, the overall reduction in waste means that the sale price must go down and the Take-Home Pay goes up.

In this alternative society without profit, everyone wins and that is surely a true improvement. Discouraging the formation of very large businesses will also create more room for smaller and medium-sized businesses to continue operating and thrive. It may even remove the need for a Monopolies and Mergers Commission, so instead of attempting to control the morals of the large corporate profit-making machines, they would be available to do something more productive. Finally, being a measure of performance, the Business Rating would help the government and others decide the best choice for future work, as well as providing any prospective employees with a good indication of potential Take-Home Pay, both providing small additional incentives to perform well, creating a natural drift towards better performing businesses. Eventually the worst ones will not have sufficient employees or customers to provide good wages and will naturally die.

In this respect, this alternative society maintains today's healthy competition between businesses, but now the competition is the number of customers and reducing waste, not a never-ending profit-generating treadmill. Here, businesses only need to concentrate on limiting their 'waste costs' and selling their 'waste cost' on to enough customers. However, if this all seems a bit too good to be true, it's because it is. Using an approach where businesses don't pay wages provides a golden opportunity for corruption and exploitation. The solution to this is explained later, in the 'Potential problems' section, leaving some time for the more inquisitive readers to discover how to 'beat the system', by allowing employees of corrupt businesses to get reasonably well paid for doing next to nothing (like those who get well paid today to endlessly regurgitate the same useless, empty, business and political gobbledygook phrases all day). By way of a clue, the problem involves yet another self-sustaining loop, just as those in the JIGSAW chapter did (Chapter 14). This now ends the mathematical diversion needed to explain how business performance is measured, so we can now take a closer look at the job roles that this calculation would not serve well and how self-employment might be a valid alternative for them. After that we can return to that much more important question of "How much will I earn?"

Self-employed

Some roles, such as an architect designing a building, lawyers working on long, complicated cases or an artist working on a large item, would require a large amount of time working for individual customers without purchasing too much. These types of individual, intellectual service roles would produce unfairly low Business Ratings, so require a different approach, one that is closer to self-employment today. Here, self-employed people don't have any Business Rating and only receive the Basic Allowance. Just like today, the customers of self-employed work must therefore pay for both the waste cost of any materials used and the wages of the self-employed people. In this alternative society, this makes self-employed people much more expensive and less appealing than a small business or an equivalent 'one employee business' who is content to live on the relatively low Business Rating. It is therefore unlikely that self-employment would be a suitable or competitive option for any jobs that could be set up as small or medium-scale businesses, with several employees serving numerous customers, including plumbing or electricians.

For those individual customers wanting dedicated attention or something very specific from a particular skilled individual, perhaps it is correct that they should cover all the expenses. After all, they are not really serving anyone else. This option would leave many niche skill groups, such as portrait painting, restoration work or very high-performance car tuning etc., to be provided by relatively expensive self-employed people. Perhaps this is no different from today, as I'm not aware of any nationwide high street brands like Portrait-While-U-Wait, Re-Store or REVS-R-US. Naturally this style of self-employment could cover any other skills that people were willing to pay for. It may even extend to cover singers, performers and sports stars etc. in what might approximate to a watered-down version of today's very highly paid celebrity culture. Watered-down due to the absence of large business profits to pay for big-name endorsements and large sponsorship deals. Without profit, the need and amount of advertising would generally reduce.

Take-Home Pay

The majority of employment will be within businesses and other organisations where Take-Home Pay is calculated like this:

$$Take\text{-}Home\ Pay = Basic\ Allowance + (Basic\ Allowance \times Job\ Rating \times Business\ Rating)$$

Whilst the Basic Allowance is paid to everyone, extra pay is based on your own personal 'Job Rating' (a value between 1 and 18 based on what job you do and your experience) and the Business Rating (a measure of business performance between 0 and 1, which is the same for every employee of that particular business). Multiplying these produces a number ranging from 0 to 18, which is multiplied by the Basic Allowance to calculate your extra pay. Therefore, total Take-Home Pay can range from only the Basic Allowance (for those with a Business Rating of zero and no extra pay) to 19 times the Basic Allowance (a maximum of 18 for work done + 1 for the Basic Allowance that everyone is paid) for anyone with the highest 'Job Rating' and a very good Business Rating. As this gap between highest and lowest paid people is much smaller than it is today, money is much more evenly distributed across the working population and is paid directly from the Central Administration, whose wider role is explained later. By way of a minor detail, the pay of part-time workers would be proportionally scaled down, like today.

This calculation means that poor business performance (and a low Business Rating) affects every single employee of that business. Therefore, any employee who is unhelpful and hinders progress, production, sales or waste reduction will reduce their own wage as well as that of every other employee. That is a real incentive to be more helpful and less obstructive at work. It encourages real teamwork and enforces the attitude of doing things 'for two' and helping out immediately. It is also different from today, where unhelpful obstinate employees still get their full pay, whilst disrupting the work of other employees, building obstacles or passing the burden, and there is more on this later when idea of 'culling' is explained.

Below are a few examples that start to test this thought experiment, to see how it would work in practice. These examples demonstrate and quantify how different Business Ratings affect Take-Home Pay under a few different circumstances (note that both Service Level and Research Level are zero in these cases).

Small local business

This business only has two employees, relatively low purchases (30% of the fixed Cw value), 100% sales and 20 customers, so its Business Rating would be 0.669 (67% of the maximum pay available for that role). Below are some changes that might occur to affect this rating.

Change	Approximate pay change	New Business Rating
Employ an extra person	−10%	0.570
Attract 10 additional customers	+7%	0.739
Keep the original 20 customers, but lose half of the sales	−8%	0.591
Lose half the customers and half the sales	−22%	0.455

Medium-sized business

This business has 50 employees, relatively high purchases (10 times the fixed Cw value), 100% sales and 1000 customers, so its Business Rating would be 0.658 (65.8% of the maximum pay available for that role). Below are some changes that might occur to affect this rating.

Change	Approximate pay change	New Business Rating
Employ 5 more people	−1.3%	0.645
Lose 30% of sales	−17.5%	0.482
Lose 25% of customers and sales	−15%	0.507

A short break

At this point it is probably time for a short break. You have just been immersed in a strange alternative society with no concept of how it works. You may be awash with questions or even be totally confused? If this is the case, it is probably best to return to the point at which everything was reasonably well understood and recap. Three quarters of this book have been spent moaning and ranting about things that do not seem right with the modern Western society. Although this kind of moaning can be quite therapeutic, it is not overly helpful, and it is much more productive and satisfying to think of possible alternatives or solutions. What you have just read represents a completely different approach centred around providing what people really want and need, in contrast to focusing on profit and economic growth. Parts were based on maths, which may have added to the confusion for some, whilst for others it can provide some structure and rigour that helps to demonstrate, validate and quantify the ideas much more clearly than any collection of words can ever do. This alternative society may be utterly unpalatable to you, especially if you work in the finance industry, which was first accused of being a source of problems and bad influences and has now been completely obliterated from existence altogether.

For those still struggling with the concept of funds and wages appearing like magic from fresh air, then get used to it. As explained at the start of Part 3, this is just how every bit of new money is created today. Where on earth do you think the trillions of dollars, pounds and euros were created from in 2008 and 2009? It certainly wasn't the piggy bank of some cautious and prudent global bank that was saving for a rainy day; it all came from fresh air, as does credit creation, economic growth, quantitative easing and national debt etc. All that has happened here is that the financial intermediary has been removed, and the fresh air has not been packaged up with the constraint that you must pay it all back with a bit of extra interest from someone else's package of fresh air. Having now slightly adjusted back to the main storyline, it is now possible to continue and attempt to answer some of those questions about this strange alternative society. This is not done gently but is more in keeping with jumping straight back into the cold lake, by introducing the controversial concept of employee culling, which you were warned about.

Employee culling

It has just been explained how Take-Home Pay is strongly influenced by the varying performance measurement, labelled Business Rating. This means there is no true concept of a fixed-salary job. In an environment where a fixed salary is guaranteed each month and is not affected by slow production or poor sales, all the 'jobs-worth', 'finger-pointers' and 'process-slaves' can flourish, wrapped up in their waffle-wordy comfort blankets, wallowing in their protective process-pits, day-dreaming of continual improvement and constantly 'passing the burden' onto others in blissful ignorance of the real world around them. They can do this safe in the knowledge that they will get paid the same and that other employees will have to absorb all the extra work and inefficiency they are generating. (Note that following the rather dry mathematical interlude, the normal service of cynical ranting and rambling has now been resumed.) In this alternative society, any unproductive work will not cost the company in time (as time is free), but anything that adversely affects production, sales, waste or the number of customers will directly affect the Take-Home Pay of every single employee equally.

Under these conditions, your individual pay is just as reliant on the work of others as on your own work. This creates more incentive to actively help fellow employees directly and immediately. This is true teamwork in action, rather than just glibly telling people to follow a process and to sort it out for themselves. Equally, there would be much less tolerance for those who don't contribute as much or are seen to be reducing the Take-Home Pay of others. There will always be some of these, it is an unavoidable product of the spectrums of laziness and selfishness described in Part 2. It would be beneficial to the majority if this unhelpful, unproductive, lazy minority could be removed or culled from the business. Is that a scary thought or are you already forming a list of those you would nominate? This culling could be achieved via continual nomination, where those nominated many times, by several different people, would first be warned and checked, before eventually being sacked if the nominations continue. No dispute, no litigation, they just lose their job and leave. As an additional deterrent, the culled employee could also receive a small reduction in any future Take-Home Pay, by reducing their Job Rating experience value each time they get culled (harsh but fair?). This harsher environment will install is a true sense of effort, action and teamwork, where it is always better to properly help a colleague immediately, rather than let them struggle with a few unhelpful empty words like "Follow the process in the company database". It will also deter people from generating more unnecessary work or introducing new unnecessary or unhelpful processes, as that could attract some nominations for culling.

Health and safety

Previous chapters have provided multiple onslaughts on the problems of litigation, processes and Health and Safety, and this section looks at how an alternative approach might solve these problems. Firstly, every person would be explicitly taught and told that their own Health and Safety is their own responsibility and that under no circumstances should they do anything they are not willing to be responsible for themselves (climb a ladder, use a tool, work with a solvent etc.). To put it another way, they absolutely don't have to do anything they don't want to, but everything they do is their own responsibility. In order to claim any type of compensation they would need to show that they were actively coerced into doing something unsafe (in other words, the business remains innocent until proven guilty). Inevitably this means that some things won't get done and people will rightly say when they are not willing do something until it is safer. This is where the Health and Safety employees start to earn their wages, in a helpful and practical way. Here all Health and Safety roles will be practical, active and helpful. Instead of the waffle-wordy, finger-pointing, process-promoting, suit-wearing, Health and Safety wordsmiths who instruct us to write a risk assessment or follow a process, in the false belief that all these wonderful extra words will magically make everything physically safe, they would be the ones who actively solve the real problem. They would act like on-call Health and Safety police, providing practical equipment, actions and solutions to any Health and Safely problems. It is these Health and Safety employees who would source the right harnesses and correct chemical containers, dispose of oil properly, replace a broken ladder or find the correct information and data sheets for people. When not actively providing this practical help, they would be out on patrol, searching for problems, advising, teaching and actively looking for other problems that need solving. These people chose to get paid to do Health and Safety work, so here they can do active, practical Health and Safety work, instead of just sitting behind desks, spending a couple of minutes glancing at spreadsheets that skilled doctors, teachers and engineers have had to spend hours and hours creating, before shuffling some paperwork, claiming that it all needs to be improved yet again and then relying on others to solve everything and do it all for them, by creating a slightly different set of words and processes. Put more bluntly still, in this alternative society Health and Safety people will act not talk. Apologies to any practical or hands-on Health and Safety representatives who are reading this, but unfortunately, I haven't encountered very many like you. Instead, I have had to endure plenty of the smartly dressed, finger-pointing wordsmiths, whose best and most helpful advice seems to involve regurgitating some unrecognisable process number and adding the words "with a risk assessment" to the end of every sentence. If they already understand it, if they know what needs to be done, then they can act and do it themselves and just start being a bit more helpful.

Full pension

The Basic Allowance, which is paid to everyone, acts as both a 'unemployment benefit' and 'basic state pension'. However, a person's full pension is based on an accumulative measure of how much benefit they provided to society over their whole working career. It is incredibly simple monitor each person's Job Rating x Business Rating for each year and record the accumulative total. Dividing this total by a standard working life (say 40 years) gives you their 'Average Annual Rating'. Their full pension will be the simple calculation below.

Annual Pension = Basic Allowance + (Basic Allowance × Average Annual Rating)

This approach directly relates to a person's overall contribution to society. It is simple to understand and administer and, in contrast to today, it does not depend on paying contributions, inflation, volatile financial markets or fluctuating share prices for its value. It also means that someone who works for only 20 years will get less than half the full pension of someone who works for 40 years (noting that if you only work for 20 years then your experience rating will not rise fully either). Similarly, someone who chooses to work for a few extra years and so contribute a bit more to society will then be rewarded with a higher pension when they eventually choose to retire.

Central Administration

The role of the Central Administration is similar to parts of the civil service today. Instead of monitoring tax and state benefits, it will monitor and record the following numbers for each business, so that it can calculate their Business Rating.

- Purchases (P)
- Sales (S)
- Number of customers (Nc)
- Number of employees (Ne)

This Administration will also monitor and record the following numbers for each person, to calculate and provide their Take-Home Pay or full pension.

- Business Rating
- Employee Job Rating
- Employee Take-Home Pay

As the Business Rating provides a performance measure of each business, it can be used to compare similar businesses, allowing new work to be awarded to the higher performing businesses, with less waste or more customers. In this way, both sale prices and waste will naturally fall and settle to the lowest possible level. It will also help to find anomalies, such as business that are struggling or are perhaps corrupt in some way, so that they can be investigated or helped if needed.

Therefore, although this Administration task remains an important one, it is also relatively simple, when compared to the operation of finance and business today. This Central Administration could effectively replace the role of today's banks, financial authorities, fraud checks, accountants, unemployment benefit, pension schemes, contract bidding etc. In this version of society, most of this finance and administration work would disappear in a puff of smoke and be replaced by a few simple numbers and calculations. There are two opposing ways to look at this. Today's view would be, "How can we possibly survive without it? All those people will be unemployed". The alternative perspective would say, "All those people are now available to do something more practical and helpful". In this version of society, these people would be available to become well-paid teachers, police, doctors, nurses, engineers etc. This central Administration would also replace all the insurance companies, as explained next.

Insurance

Insurance is a concept based around many people contributing a relatively small amount of money, so that those who need to replace expensive items can do so at no extra cost, because the insurance covers it. The insurance business is also a very good way to make a lot of profit, which is why you are always asked if you want insurance when you buy the products that are advertised as being well made, high quality and very reliable. Although a non-profit version of insurance would be possible, there is a more radical alternative, where insurance payments do not exist. Instead, when something needs replacing (like a car after a crash) you would simply request funds from the Administration to pay for a new car (or any other product). At first sight this approach seems open to all sorts of corruption unless some type of deterrent is involved. Again, a very simple approach is used, in the form of a decreasing percentage of funds for each claim. The first claim would pay 90% of the value, followed by five successive decreases of 15%, meaning the second claim would only provide 75% of the replacement cost and a sixth claim would only provide 15% of the value. This approach would mean a family could choose to make the following claims.

- First claim, for a new sofa, would give you 90% of an equivalent new sofa.
- Second claim, for new carpet, would provide only 75% of an equivalent carpet.
- Third claim, for a new car, would provide only 60% of the equivalent new car.

Now the incentive not to make unnecessary claims for small items is clear. For each small claim you make, you put yourself at a higher risk getting low percentage of funds for the much bigger items later and not being able to afford a new car. If you made the three claims above but were then unfortunate enough to have a house fire, then you would only get 45% of the house value. Perhaps this is too harsh, but it certainly provides an incentive not to claim unnecessarily. For house claims, perhaps a lower percentage drop of only 5% could be used, so in the example above the fourth claim for a house would now give a fairer 80% of the value. Either way, this approach is very simple. Naturally each claim would need to expire after some time span, so maybe after

2 years without a claim, you would move back up one level. In this way, insurance as we know it would not be necessary and everyone would be guaranteed replacements for damaged items, whilst having to carefully consider which items it is important to replace using these freely available insurance funds.

People of a cynical, questioning or corrupt manner will quickly spot that this is open to fraudulent claims, but these could be prevented by the following set of two rules.

1. Insurance only applies to digital purchases which have both proof of purchase and a record of the price paid.
2. The value will be the lowest of the 'price paid' or the price it can now be purchased for new.

Alternatively, a non-profit version of today's insurance could be used. Here small insurance payments would still have to be made, but any insurance company charging too much would need to either refund some premiums or pay out more. If they didn't do this then any excess sales (e.g. 110% of what was paid out) would be treated as 90% sales and so reduce the Take-Home Pay of all employees.

Harm Rating

Now that the basic outline and operation of this alternative society are known and to some degree quantified, there are a few anomalies to take care of. Some industries may be essential (so have good Job Ratings), require very little energy and produce little waste (so have good Business Ratings) and so provide attractive, well-paid jobs with a cheap product. In many cases, this is precisely the intention, but for some industries the product may have some harmful or detrimental effect, such as sugar, coal, polystyrene etc. However, so far there is no discouragement for their production, sale and consumption. To resolve this, an additional number called 'Harm Rating' is introduced, which is only applied to the sale price at the point of sale, not unlike the tax imposed on cigarettes today. The price increase is to deter non-essential sales and help promote less harmful alternatives.

Final Sale Price = Harm Rating × Business Sale Price

For the vast majority of products, the Harm Rating will be 1 and have no influence at all, but values higher than 1 can be applied to industries that are known to be detrimental or harmful in some way. In this way, industries which are essential but also detrimental in some way will have a balance between a high (essential) Job Rating and lower Business Rating due to lower sales or fewer customers due to the higher sale price. Similarly, applying this Harm Rating to some non-essential industries which already have a low (non-essential) Job Rating, such as tobacco and gambling, would make them even less attractive as an employment option. Isn't this exactly how it should be for non-essential, harmful industries? Hopefully this seems like common sense, but it is again in stark contrast to today, where hugely profitable gambling and tobacco industries cannot be quickly or easily reduced because of the large tax income they generate. In government today there is a conflict of interest (or contradiction): "We want the tax revenue, but we can see the harm". As a complete aside, the growth of online gambling is a new and vibrant social cancer, growing on the fertile soil of a profit-seeking society that will undoubtedly start to generate more and more debt related social problems, if it is not significantly limited and curtailed in some way (but try doing that while it is generating lots of tax revenue).

How would all this affect people and businesses?

This alternative version of society is intentionally very different from our current version because it has been designed to be consistent with the real world. It aims to provide a framework or structure which benefits both people and planet, instead of the world of finance, whilst maintaining the need for competition and the rewards for ambition and real improvement. Hopefully the descriptions and explanations so far indicate this has been achieved, at least to some extent. However, as indicated in the IMPROVEMENT chapter (Chapter 3), in our wonderfully complex world there are downsides to almost every change. Therefore, it is now time to investigate or test this thought experiment, by assessing what would happen across a wide, almost random, selection of examples, looking at a few of the more interesting details, both good and bad. As this cannot cover everything, you may want to supplement it with similar assessments of interest to you.

Bank loans

The absence of profit, banks and interest rates suggests that there is no equivalent of a bank loan, but it would be possible for the Central Administration to provide additional funds to help people buy expensive items such as homes, cars etc. when needed. As this Administration already provides everyone with their Basic Allowance, Take-Home Pay or Full Pension, then any monthly repayments can be taken directly at source, without any interest payments. People would pay back only the exact waste allowance they borrowed. In this way, personal debt could be limited by the Administration to a level that can be repaid at source and not left to the individual person to build up to an uncontrollable level. Unlike today's banks, credit cards and pay-day loan companies, here there would be no way to profit from excessive uncontrolled lending.

Sporting events

As the Business Rating calculation removes the incentive for huge numbers of customers and forces any unnecessary purchases to reduce Take-Home Pay or increase sale prices, it would be unlikely that any businesses would make large payments to sponsor sporting events. An alternative source of prize money would be needed (remember that sportspeople are already being paid, but prizes are what makes it competitive). This could be done by simply adding some cost onto the price of tickets (as would be done today), but this breaks the principle that any 'purchase cost' should only represent the 'waste cost' and it could be the first crack back into the realms of over-charging for profit and the benefit of others. Another preferable option would be for the Central Administration to provide even more funds as prize money for sports and other competitions. In keeping with the original principles of providing what people want, the prize money (or prize fund) would be directly proportional to the number of spectators or customers, so the sports which attract the highest crowds and so benefit the most people, would become the sports with the highest prizes. This approach could be fully consistent across all sports, so it would not be the sport, the game, the duration or the difficulty that determined the prize money, only the amount of people that pay to watch it. In case you haven't worked it out yet, the ticket price for all sport events would simply be a share of the total waste cost of hosting the event, in other words relatively low in many cases.

Software industry

Software often takes a lot of time to develop and test (or debug), but other than all this time, the software industry tends to have relatively low levels of purchases and running costs, such as computers, cables and some electricity. Therefore, a software business with enough customers will have a good Business Rating and well-paid employees. However, if sales of their software are good and the waste costs of developing it are covered quickly, then additional sales will start to create an excess of sales and reduce Take-Home Pay (as explained earlier at the end of the Business Rating description). This problem of excess sales arises because software can be easily copied and sold again and again, with almost no waste (just a bit of electricity). This situation is much less likely when producing physical products such as cars, phones, toys, clothes etc. where each item must be made. In this sense, these excess sales of software would be creating some kind of impossible 'negative waste' and no longer represent anything real. This anomalous effect would not be done intentionally or out of greed (because it would also reduce Take-Home Pay), it would only occur unintentionally by selling more copies of software or computer games than was originally anticipated in the pricing. In this respect it could be a common occurrence.

The solution is both simple and beneficial. As the level of sales (S) approaches the level of waste or purchases (P) used to produce the software, the waste costs of production will be almost covered, and so further sales of the software would reduce in price and it would eventually become free. Here costs would not increase with demand as today, but reduce with demand, as the production waste cost is spread more thinly across more customers. This does mean that those customers who buy the software first could pay a higher price than those who buy it later, if and when the sale price starts decreasing. This is acceptable, as presumably those who buy it first will be those with the most urgent need or have most to benefit from it.

One final point to note is that, although most software engineers will have the same Skill Rating, those who produce software for games would probably have a lower Job Role Rating than those producing the software needed by the more essential machines such as medical equipment and transport etc.

Hiring equipment

This situation is very similar to sales of software, where the initial purchase cost of the equipment will be spread across the estimated number of times it will be hired. If this estimate is too high, then not enough sales will be made, so either employees will get paid less or the hire price will need to increase. However, if the original estimate is too low then, just like software, the hire price will start reducing as the original waste cost is covered. Again, this benefits more and more customers, with cheaper and cheaper hire costs, without reducing the Business Rating or Take-Home Pay of employees. It may even increase slightly with increased number of customers.

There is no suggestion that either the software company or the hire company (or any other business in a similar situation) need to do this for each individual item or product. The assessment of Business Rating is only done at the overall business level, meaning that somethings may be under-priced, whilst others may be over-priced. However, each business and employee will know that it is impossible to benefit or profit from repeated over-pricing and doing so will only result in a reduction in Take-Home Pay.

Lawyers

I have already insinuated that lawyers who are paid by the hour or letter are on to a 'good little earner' and have an incentive to take things slowly or write one more letter. Meanwhile, the less-moral, ambulance-chasing, "no win no fee" breed just get paid for blaming others in the litigation loop. In this alternative society, most lawyers will be paid like plumbers or hairdressers, using the Business Rating. In their predominantly intellectual, low-waste industry their Take-Home Pay will be dominated by the number of customers, creating an incentive to resolve cases and help customers more quickly. The natural limiting that was designed into the Business Rating calculation means that at some point the extra effort of chasing more customers won't be worth it, especially if their reputation is damaged by rushing cases through.

School teachers

A similar case applies to teachers. The Business Rating calculation allows significant increases in Take-Home Pay for increasing customers (or students) up to about 20 or 30 per employee. After that there would be diminishing rewards for increasing class sizes to 40 or 50, where the extra effort simply isn't worth the reduced rewards. If necessary, class sizes could also be restricted by regulation.

Research and technology advancement

It has already been explained how pure research does not have to be reliant on profit and how the Research Level would allow scientists to be paid. However, a huge amount of research is done within technology industries. In this version of society, if a business wished to do research, it would need to have more employees and purchase more equipment without increasing sales immediately, both of which would reduce Take-Home Pay of every employee, but by how much?

Let's use the same example as before of a medium-sized business which has 50 employees and 1000 customers, with purchases equal to 10 times the fixed Cw waste value and 100% sales, producing a good Business Rating of 0.658. If this business was to recruit five more employees just to do research work and increase purchases by 10% to buy research equipment for them, without any increases in sales or sale price, then the Business Rating would reduce to 0.608 and reduce Take-Home Pay by about 5% (the reduction would actually be slightly less than this due to the fixed Basic Allowance contribution). Although this would not be suitable for all businesses and the pay reduction might be unpalatable to some employees, research is an essential and expected part of many high-tech industries and five full-time researchers and a 10% budget is something many current businesses can only dream of being able to afford today. Essentially this approach is like opening up large-scale government-funded research to any businesses willing to accept a relatively small reduction in Take-Home Pay and would be beneficial for many larger high-tech businesses and technology advancement as a whole.

Exclusive fashion

It is difficult to see how this version of society could sustain an exclusive high-price fashion industry, primarily because the price of the clothes could only be a measure of the materials and waste used in their manufacture and the seller could not obtain any profit from excessively priced products. The only way for this type of industry to flourish would be via self-employment, where handmade clothes could be sold for any price, almost like works of art or similar, whilst the vast majority of the clothing industries would compete on reducing the waste cost of the clothing they produce and maintaining sufficient customers.

Charities

Strangely, the first question to ask is whether charities will be needed as much in this alternative society, or even at all. Care work will be well paid, homeless shelters, care homes and youth centres etc. can all be funded directly by the voting allowance and important medical research work can continue to pay reasonably good wages. So, assuming that there is still a place for charities, and they cannot generate any profit, how would they operate? The first point to make is that the 'high street charity shop' is a great way to reduce waste. Instead of just throwing something away, donating it allows someone else to use it, a common sense approach that should not be hindered or prevented. As with businesses, the charity does not pay wages and so the price of the items only needs to cover or match the waste cost of running the shop, as the product itself is donated freely and has no waste cost. However useful and sensible this is, there is still no incentive or reward (extra money) for the charity itself. The incentive could come from each customer having to donate directly to the charity before they can take any of the free-cycle goods away with them. Furthermore, altruistic donations can sometimes be far higher than paying a marked monetary cost, simply because the feel-good factor is far greater. You are doing it because you want to not because you have to, just like giving blood.

National emergencies

National emergencies tend to disrupt the normal operation of society, with no better example than the recent COVID-19 pandemic. In our current society, which is optimised to operate only in the direction of growth, this type of disruption has a dramatic effect that is described in terms of "economic slowdown", "downturn", "unemployment", "bankruptcy" and "increased debt". How would a national emergency affect this alternative society? Using the COVID-19 pandemic as a recent and well-understood example, exactly the same physical real-world constraints would be needed, such as shops, bars and theatres closing etc., resulting in the same reduction in sales. This would reduce Business Rating and Take-Home Pay for many employees. In the worst-case scenarios, pay would reduce to the Basic Allowance only, for the duration of the emergency. Meanwhile, all the essential keyworkers such as hospital staff, carers, supermarket workers and delivery drivers would continue to be fully paid and even see small increases, for those who start to have more customers or benefit more people (such as hospital staff). To my mind, this approach contrasts very favourably to the big-fat-round-zero that keyworkers got during the actual pandemic, whilst simultaneously many non-essential profit-making businesses got furlough payments for not working at all. In other words, our affluent, efficient caring society looked after the economy (to which it is addicted), more than it looked after those who risked their own wellbeing and worked flat out to look after and save the lives of others. In this alternative approach, there would be no bankruptcy or failed businesses, because there would be no debts, loans, interest payments, shareholders or financiers to pay and keep happy. Crudely speaking, businesses would simply slow and pause and then simply start up and continue as normal as the national emergency eases. This demonstrates yet another very important contrast with today's society: this alternative society has a natural ability to slow down, pause and even stop whilst remaining stable and functional.

Concerts, festivals and events

Concerts, festivals and events provide and sell an experience as opposed to a physical product, but still need to hire or purchase equipment, all of which contributes to the waste cost of the production. As with physical products, the sale price of the tickets will need to cover the full waste cost of hosting and running the event. This might be very significant for a one-off event with only one show, whilst long-running theatre productions could have relatively low ticket prices, if many customers are expected over several weeks or months. In this respect, some theatre shows could be similar to software sales, as higher-than-expected ticket sales would ultimately lead to reductions in ticket prices and possibly even 'almost free' tickets once the entire waste cost has been covered. This is another case of those who want to see the show first potentially paying more, but in the long run, more and more people will be able to benefit and see the show. Just to reiterate, in this alternative version of society, these events are there to benefit and entertain the population and not to generate profit as they are expected to do today.

Politicians

In this alternative society, there is a lot less opportunity for politicians (or anyone else for that matter) to benefit from biased or selfish choices and decisions. They could still provide large contracts to the businesses of friends and family, but there is no method for either politician or friends to profit as their Take-Home Pay will be calculated and paid in exactly the same way as all other businesses. Any small benefit due to increased work or number of customers will also be shared directly across all employees of that business and not just the friends-in-high-places. In other words, removing the ability to profit also removes the temptation and incentive to be selfish or biased towards those you know.

Recycling

Recent environmental problems and a far better global awareness have led to a large increase in the recycling of materials. Much of this is under legislative control and at the expense of the business, which can inevitably lead to a few unscrupulous businesses disposing of rubbish illegally (like fly tipping) or just shipping it to a country where no one will notice it being burnt. In order to promote (and not dissuade) recycling in this alternative society, there would be no charge for waste collection or waste delivery to any recycling centre. Once collected and sorted, it will be available to those that want it. Today recycling can be very expensive due to the time-consuming sorting and cleaning etc., but here it is all done by a recycling business, doing an essential (well-paid) role where the time of employees is free. This makes recycled material and new raw material direct competitors. The one that is cheapest (less wasteful) to convert back into useable material will automatically be the most environmentally friendly with the lowest overall waste cost.

Opportunity for crime

A lot of crime is based on being able to provide something people want more cheaply than the legal method, such as not paying enough tax, not paying wages or simply copying an idea and selling it more cheaply. This type of crime is not possible in a society where the cost of products and services are naturally already as low as possible, consisting only of the waste cost. In this situation, it is much harder or even impossible to produce a similar product more cheaply, but if it were then this would simply become a legal, less wasteful and therefore better alternative to the original. However, other crimes such as theft will still occur and these can only be prevented by strong law enforcement. With high Job Ratings for essential services like police and voting funds available to boost local crime prevention where needed, in this alternative society there is no reliance on a politician who lives 300 miles away having to choose if your area could do with a few more police and whether they are affordable. Although not initially considered or intended, this alternative version of society seems to have some natural and very beneficial side-effects for crime prevention. Another indication that it might be a sensible solution.

Economic growth

As this version of society does not have any financial industry to drive economic growth, it is difficult to see how it could increase standard of living or cope with a growing population. As indicated earlier, reducing the level of waste that a business needs to operate does two things simultaneously: it reduces the waste cost (sale price) of the product, and it increases the Take-Home Pay of the employees of that business. Collectively, as businesses become more waste efficient, earnings increase and prices reduce, everyone will be able to buy a bit more. That is an increase in the standard of living which is directly related to reality and how energy efficient we can become. However, it does not solve the issue of increasing population. As each extra person will automatically receive the Basic Allowance, and more if they work, then they can buy more products, which will generate more waste. Therefore, to keep pace with population growth all that is needed is an increase in energy provision. In a situation where the energy needed to mine materials, harvest and make products does not match the population growth, then there will be a surplus of money and not enough products to buy. Therefore, all this alternative society needs to do is to ensure that the amount of energy available grows at the same rate as the population and this will maintain the standard of living for a growing population.

Home carers

As mentioned earlier, in this alternative society care work is relatively well paid and voting funds can pay for more care homes if needed. However, neither this nor the Take-Home Pay calculation would help those who choose to prioritise caring full time for a family member or close friend at home: so far they would only receive the minimum Basic Allowance, similar to today. Here this altruistic act should be better rewarded – but with plenty of other care options available, it should also be recognised that this would also be a personal choice and not necessarily an essential need in the way that it can be today. Therefore, one option could be to use the Service Level to increase Take-Home Pay, perhaps up to a maximum of 0.25 depending on the level and amount of care needed. Alternatively, the carer could operate as a small care business with only one employee, earning a Business Rating of around 0.3 for caring for two people, increasing to around 0.5 for caring for five people.

Possible potential problems

As indicated earlier, this weird alternative is not without some problems. The first and simplest of these is labelled 'experience inflation'. As businesses do not pay wages, it would be very easy for them to just keeping increasing the experience value of the Job Rating every time an employee said they wanted a pay rise. One possible solution to this would be recognising that generally experience comes with age, so for larger organisations the experience profile should broadly match the age profile. Another option would be to make employees' experience level available to all employees, allowing any unpalatable anomalies to attract nominations for culling.

The next problem is much more complicated and returns to the problem set earlier, involving a loop that corrupt businesses could exploit to provide good Take-Home Pay by doing almost nothing. It starts with Company X buying a large number of products, which are then all sold to Company Y, giving Company X good sales, a high Business Rating and good Take-Home Pay. Meanwhile Company Y is busy selling the same large batch of products to Company Z, also achieving good sales and good Take-Home Pay. This purchase could then continue around a ring of corrupt companies until eventually reaching Company X again, in a corrupt version of pass-the-parcel. All employees, of all companies in the ring, would get good Take-Home Pay, except the one left holding the large purchase. This problem is not possible today, as the salary of each worker would have to be added on to the cost at each step, making it unviable as a loop.

Several options were considered to overcome this tempting pass-the-parcel loophole, two being deterrents used today. One was based around auditing, checking and administration (things that a really nice society could do with a bit less of). However, this approach wouldn't be able to prevent some smaller-scale, better-hidden version of the same practice being used to just enhance Business Rating a bit. Another option relied on increasing the sale price at each step, as the need to pay wages does today, but this broke the philosophy of keeping sale cost equal to only the waste cost. The chosen solution maintains this important philosophy and has the big advantage of flipping the opportunity for exploitation directly into a deterrent against it. However, this solution requires a complication: it introduces two versions of the same currency, something like having two sets of coins, one red (for business use only) and the other blue (for people and governments), but otherwise the two currencies are the same in every way.

Under this modification, the Business Rating calculation would remain exactly the same, with all business purchases (P) using only red money, but sales (S) consisting of a mixture of red money for sales to other businesses and blue money for sales to people or governments. Using this solution, every single business purchase (including any continual pass-the-parcel purchases) use only the red money and so it is possible to keep an accumulative 'total red spend' value for each business. This new value would be used to reduce the Business Rating by using an additional factor of the form below, which is very close to 1 when 'total red spend' is small relative to the Fixed Value, but reduces towards 0 as 'total red spend' increases, as it would in the corrupt pass-the-parcel loop.

$$Red\ Spend\ Factor = \frac{Fixed\ Value}{Fixed\ Value + 'total\ red\ spend'}$$

The only way to reduce this 'total red spend' is by sales made with blue money – sales to people or the government. This blue sale is precisely the point at which the product or service becomes useful or beneficial to the population and not just another business transaction.

For example, assume Business A spends a value of 20 (red) and Business B spends a value of 30 (red) to make two different components. Both are purchased by Business C (for 20 red and 30 red respectively) and combined into a single product to be sold for 50. At this point, both A and B have a good Business Rating because their sales (S) still match their purchases (P), but all three businesses have now accumulated some level of 'total red spend' and as yet Business C has no sales either. If people or government then buy this final product (of value 50) using their blue money, Business C now also have sales (S) matching their purchases (P) and a good Business Rating, but all three still have their 'total red spend'. These 'total red spends' can now be cancelled out by this (non-business) blue spend, in the following way. First the blue spend, of value 50, removes 50 from the 'total red spend' of Business C, before splitting and following a waterfall down, 20 going to Business A and 30 going to Business B to remove that amount from their respective 'total red spend', which in this simple example would reduce the 'total red spend' of all three businesses to zero.

In more complicated cases, the blue funds would continue their waterfall journey, splitting and filtering down further and further, following the paths of the business red money purchases, cancelling out all contributions to any product or service purchased using blue money. As this is still only a thought experiment (albeit a complex and prolonged one), the details of how the blue funds are split, directed or prioritised are not important here. It is only necessary to understand that this solution means that only those businesses that contribute to the beneficial blue sales that provide benefit to people and government will be able to reduce their 'total red spend' and maintain a reasonable Business Rating and Take-Home Pay. Conversely, any unnecessary business transactions (using red money) will be detrimental to employees of that business.

Although being a little unusual (like many things in this strange alternative world), this solution has a few interesting and beneficial consequences. Firstly, a rise in the collective 'total red spends' of all businesses would be a clear indication that the businesses are producing or using more than the public's blue funds can or want to buy. Equally, a rise of the 'total red spend' of any individual business would indicate they are not receiving their fair share of the blue fund waterfall or that their work is simply not benefiting the population. It is worth acknowledging that, with this added complication, there will probably still be a role for accountants in this alternative society, albeit far simpler than dealing with shares, dividends, inflation, interest, exchange rates and tax. This solution may be very different, but it is definitely not more complicated than accountancy today.

Very real problems

There are two further problems, which technically fall outside the original scope of this thought experiment to find an alternative version of society. Both relate to how this alternative society could interact or operate with our current real version of society, effectively making them more practical 'real-world' integration problems, but they are significant enough to be worth the briefest of explanation (otherwise this book will never end).

The first is, would it be possible to convert from our existing society into a something so radically different? The suggestion here is that a transfer may be possible by running both systems in parallel for a good number of years. During this period of duality, society would continue to use only our current version of prices, but everything would also be given second waste-only cost which will initially be strongly contaminated with 'non-waste costs' of time etc., which would need to be gradually flushed out over the long period of duality. Towards the end of the duality period when the waste-only costs are quite representative and valid, estimates of the Basic Allowance can be made, before finally having a 'switch-over day' when the new prices and wages are provided. Obviously, there would be many more complications to be considered, such as the significant problem of large sums of (old) money stored in bank accounts and investments, and the mere mention of this indicates how far this book has stretched beyond the original moans and groans of Parts 1 and 2.

The second 'real-world' integration problem is, how would two countries with these two completely different versions of society and methods of valuation be able to trade with each other? Again, by way of the briefest suggestion, this could be overcome with some good old-fashioned direct trading of products and services, such as 500 cars for 10,000 vaccinations or 500kg of apples for 100kg of fish etc. This would be a far from perfect solution, but provided both sides considered the trade to be fair, by their own needs, standards and methods of measurement, then the trade could go ahead.

What has all this achieved?

Having trawled through the strange and weird concepts of this alternative version of society, been bombarded with new ideas and even dragged through some maths, what has all this achieved? There are at least three answers to this question depending on the perspective and viewpoint. The only real and valid answer is from the perspective of the real physical world, in which case the answer is "absolutely nothing at all". This chapter is nothing more than just another set of silent words that do nothing, except perhaps provide a bit of entertainment or some food for thought. From my own personal perspective, this chapter is nothing more than my best solution to this rather profound and complex puzzle that I chose to set for myself, before getting too tired to think about it any further. In the context of this book, this chapter paints a picture of an undoubtedly different society, providing another important and very useful tool to judge and compare our current society against. It is another way for us to see our society from a very different perspective, by helping us to step even further back from our daily lives and to see an even bigger picture more clearly.

There is no pretence that this thought experiment solves any problems or provides any solutions but, mostly via conscious design choices, this strange alternative society does attempt to remove the worst parts of today's society, whilst maintaining the better aspects listed here.

    a) Competition of prices and products.
    b) Wages based on contribution and performance.
    c) A monetary system for exchanging goods and labour.

d) Opportunities for pure research and technology advancement.
e) Central government control of national interests.

Whilst some of the differences with today's society were intentionally designed into the solution, others were just unexpected natural consequences of this particular solution. These pleasant surprises included prices being driven to zero, the cheapest products being the most environmentally friendly, less opportunities for crime, and rubbish becoming a direct competitor to new raw materials (by removing the cost of the time-consuming sorting and cleaning). Intuitively these natural, unintended side-effects suggest that there is good amount of common sense and a consistency with the real world contained within this solution. The next list summarises the main differences with today's society.

a) Funds (or money) are based on the real measure of waste, rather than being a purely abstract measure dominated by the cost of our time.

b) Prices are driven down towards natural minimum limits (instead of relentless, unlimited increases).

c) Rewards are based primarily on benefits to others (rather than rewarding selfishness or gaining profit from others).

d) More jobs are paid well (but with less opportunity to become very rich).

e) A lot less administration and litigation.

f) More democratic voting, giving more direct democratic control of local decisions and actions.

g) The whole finance industry is reduced to the few relatively simple GCSE maths equations below (rather than needing a maths PhD to understand financial markets).

$$Job\ Rating = Role\ Rating \times Skill\ Rating \times Experience\ Rating$$

$$Business\ Rating = RL + SL + \frac{Nc * Cw}{(Nc + 5Ne) * (Cw + P)} + \frac{S}{\left(\left(1 + \frac{3}{Nc}\right) * \sqrt{Ne} * Cw\right) + P}$$

$$Take\text{-}Home\ Pay = Basic\ Allowance + (Basic\ Allowance \times Job\ Rating \times Business\ Rating)$$

$$Annual\ Pension = Basic\ Allowance + (Basic\ Allowance \times Average\ Annual\ Rating)$$

$$Insurance\ Payment = Minimum\ of\ (New\ Cost\ or\ Purchase\ Cost) \times$$
$$(1 - (0.15 \times number\ of\ claims))$$

This gross simplification of the finance world, and the removal of a lot of administration and bureaucracy, mean there will be more people available to fill the practical, beneficial, highly paid roles of teachers, doctors, nurses, police etc. In short, this simpler, alternative society aims to provide what people really want and need, without wasting the finite resources we have available to us. It tries to ensure that all financial decisions are naturally and inherently consistent with the real physical world and, instead of putting barriers in front of our altruistic side, it attempts to reward altruism and helping others, whilst limiting the rewards of selfishness.

An alternative view

Although all this started with the pessimistic moans, groans and frustrations of Part 1 and a desire to understand the reasons behind them, the intention was not to be negative. It is hoped that those earlier pessimistic moans, and this more unusual optimistic thought experiment, combine to provide some very different perspectives of our society and, crucially, that is the real aim of this book. It has attempted to present a very different set of views, intended to provoke thought, see things differently, understand more and question the more commonly accepted views, in order to get a clearer view of what something actually is or isn't. These types of direct comparison make it possible to see differences, alternatives, flaws, problems and changes in our current society that would otherwise be invisible, lost or difficult to recognise in the detail, complexity and accepted normality of everything around us. It is hoped that these different and unconventional perspectives can allow people to see, question, understand and judge our society differently than before.

Perhaps our society is not as comfortable, affluent, efficient, democratic, concerned or caring as it is commonly promoted and accepted to be. Conversely, some may believe that all is well, nothing is broken, nothing needs fixing and our current financial system will drive us all to a bright and prosperous future. Others may consider that this type of questioning and outspoken outbursts against some of the more commonly accepted and normalised views come close to some kind of modern-day heresy. Whatever your own personal view and perspective, it is not until something is recognised and accepted as broken or flawed that any attempts can be made to fix it. Within the context of this book, these different perspectives allow people to decide for themselves whether the frustrations of Part 1 are just the indulgent, opinionated moans, groans, rants and rambles of another grumpy old man with something to say or whether they are a consequence of some significant, underlying systematic problems and influences within our society.

"Following the rules of the game will not change the game. To change the game, you must first show that the rules are wrong."

17

BACK TO REALITY

*"We have now sunk to a depth at which the restatement
of the obvious is the first duty of intelligent men."*
(George Orwell, 1903–1950, author)

Whatever your views of our current society and that alternative version, we all live in the same single physical reality. It is a reality constrained by physical limits and laws, where even the energy from sunlight is limited by how much we can capture each day. It is only our perceptions of that single reality that differ; we all perceive the same single physical reality differently. However, it is not these perceptions that decide what happens, it is physical reality. It is physics that decides if a bridge will collapse, not the perception that it is big or strong enough. It is reality that decides if your car breaks down, not the perception that you were sold a reliable car or your desire to reach Leeds by 3:30pm. Changing our perception of reality only changes what we think of it, it does not change the reality itself. If people are hungry and cold, saying they are not, just looking away or claiming it's their own fault does not change the reality that they are hungry and cold. Physical reality is totally unaware of what we say, think, believe, perceive or expect, and it will only respond to our actions. We experience physical reality all the time and it is the foundation stone of everything we intuitively understand as common sense.

Financial lens

In stark contrast to this physical reality, we live in a society dominated by economic forces and financial influences. I have tried to demonstrate, in my own crude and opinionated way, how this abstract, unlimited, unstable financial system is detached from the real physical world. It is utterly incapable of measuring, judging or comprehending human values, the physical limits of planet Earth or the needs of its population. Instead, finance creates a contradiction with the limited physical world by constantly and single-mindedly demanding "MORE" growth from us, from our society and from our planet. It achieves this by rewarding those who can generate the most profit, encouraging us to charge as much as possible for providing as little as possible, tempting the selfish side of our nature to the surface. Simultaneously, this need for profit and growth passively discourages anything that isn't profitable, such as helping people. The love of money is accused of being "the root of all evil" because it can affect our morals and judgements.

The human invention of money has become the single abstract measure of materials, transport, medicine, food, education, land, energy, services, sport, work, shelter, entertainment, care, waste and, more recently, even the gases in our atmosphere. Even our time, happiness and success are measured in monetary terms. It is simply incomprehensible that a single abstract unit of measurement is the best way to measure all these different things, yet we simply accept that it is, every single hour of every day. Increasingly we see the world through a financial lens. Increasingly our perception, measurements, understanding, judgements and reasoning are switching away from the shared physical reality, towards a more abstract monetary invention of our own making – one that our society has become increasingly addicted to and dependent on.

This monetary abstraction distracts us away from what people need now, towards what is affordable or how that same money might grow in future. Economic sense turns our decisions away from what is needed now. Even though we have all the materials, knowledge, skills and time needed to build a new hospital, prison, school or bridge, it is money that says we can't. Money says it is not affordable. Money says it is not profitable enough. It is money that says people cannot have what they want or need. From this perspective money, profit and finance are not the provider of all things good, they are the shackles and constraints, the ball and chain that prevent people from making the right decisions, that prevent people doing the right thing and prevent people getting what they need or want. The fundamental measure of better or worse is switching away from what is beneficial for people and the planet, towards what is better for money, profit, finance and economic growth. Economic sense has started to overtake common sense as the dominant factor in our decision making. As a minimum, this distorts our decision making in favour of money and profit. At worst, it allows money and profit to decide and dictate what is possible and what is not. It creates a 'wedge of contradiction' that is driven into each major decision, abstracting and distorting our decisions away from reality.

Battle against abstraction

For a century or more, our decisions and common sense have been under assault from this financial abstraction, battling against the growing pressures of finance and economic sense. This is a tough battle to fight – economic sense says batteries should not be replaceable and that we should make ultra-processed foods that are addictive. Over the last few decades this economic attack has been aided and abetted by a more modern toxic concoction of additional abstractions, each disabling our common sense a bit further.

- The use of empty, bland meaningless language to avoid, ignore or dismiss problems and contradictions is becoming more common and accepted.
- Computers remove context and understanding from the information we use. We have far more information but understand it less. We use more information blindly. Having and storing information is becoming confused with having knowledge and understanding.
- Processes abstract our actions from what we do and why. They demote, prevent or exclude other valid or sensible alternatives from being considered or used. We slavishly follow them without understanding or questioning if they are suitable for that situation.
- The recent fashion and obsession for continual improvement allows anything labelled as feedback to be interpreted as

an unquestionable guarantee of yet another improvement, without thinking about who the change will affect or what it will disrupt.

These more recent abstractions from the real world further reduce our ability to shout, "This isn't right". They help contradictions sound plausible; they allow false logic to remain hidden for longer; they help bad decisions sound correct or at least more tolerable. More than ever before, people are allowing these abstracting influences to make decisions for them. "We can't afford it", "I followed the process", "I copied the information from the screen", "The feedback said change it." Along with some of our ever-present laziness and selfishness, people don't need to understand or feel responsible, they can switch off and let go, letting money, profit, information and process decide for them. It is in this dense fog of abstractions that groups of smartly dressed, intelligent people nod in agreement that "not buying new medicine", "closing a community hub" or "not providing more education facilities" is the sensible and correct decision to make. Life in this fog, where people are unable or unwilling to decide for themselves, means that exchanging four pound coins requires two machines, a laptop, a piece of paper a human and three queues. It means you can't swap two appointments at the same venue on the same day and it becomes impossible to donate some left-over balloons to a junior school. It is this 'fog of abstraction', this detachment from reality, that makes it hard to do the right thing, to make sensible decisions or to help other people. In short, it makes the simplest of things difficult.

Doing the right thing

All those altruistic, selfless people who volunteer their time and energy to provide and promote a wide range of activities like clubs, sports and social gatherings for the benefit of others must now struggle and swim against the tide of influences that society imposes on us. Our modern society builds an obstacle course of process hoops, Health and Safety hurdles, payment obstacles, computer barriers and informational dead ends, to jump, crawl, climb and navigate through, in the form of the following:

- "You need to apply for permission."
- "You must get an agreement before you can do that."
- "You can't until you complete an application form and have it checked and accepted."
- "You need to follow the process online."
- "Sorry you are not allowed because we are not insured for that."
- "You will need to obtain consent from everyone first."
- "You need to maintain records of all your activities."
- "You will need to get insurance for that."
- "We will need to have everyone's full contact details."
- "Only if you have done full risk assessments and had them authorised."
- "You need to pay for an independent assessment before you can do anything."
- "You have to set up an online account and get everyone to register."

All this so-called help and advice is just 'passing the burden'; it can hardly be considered as helpful, active, practical encouragement. Collectively, it provides few or no tangible incentives for those altruistic people who want to help. All the effort involved in completing this arduous, time-consuming obstacle course is before you can even start to contemplate how you might provide the first bits of any actual practical, useful help or service for those who need it. Our society is effectively deterring efforts and attempts to help and benefit others. Filling in forms, feeding the 'binformation machine', recording, checking, reviewing and collecting fees and payment is now far more important than doing something or providing practical help for those in need. This is why it is almost impossible for a business to donate unwanted furniture and computers to a school. The combination of this costly, time-consuming obstacle course and the risk of being sued just make it a lot easier to not even bother trying to help, or to just throw away perfectly good equipment.

Today, decisions are not based on what is best for people or what they need, they are based on what is affordable, what is profitable, what is quickest or most efficient, what is in line with process or what the computer tool dictates. It is becoming increasingly difficult for people to make decisions that deep down they know are right, that are just common sense, that are for the benefit of people. Genuinely helping people takes time, so it doesn't save or generate money and often it is costly. This is the reason why the modern Western world is so frustrating and why simple things are difficult. We are living and coping with all those decisions that are not made for people's benefit, that are not made in the best interests of people. Decisions that are abstracted or detached from reality.

Living with abstraction

For many people this is all acceptable and normal, especially those born into this most recent 'have a conversation', 'information', 'feedback', 'continual improvement', 'process pit' evolution of our society. It is just how things are, it is encouraged and apparently it improves things. There is a naïve assumption that all the best intentions will miraculously manifest themselves, whilst there is little regard for any of the real practical disruption and consequences. It is the real physical world with all its limitations and constraints, along with our natural unreliable human behaviours, that steadfastly refuse to let these hypothetical high expectations and theories work in practice. It is our one shared physical reality that ultimately decides, not our perceptions, expectations or beliefs.

Today the following list of behaviours are commonplace and acceptable.

- People talk without saying anything meaningful.
- Having yet another 'useful conversation' replaces any decisions and action.
- Copying a file of information is assumed or considered to be the same as understanding and knowledge.
- Computer tools say it must be 'this' or 'that' (but absolutely nothing in between or anything different).
- Processes exclude other sensible alternatives.
- Anything labelled as feedback generates yet another change (or improvement?).

This is what generates delays, continual change, inefficiency and frustration. This is why simple things are becoming more difficult. This gradual growing abstraction and detachment from reality means people are starting to forget some of the more traditional, important truths, such as the three below.

- It is not feedback and raw information that makes good decisions, it is knowledge, understanding, context and common sense.
- It is not processes that make things better and more efficient, it is people's understanding, experience, willingness to help others and ultimately their actions.
- It is not money that makes things better, it is people's decisions, behaviour and actions.

We are slowly, gradually, incrementally squeezing common sense, human values and physical reality out of the way we make decisions and our choice of actions. That is why things are so frustrating and why even the simplest things are becoming difficult. That is why the cracks are starting to show and ultimately why our society is fundamentally flawed. These types of abstracted decisions are starting to make us look like idiots (incidentally, the economist Yanis Varoufakis has a similar sentiment about finance at the end of his book on capitalism referenced in Chapter 9). This must be the wrong direction for our society to be heading in, or, more disturbingly, the wrong direction for our society and economy to be leading or dragging its addicted dependents, followers and believers, without people having control over it.

The cracks

In this fog of abstracted, distorted decisions, the problem of women being unfairly pressurised to buy beauty products is met with the ridiculous solution of doubling the problem and pressurising men to the same extent, economic sense says that destroying food harvests is the best thing to do (as in the book *The Grapes of Wrath*[1] and the *Time* magazine article on crop destruction[2]) and the clothing industry has used the same type of wilful destruction to keep demand and prices high. Economic sense also says that light bulbs that are too reliable must be replaced with unreliable ones, computer software should be made slower on purpose to make it unusable, and ultra-processed food is made so addictive that you can't stop eating it.

In a society where this is accepted, even encouraged or promoted, then the judgement and common sense must be questioned. These and the other examples scattered throughout the book suggest that the erosion of our common sense has already started, that the cracks are starting to appear, that the world really is starting to go slightly mad. Some people have even invented and sold a way to make wiping your arse more difficult and frustrating than it needs to be! Toilet paper is manufactured flat, sold flat, delivered flat and it is flat when it is put next to the toilet waiting to be used. We then use it while it is still flat. So, who the hell thought that a good way to dispense it to people sat on the bog, would be to scrunch it up tightly and squeeze it through a tiny hole, one sheet at a time! If someone asks to read a page of notes or have a blank sheet of paper, I don't say "Yes of course" and then immediately screw it up into a ball before giving it to them, because that would be extremely unhelpful, rather stupid and be a waste of their time. More astonishingly other people then buy this ridiculous idea and install it in the toilets of public buildings and places of work. How did they decide this was the best way to dispense toilet paper? What were they thinking? Was it just the cheapest option? It is certainly not the most useful, efficient or convenient. Doing reverse origami on each and every individual sheet of tissue paper to make it flat again is a very time-consuming exercise. It is certainly not a 'public convenience'.

More and more of our decisions and choices are starting to look absurd, as collectively we drift away from what is good for people, away from reality, towards the abstracted demands of money, processes and computers. If this rather frightening thought is true, then perhaps it is time for people to start thinking of alternative ways for society to operate before we lose even more control over decisions and judgements and things become even worse. The financial influences that have steered the direction of society and encouraged these types of bad decisions for a century or more will not change or reduce. Neither will the additional more recent concoction of abstracting influences. The self-feeding loops within our society will continue to encourage more profit hunting, which will continue to benefit the fortunate sections of the population and entice the more selfish parts of our human nature to the surface. They will continue to constrict funding of public services, continue to feed the debt, misery and suffering of the less fortunate sections of the population and continue to widen the gap between the haves and have nots. And all this will necessitate even more empty words and contradictory claims to cover up and disguise the growing contradiction layer between the worlds of finance and reality.

At this point the process advocates can jump in and save the day yet again with yet another process that says something like, "Everyone will help everyone else". Give it a reference number, record it, job done, no more problem. Please feel free to laugh and ridicule this world-saving process, because it is just as ridiculous as all the other processes, which all suffer exactly the same flaw. There is a huge, massive, immovable, indestructible dose of reality in the way. Alternatively, you can believe that everything is just fine and by collecting a bit more 'feedback', we can 'improve' further and make things even better for everyone. In the real physical world, you do not get something for nothing, true improvements aren't that easy, and so it is very difficult for me to see how today's version of society can lead to the fair, stable, sustainable future that it constantly claims to be striving for. It is like constantly listening to society saying, "I'm going on a diet to make things healthier, better and fairer for everyone, but I'm just going to continue eating all the chips, crisps, cake and chocolate while I'm on my diet". It is simply absurd. The alternative society in the previous chapter attempted to break these loops and influences. By making money a measure of waste only, it ensured that all financial decisions were naturally and inherently consistent with reality. It rewarded altruism, by providing the biggest rewards to those who help and benefit society and other people the most, whilst limiting the benefits of human selfishness. In other words, it allowed (or enforced) decisions to be consistent with the needs of the planet and the population.

Perhaps unsurprisingly, I think I would prefer a future in that alternative society, compared to a dystopian future version of our current society. A future where an unstable financial Frankenstein Santa dictator constantly demands "MORE", by forcing an army of profit- and process-driven businesses to "deliver continual financial improvement, maximising the risk averted profit potential by utilising an optimal synergistic convergence of digital intelligence with a biological procedural workforce", in which people do little more than blindly type numbers they don't understand into a computer, so that AI can be used to make judgements and decisions to increase profits, that no one understands the consequences of, but will affect loads of people, who are sat in their homes full of sick and elderly relatives, because the care system has completely crumbled, after those same profit-hungry businesses have finished bleeding dry every available drop of equity and value from people's homes and property and can no longer think of a way to generate enough profit from providing any kind of medical or compassionate care!

Admittedly that tirade is quite a large exaggeration, but an exaggeration is all it is. Everything in that extreme and rather cynical outburst has a strong element of truth in it, even today. The obsession, addiction and dependence that modern capitalist market societies have on economic growth is making profit and growth more important than either common sense or common good, and it will only continue to do so. Put very simply, economic sense is overtaking common sense. My generation will not escape this financial net, we are trapped in it and will drown in it. We will sell our homes to private profit-making businesses, to pay for our last few years of expensive, time-consuming care, instead of leaving our homes as a financial foundation to our children or grandchildren. They won't be protected from the even greater financial pressures they will face in future, such as education fees, extortionate house prices and rent, unaffordable childcare and probably higher medical and health care costs by then as well. The generations beyond that will have a bit more time and a few more options for a change, but none will be easy. In the meantime, our society will continue to bring comfort and happiness to many, in the form of money, wealth, choice and consumerism and this is what is considered next.

Money and happiness

It is commonly believed that money brings happiness. This is certainly true up to the first threshold where you need only enough money to be fed, safe and warm. For those who unfortunately don't have enough of these three essentials, more money can make a huge difference to their lives. In the worst cases, it may only provide some temporary relief from hunger, pain or cold, whilst more money could help to change their circumstances and provide some longer-term level of happiness and comfort. Once you pass this first financial comfort threshold, the relationship between money and happiness changes. Now the extra cash provides some new possibilities, some nice new clothes, a bigger car, an extra holiday, more meals out in restaurants or a nicer house.

However, people quickly acclimatise to these nice enjoyable extras and stop appreciating what they have (I certainly appreciate my house and car less than I did in the first few years of ownership). What initially made you happy quickly becomes just the new accepted normal. The happiness is now only temporary and, after this natural acclimatisation, future happiness means another bigger, better or newer product. This effect is greatly exploited and exaggerated by advertising, with claims that the latest and greatest new product will significantly improve your life and make you happy (selling the dream, not the reality). This very comfortable level of money allows people to get a little temporary kick of consumerist happiness whenever they want. Those who are more competitive, can choose to play "Keeping up with the Joneses" where money buys the very latest TV, phone or car etc. and earns bragging rights or status. Despite being incredibly common, I don't think I've ever heard anyone admit that this is a reasonable or sensible pursuit in life.

Beyond this second very comfortable threshold, the relationship between money and happiness changes once again. At this level, you have more money than you need or can reasonably spend and now money becomes merely status or success. Money is now a constant competition, a battle to selfishly gather more and maintain your rank and status. In all three layers, there is a desire and a want for more, so just like our economy you will never be satisfied. That is one certain way to never truly be content or happy – unless you learn to appreciate and be content with what you have, unless you can reach a 'that is enough' moment.

On a recent holiday, I was chatting with the tour guide about what makes people happy, a topic that greatly interested him. He started to describe a large academic study that was done to work out what made people truly happy. To cut the long and detailed explanation short, the top five things are listed below (note that it does not include money):

- Appreciating the things you have.
- Helping others.
- Variety.
- Being active.
- Company of other people.

If this academic study and list is correct, then the opposites of this 'happy list' can be assumed to be the equivalent 'unhappy list' below:

- Always wanting more (adverts and economic growth).
- Being selfish (money, profit, competition and business).
- Doing the same thing (following process, do everything on a computer screen).
- Inactivity (convenience, food deliveries, computer games, social media).
- Being alone.

How does our current society promote each of the items in these two lists? In the second 'unhappy list', the contents of the brackets provide some indication of the strong and increasing aspects of our lives. Our society does promote 'activity' via gym membership, pubs promote 'socialising' and restaurants, holidays, shows and fashion all promote 'variety' and something different etc., but the true incentive is profit, not people's happiness. These do help to keep us happier, but we don't get our money back if we don't use the gym, eat the food or stay at home! Meanwhile, these doses of happiness that we pay for are offset by all those other indirect influences, the ever-increasing pressures of time, cost and processes that our society creates, the frustrations of repeatedly forcing and squeezing our misshapen round pegs through tight procedural square holes, or having our desire and ability to help others obstructed or diminished. It seems like our modern society is nudging, pushing and encouraging us to be less happy.

Perhaps it is no coincidence that mental health issues are now affecting more and more people. Perhaps it is the constant struggle against contradiction, the difficultly in trying to get anything done, the constant talk and lack of action, the frustration and exasperation when even the simplest of things are so bloody difficult (like swapping four coins or using a tap). The continual need to follow yet another process, to do it all yourself using yet another website or another online application form that makes you repeatedly guess how many spaces and hyphens are needed to get the format of your reference number correct. Perhaps it is these recent influences of modern Western society that are increasing the levels of unhappiness, feeding the rise of mental health issues, as well as being the cause of my own personal frustrations?

Shackles and constraints

Three hundred years ago, when population and consumerism were both relatively low and resources were relatively high, this search for profit and growth was probably the fastest way to innovate, progress and increase the standard of living. Within the last century the rapid growth in the economy, technology and population has caught up with what the resources of Earth can sustain. More recently still, in the last few decades, economic growth has started to stretch and break the links between the financial world and physical reality, separating financial economic sense from common sense, creating a fundamental contradiction between the two different worlds.

We are entering an era where finance and monetary value are more dominant and powerful than ever before, where machines have overtaken our intelligence, where processes and procedures are seen as practical solutions, where we are drowning in oceans of 'binformation' and 'fake news' and where the 'fog of abstraction' is getting denser. It is becoming harder to understand and see clearly. It is more difficult to prevent our decisions being abstracted away from the real aims and intentions of society to benefit the population. Things that are relatively easy to achieve in the real physical world, like building a bridge across a busy road for the benefit of the town's population, just become impossible or totally unacceptable in the financial world. This is the financial 'wedge of contradiction' that we drive right into the heart of every major decision. It dictates that "You can't build a bridge", "You can't build a school" and "You can't have medicine" when in fact we could if we wanted to, there is nothing physical or practical preventing it. It is only prevented by a fictitious financial abstraction, which is completely of our own invention. I just don't see the sense in that. If the true role of society is to make decisions for the benefit of population and our planet, then driving this wedge of contradiction into every decision is a very poor way to start. Equally, seeing and judging reality through a thick fog of abstraction is not going to help us much either.

Therefore, in our comfortable, affluent, efficient world, it is not technology that is getting worse, it is not the comfort, convenience, energy efficiency, performance and benefits of technological advancements that are getting worse. It is simply how we treat other people and how we make decisions that are getting worse. It doesn't matter how good technology gets, because better technology will only help accelerate our society further and faster in the direction that decisions are made. Whilst those decisions continue to be financially and procedurally abstracted away from what people need and want, then better technology won't help, things won't get better. Economic sense will perpetually decide in its own favour. Our current version of society will not and cannot lead to a world where decisions are based simply on what people want and need, even if all the materials, knowledge, time, people, skills and capability exist. This dominance of economic sense over common sense is something that many people will already recognise as a very real part of our society today.

More than ever before, it is becoming important that we can clearly see and understand the structure and operation of our society, the way it influences and affects how we make decisions and the direction it is heading in. This is ultimately what this book has attempted to do, albeit in some rather flippant, exaggerated, cynical and hopefully entertaining way. In our hugely complicated world, where important decisions affect the lives of thousands or millions of people every day, why do we allow this wedge of contradiction and fog of abstraction to distort and detach decisions away from reality, away from common sense and away from what people really want or need. Yet we have no choice. Our society dictates that this is the way decisions are made, under the financial shackles and constraints, under strict processes, and this is exactly what we do every single day. People should not need to say things like "We need a bit of common sense", because all decisions should and could be common sense. But that will need some fundamental changes.

Need for change

Although there have been plenty of my individual opinionated rants and moans, this need for fundamental change is not just another one. It has already been recognised across many varied fields and professions. Recall the David Attenborough statement from Easter Island, referred to at the end of the WHEN IS ENOUGH? chapter (Chapter 15). This can be joined by the opinions expressed in the two finance books referenced earlier, along with similar books listed below written by lawyers, police, teachers, doctors and other professions (even this one by an engineer) all claiming that something is fundamentally wrong with the way our society operates and that something needs to fundamentally change.

- *The Secret Barrister: Stories of the Law and How It's Broken*, ISBN 978-1509841141
- *Tango Juliet Foxtrot: How Did It All Go Wrong for British Policing?* Iain Donnelly, ISBN 978-1785907166
- *The Education System Is Broken: Strategies to Rebuilding Hope, Lives, and Futures*, Cathy S. Tooley, ISBN 978-1475827392
- *This Is Going to Hurt: Secret Diaries of a Junior Doctor*, Adam Kay, ISBN 978-1509858637
- *Ultra-Processed People: Why Do We All Eat Stuff That Isn't Food... And Why Can't We Stop?* Chris Van Tulleken, ISBN 978-1529900057

These aren't requests for a bit more feedback on how things can be improved or suggestions of a bit more continual improvement. They are a varied collection of views from different professional corners of society, all reinforcing and backing up the claims of the do-gooder activists, that a fundamental, significant and effective change is needed to fix the underlying flaws in the way our society operates. Armed with our current level of scientific knowledge and our understanding of our planet, there are many people who already accept that something isn't right, that things are not going well within our society and that now is the time to fundamentally change.

Until something does change the direction in which our society is heading, we will continue along the same well-trodden path. Human psychology will ensure that future generations continue to copy and extend the financially rewarding, selfish, profit-making behaviours of today. Significant change will only happen when the financial wedge of contradiction is removed, and the fog of abstraction can be lifted from around the big decisions of business and government. Only then, when some good old-fashioned common sense dominates their decision making, will our society be consistent with the needs of the population and planet. Only when our society provides bigger rewards for helping others and removes the temptation of selfish personal profit will the direction of human behaviour and our society change. The alternative society in the previous chapter aimed to do just this, by providing the biggest rewards to those who benefit the most people and create least waste. It was designed so that the time-consuming jobs of care, teaching and recycling were encouraged and well rewarded. Funds were spread much more evenly across society, especially across the wide range of essential roles that we cannot live without, such as all those COVID-19 keyworkers, health workers, refuse collectors, cleaners, food producers and suppliers, etc. These are the essential roles and people that our society depends on, yet our current prosperous, efficient, caring, affluent, financial society could only reward them with a word (thanks), a label (keyworker), a noise (clap) and an image (rainbow) during the COVID-19 crisis, because apparently there was not enough money available to reward them financially. It really is a mad and topsy-turvy world we live in!

The alternative society thought experiment attempted to look at what might be possible, but it does not pretend to provide the answer or even suggest a solution. There are no quick, simple or perfect solutions, our society is just far too complex, and people will always have different views and opinions. It is not possible to please all the people, all the time and every alternative option will have advantages and disadvantages. Despite this, the previous chapter may help to undermine some views and arguments that there are no possible alternatives, that there simply is no other way. If a single chapter within a flippant and opinionated book of indulgent moans and groans can generate an alternative society that has different underlying principles, a different direction and doesn't destroy today's strong incentive for technology advancement, then at the very least it suggests that suitable alternative societies could be possible.

Chance for change

Although within my lifetime I will never get to see any change in the direction of our society, all the thought and analysis involved in writing this book have convinced me of one thing. The best, the easiest and possibly the only way for society to provide the sustenance, safety and stimulation for the growing human population on an isolated planet, in a way that is sustainable, stable and fair, is to ensure that both the basic fundamental principles and the underlying operation of that society are as strongly linked to the real physical world as possible. This is simply not the case today. Somehow, someway, our society must start providing what is right for people and what is right for our planet, and start rewarding those who do it. But we are currently an extremely long way off from that. It will not be possible until we can change the rules of the game, change the way society operates. It will never be possible to escape the unlimited loops we are trapped in, reliant on and addicted to, until the unlimited demand for growth, the ability for money to make more money, and the incentive for selfish profiteering are removed from society.

As the dominant species on this planet (again ignoring the strong arguments for insects, bacteria and viruses), it is only humans who can decide, act and change things, but any type of significant change has several fundamental problems. Firstly, it is much more difficult for people to change society than it is for society to change people. This is because people are moulded and must fit within society's structures and methods to live, survive and thrive within it. Secondly, it is almost impossible to dramatically change something, whilst simultaneously continuing to obey and follow the same rules you are trying to change. It is difficult to change the rules of the game whilst you are still playing it. Thirdly, and most controversially, those people in the powerful positions, who are needed to enact or accelerate any such change, are precisely those who are benefiting the most from the status quo of the current system, so inevitably (and perhaps selfishly) have the least incentive to change it. Just as there has been almost no change in the last few centuries, there seems to be no escape from the direction in which our financially driven society is leading (or dragging) its addicted, growth-obsessed followers and believers. Therefore, this chapter finishes back in today's real world, with the question "Will anything change either now or in the near future?" The optimistic set of answers to this question can be anything you want them to be, but the pessimistic, realistic and practical answers are all approximately the same: "You must be joking!"

"The abstract world of economic sense is overtaking the real world of common sense."

18

LAST LAUGH, CLOSING THOUGHTS AND FINAL WORDS

"When a man finds a conclusion agreeable, he accepts it without argument, but when he finds it disagreeable, he will bring against it all the forces of logic and reason."
(Thucydides, 460–440BC, ancient historian)

The vested interest of the powerful institutions in maintaining the status quo will ensure that any fundamental change in society is highly unlikely. Therefore, as long as I remain compos mentis, I have got many more years of listening to people talk utter rubbish, seeing and coping with selfish behaviour, spotting contradictions and watching people not indicate at roundabouts. By now it should be blatantly clear that I get just as frustrated with these modern-day problems as anyone, perhaps more so than most, and unfortunately this is only likely to become worse as I become progressively older and grumpier.

Coping with frustration

To cope with this and put up my own miniscule, trivial bit of resistance to the inevitable social slide into dystopia, there are a few things I try to do. In the same way that I analyse things around me, I also analyse and judge myself and my own faults, several of which will be apparent from this book (but at least I do indicate at roundabouts). During 50 years of this analytical self-judgement I have learnt a few simple rules which I consciously try to follow in (almost) everything I do:

- Always be honest with everyone.
- Only preach what you already actively practise, instead of preaching first and then forgetting or failing to put it into practice.
- Appreciate what you have every day, even the small simple things like a cup of tea or a sandwich.
- Don't worry about things you can't change, laugh at them instead (just as most of this book laughs at a society I cannot change).
- Genuinely and consciously think of others before you act.
  - Consider at least one other person or group when doing things (it will help you see things differently and act differently).
  - Don't ask someone to do something unless you would also be willing to do it yourself to the same extent.
  - Don't do things unless you know what effect they will have on others.
  - Don't assume people will understand information you give them, as their mind-reading skills will be similar to mine (and remember the George Bernard Shaw quote from the first chapter "The biggest problem with communication is the impression it has occurred").
- Be a role model for others (if you do it, others will do it).
- Whenever possible, try to learn or understand and help others do the same (this is very different from just assuming you are right).
- Avoid confrontation, it is not a good way to attract attention.

This type of self-judgement requires honesty with yourself. Only you can make a self-judgement, only you can ensure it is an honest one and only you know whether it is disguised by excuses and words.

Life is complex, difficult and sometimes hard, but it is good to look for things you can appreciate about your own situation and enjoy them.

Don't continually think "I need...", "I want..." or "I will be happy when..." because it will never be enough, you will always be chasing more. If you always try to do things only for yourself, you will become increasingly frustrated when people obstruct or hinder you and your pursuits. Conversely, if you try to actively help or benefit others, in little ways, every day, then you will feel that small sense of satisfaction. In short, my approach to overcoming the frustrations of modern society is to try to genuinely be aware of people and try to act in a way that is beneficial to them, providing of course it doesn't involve setting up yet another bloody online account, following another ridiculous process or banging my head against the wall trying to explain to someone why their request is completely nonsensical. But more than all that, my coping mechanism is humour, so I would like to add that to the list of things that make me happy, both laughing and making others laugh. To that end, instead of getting more frustrated I intend to follow the advice of the Roman philosopher Seneca who said, "It is better to make fun of life than bewail it", just as I've attempted to do in this book.

The last laugh

I have always enjoyed the misdirection, contradictions, wordplay, broken logic and mind-play contained in a lot of humour and jokes and it is a true pleasure in life to laugh and make people laugh. Humour is my coping mechanism; it is extremely helpful when coping with the thought that common sense is becoming a rarity. Much of the best comedy is based on nothing more that lifting a mirror up to society and highlighting its flaws, and programmes such as BBC's *Yes Minister*, *The Office* and the Dilbert cartoons[1] do it very well. I therefore intend to continue finding humour in the false logic and contradictions of what people say or do, like in these cases where people muddle up well-known phrases.

> "I'm putting my foot down, with a firm hand."
> "When I read a book like that, it just goes
> in one ear and out of the other."
> "I don't know how they sleep with themselves."

Unfortunately, this humorous approach is unlikely to prevent me from inevitably becoming the grumpy old man that I am destined to become.

It will probably just make me a more pedantic, irritating, grumpy old man with a bad sense of humour, which is even worse.

Initial intentions and final outcomes

The original intention of this book was only to bust a few common myths and laugh at the frustrations of my generation struggling with the pace of change and modern technology, to prompt some thought about what really happens beneath the words and beyond the processes of our daily lives. However, it grew beyond this original concept into a much wider look at modern Western society, the way it operates, the direction in which it is heading and how it influences human behaviour. It therefore seems ironic that, in hindsight, a book originally intended to appeal to the frustrations of the older generations may be more suitable and relevant to the younger generations, by providing a very different view of our society and the direction in which it is heading.

Although a few political and environmental issues have been raised, this book was not written with any political or environmental agenda. I'm an engineer with an analytical mind and the only things that I am interested in are reality, truth, understanding, knowledge and common sense. By using the analytical engineering techniques of stepping back, comparing and contrasting against alternatives, and looking for self-feeding or uncontrollable loops, it is possible to see things differently and more clearly. By removing some of the confusing, complex and often distracting details, these engineering approaches can help to expose some of the underlying flaws in our society and highlight how our society differs from the more conventional, commonly accepted views. However, one of the most important aspects of this book is to emphasise and reiterate the fundamental contradiction between the financial world and the real physical world. One is an abstract, belief-based concept invented by humans, fuelled by fresh air and without any physical construct or limits, whilst the other is the fundamental physical reality and absolute truth of our world on which all our common sense is built. If the true role of society is to provide a stable, sustainable, safe and stimulating environment for the population, then driving this contradiction into each and every decision simply cannot be the right way.

It was understanding this fundamental contradiction that led to the alternative society thought experiment and a further addition to the book. The puzzle was to see if there were any possible alternative or better ways that a human society could operate. However, if the propaganda-style promotion of this alternative society (or the other little sporadic bursts of optimism) has temporarily blinded you or filled you with renewed enthusiasm, then do not be too influenced by the words and content of this book. That chapter remains exactly as it was the very first time you unknowingly picked up this book and absolutely nothing has changed. Whether my solution to this complex puzzle is suitable, reasonable, relevant, acceptable, common sense, valid or even fair is totally irrelevant, as the intention was only to provide an alternative and hopefully interesting way to view, understand and judge our own current society in a very different way and from a very different perspective. As explained in the very first chapter, any set of words, idea, alternative or suggestion does not provide a solution or make things better – only good decisions and actions do that.

What do you think?

You now know my somewhat unconventional, analytical opinions on the society we live in and hopefully this urge to "say it all" has provided some interesting views and plenty of food for thought. I have tried to explain my views in a way that at least makes them justified opinions; maybe that was sufficient for you to accept them or maybe not. If you happen to agree with my opinions then all I have done is state the obvious, confirm that the world really is going mad and that some kind of dystopia awaits future generations. Conversely, you may disagree with everything that has been said, which probably means that I'm an incompetent idiot or that I've already become an out-of-touch grumpy old man far sooner than I'd wish. Much more likely is that there is some element of truth in my opinions and thoughts, but plenty of other opposing views to consider. This alone is a worrying sign, because it indicates that there are enough problems, enough bad decisions, enough ridiculous solutions and enough visible cracks appearing to suggest that we are starting to drift away from common sense and reality. It suggests we need to be wary, careful not to drift or be dragged further in the same direction, where the influences of money, profit and markets choose on our behalf without limits and without our control, where people must increasingly bend to the demands and constraints of computers, machines and processes, instead of them being there to help and aid people.

Whatever your own opinion and views, I hope this book has provided a thought-provoking or entertaining read. All the time and effort spent writing it will have been very worthwhile if it has achieved any of the following. However, please "DO NOT provide feedback on the book, it is NOT important, and it will NOT be used to improve this book".

- It was to some extent relevant, factual, correct or interesting.
- It was enjoyable, entertaining or amusing to read.
- You learnt something new or now understand something better than before.
- You now see or think about some things differently than before.
- It has made you think about your own use of words and, more importantly, your actions.
- It has made you think more about other people, your awareness of them and trying to help them more.
- It has made you start using your indicators at roundabouts and road junctions.

If it has achieved none of these, then I apologise for wasting both your time and your money. At least your money has not gone straight into my pocket, but is going to help those in a far worse situation who need it far more than you or I. Despite the many suggestions and indications that modern Western society encourages the worst of our natural human traits and constricts our more altruistic nature, everybody could change a bit if they chose to. You can always choose how much to be aware of others around you and how much to help them, you can choose how to judge and measure real benefit (and it isn't money), you can chose how you make decisions (do you just follow the process or do what is helpful or right?) and you can definitely start by considering others and lifting a finger to help other road users by using your indicators.

The last question

In the preface, this book started with the rather superficial question of whether this collection of opinions are just the moans, groans and rants of another grumpy old man or whether they are a valid, but perhaps exaggerated, representation of the way we live today. The last question of this book is far more important and much more worthy of your consideration. It is whether the influences within our society are starting to distort, detach or corrupt our judgements, decisions, common sense and actions, away from the real world, away from what the population and planet need.

A closing thought

For thousands of years our societies have been based on various belief-based systems, such as gods of weather and seasons, mythical monsters, magical witches and demons, formalised religions and omnipotent beings, royalty, noble blood and most recently a belief in the abstract concept of money, markets and profit. Meanwhile, humanity has evolved to learn that physical reality is controlled by the laws of nature and physics, which we continue to research, understand and learn more about. We already know we cannot beat these physical laws and yet we still choose to run our society on principles and theories that are completely detached from them. Our society remains precariously founded on nothing more than belief and abstraction, in exactly the same way it has been for many thousands of years. With our current level of scientific knowledge how can this, in any sense, be the correct thing to continue doing? Deep down don't our understanding of scientific physical laws, our intuition and our basic common sense dictate that the fundamental principles of a society should be based firmly on the physical reality of the world we live in and not on some fictional, abstract belief system?

It is not until all decisions are based firmly on physical reality that we stand any chance of a stable and sustainable future society. Physical reality will not bend to society's rules and principles, it will not comprehend the human invention of money, profit or economy, it will not hear anyone's overly optimistic words, theories, procedures, policies or predictions. Physical reality will always make us bend to its rules, it will eventually win every argument and will always continue to do so. Physical reality is something we experience every single day of our lives, it is the best and most reliable form of feedback we have and it is the foundation stone of everything we intuitively understand as common sense. So why on earth would we choose to base our society and our decisions on anything else? Why on earth should we hide it in a fog of abstraction or drive a wedge of contradiction into it? Would it not be sensible, for the first time in human history, to base the foundations of our society on something real, on something stronger than our changing beliefs, on something which is more stable and permanent than any society we could build, on something which will outlive everything we know and understand? Isn't it time we based our society on physical reality itself? Once the technological miracles of the current Information Age have filled our minds with more information than the human brain can comprehend or cope with, wouldn't it be sensible if the next stage of human evolution could honestly and truly be called the Reality Age? That just seems like basic common sense!

Final three words

This is finally the end of the book and the fact that you are reading or hearing this means that a wide range of people now know what I had to say. It concludes the "SAY IT ALL" phase of my life and some (or many?) will disagree with it. I can therefore now look forward to learning and understanding something new from all the opinions, explanations and reasoning that differ from my own. Finding out why and how you are wrong is an excellent way of learning and understanding something new, as implied by these two quotes.

> *"Doubt is the beginning, not the end of wisdom."*
> (George Iles, 1852–1942, author)

> *"It is better to change an opinion, than*
> *persist with the wrong one."*
> (Socrates, 469–399BC, Greek philosopher)

Being exposed to different opinions, alternative approaches, structured reasoning and theoretical thought experiments is an excellent way to see, learn and understand more. Equally, being involved in open, structured, reasoned debate and learning from other people's views and experience is an enjoyable part of my life. This is especially true when it is over a pint or two, and within the context of the WORDS chapter (Chapter 1), knowing that all these interesting opinions, enjoyable debates and collections of words are in fact all completely silent and will not change, do, fix or solve anything at all without action. Now that I have said it all,

I can start looking forward to the inevitable "sod it all" stage of my life. Although I still hope to learn and understand more from others in future, I can now attempt some different kinds of thought experiment, ones where I attempt to relax a little more and allow myself to experiment using the words "SOD IT" occasionally.

"SOD IT ALL"

ACKNOWLEDGEMENTS

I must start by thanking all those good, considerate people, who think of others and help them by using their indicators at roundabouts (unlike the other selfish, lazy or ignorant people who don't). More seriously I would like to thank my parents and extended family and several other influential people I have met over the years, who have taught me that morality and truth are much more important than deceptive words and selfishness.

Special thanks to my wife for tolerating my reduced contribution to home life during the 5 years it took to compile and write this book, and also to Paul Grimsey for having the willingness and perseverance to read several of the earliest, barely legible, draft versions from cover to cover. Additional thanks and appreciation for all those who helped to refine the content at various stages, including Marion Higgins, Jane and Liv Barrett, Celia, Tom Moss, Olivia Howard, Tony Ireland, Steve, Clare Higgins and Jo. It is this group that helped convert around 150,000 rambling words into this more presentable version. Gratitude also to Ken Abbott who has listened to and added to my moans and groans over many years. Thanks also to those who provided moral support and encouragement, including my mum and dad, Ian Malcolm, Kate and Jo Williams and Dave Murphy, who have collectively fuelled my motivation to continue and finish.

I must also thank the publishing team at SWATT Books, including Sam Pearce and Rosie Stewart, for all their help, and for clearly demonstrating how true knowledge, experience and expertise can make some difficult things simple. Finally, I'd like to thank you, the readers, for your donation to charity through the purchase of this book and for tolerating all my moans, groans, rants and everything I had to say. I hope it was worthwhile, but, if not, then at least your money has gone to the good causes, so thank you.

My usual preference for charity donations tends to be cancer related, as it has directly affected my personal life more than other issues and problems. However, regardless of how relentless and devastating the nature of cancer, it is exactly that – natural. Cancer is just a natural biological consequence of our DNAs' ability to mutate and evolve and it is not attributable to human mistakes or the other influences of our society. Therefore, more in keeping with the content and conclusions of this book, the profits from this book will be donated to help those people who do suffer at the hands of society's flaws and problems, those people who our affluent and caring society struggles to support sufficiently, because they provide the least prospects of a profitable return on financial investment.

Therefore, in buying this book, you have helped charities that altruistically swim against the prevailing currents of our financially driven society, to provide much-needed care for those who need it, including the homeless, elderly and ill. My original intention was to provide the list of charities here but unfortunately, I could not generate it in time for publication. It seems that even donating the profits from the sale of a book to charity is not that simple either!

_____

"Don't forget to use your indicators, but if
that's not for you, then do it for others."

References

1 DON'T BELIEVE A WORD

1   Kate Kershner (30 November 2023), "Did that astrologer read you right? That's the Forer's effect", Howstuffworks: https://science. howstuffworks.com/life/inside-the-mind/human-brain/forer-effect.htm
2   Saul McLeod (16 June 2023), "Loftus and Palmer (1974): Car Crash Experiment", simplypsychology.org: www.simplypsychology.org/loftus-palmer.html#:~:text=Findings%3A%20The%20estimated%20speed%20was,asked%20the%20%E2%80%9Chit%E2%80%9D%20question
3   Ralph R. Ortega (5 March 2020), "Shocking moment California health official LICKS her finger during coronavirus press conference – just seconds after warning people not to touch their faces", *Daily Mail*: www.dailymail.co.uk/news/article-8077049/Health-official-licks-finger-warning-people-against-touching-faces-avoid-coronavirus.html

2 SOME FEEDBACK ABOUT FEEDBACK

1   Dave Gorman, *Life Is Goodish*, Series 3 Episode 8, "A German tradition", UKTV.
2   *Room 101*, Series 3 Episode 1, BBC, with guest Joan Bakewell who nominated customer surveys: www.bbc.co.uk/programmes/b03sblyw

3 WHAT IMPROVEMENT? (OR WHAT IMPROVE MEANT)

1   Tom Coyle (26 February 2015), "The inefficiency of change", LinkedIn: www.linkedin.com/pulse/inefficiency-change-tom-coyle

4 FALSE LOGIC

1   Douglas Hofstadter (1999), *Godel, Escher, Bach: An Eternal Golden Braid*, Penguin.
2   *Yes, Prime Minister*, "Power to the people", BBC, episode in 1988.
3   *The Last Leg*, Series 5 Episode 6, 13 February 2015, with guest David Mitchell, shown on Channel 4, Open Mike Productions.

5 BINFORMATION

1   Mark Ziemann and Mandhri Abeysooriya (26 August 2021), "Excel autocorrect errors still plague genetic research, raising concerns over scientific rigour", The Conversation: https://theconversation.com/excel-autocorrect-errors-still-plague-genetic-research-raising-concerns-over-scientific-rigour-166554
2   Met Office, "The Great Storm of 1987": https://www.metoffice.gov.uk/weather/learn-about/weather/case-studies/great-storm#:~:text=The%20highest%20measured%20wind%20speed,at%20several%20other%20coastal%20locations.
3   Tim Harford (2020), *How to Make the World Add Up: Ten Rules for Thinking Differently About Numbers*, The Bridge Street Press.
4   BBC News (24 November 2022), "Post Office scandal: Horizon contract was 'fatally flawed'": www.bbc.co.uk/news/business-63748812

7 LIABLE TO BE UNRELIABLE

1   Sergio Leone (dir.) (1966), *The Good, the Bad and the Ugly*, produced by Alberto Grimaldi, United Artists and Produzioni Eurropee Associate.

8 LIFTING A FINGER

1 Cara Flanagan, Matt Jarvis and Rob Liddle (2020), AQA *Psychology for A Level, Year 1 & AS*, 2nd Edition, Chapter 4 – Approaches in Psychology.
2 Derek Sivers (2010), "How to start a movement", TED Talk, YouTube (also YouTube clip called "Lone Dancer"): www.ted.com/talks/derek_sivers_how_to_start_a_movement?language=en

9 FINANCIAL PLAYGROUND

1 Yanis Varoufakis (2019), *Talking to My Daughter: A Brief History of Capitalism*, Vintage.
2 John Lanchester (2010), *Whoops! Why Everyone Owes Everyone and No One Can Pay*, Penguin.
3 Rory Kennedy (dir.) (18 February 2022), *Downfall: The Case Against Boeing*, produced by Rory Kennedy, Keven McAlester, Mark Bailey, Justin Wilkes, Sara Bernstein, Amanda Rohlke, Brian Grazer; distributed by Netflix; Imagine Documentaries, Imagine Entertainment, Moxie. View a trailer here: www.youtube.com/watch?v=vt-IJkUbAxY
4 Wikipedia, "History of coins": https://en.wikipedia.org/wiki/History_of_coins
5 2020 BBC Reith Lectures: *From Moral to Market Sentiments*, Episode 1, "Mark Carney: How we get what we value", BBC Radio 4: www.bbc.co.uk/programmes/m000py8t#:~:text=In%20this%20lecture%2C%20recorded%20with,values%20and%20constrain%20our%20choices%3F

11 WHO DECIDES

1 BBC Scotland, *Burnistoun*, Series 1 Episode 1, "Voice activated elevator": www.bbc.co.uk/programmes/p00hbfjw
2 Google DeepMind, "AlphaGo", beating world Go champions Lee Sedol and Ke Jie at the boardgame Go: www.deepmind.com/research/highlighted-research/alphago
3 Nadia Jaber (22 March 2022), "Can artificial intelligence help see cancer in new, and better, ways?" National Cancer Institute: www.

cancer.gov/news-events/cancer-currents-blog/2022/artificial-intelligence-cancer-imaging

4   2021 BBC Reith Lectures, "Professor Stuart Russell: Living with artificial intelligence", BBC Radio 4: www.bbc.co.uk/programmes/m001216k

5   Nick Bostrom (2014), *Superintelligence: Paths, Dangers, Strategies*, Oxford University Press.

12 THE SEWER SYSTEM

1   Wikipedia, "William Jennens", on the Jennens vs Jennens court case: https://en.wikipedia.org/wiki/William_Jennens

2   UK Government, National Statistics (25 November 2023), "Police workforce, England and Wales: 30 September 2022": www.gov.uk/government/statistics/police-workforce-england-and-wales-30-september-2022/police-workforce-england-and-wales-30-september-2022#:~:text=As%20at%2030%20September%202022%2C%20there%20were%20142%2C145%20FTE%20police,police%20officers%20in%20September%202021

3   Owen Bowcott (4 April 2011), "Number of solicitors triples in 30 years", *The Guardian*: www.theguardian.com/law/2011/apr/04/number-of-solicitors-uk

14 THE JIGSAW

1   YouTube, "Bill Nighy video backing Robin Hood tax on banks": www.youtube.com/watch?v=ZzZIRMXcxRc

2   Charity Commission for England and Wales, Charities in England and Wales – 19 March 2024: https://register-of-charities.charitycommission.gov.uk/sector-data/sector-overview

3   Reuters (11 January 2020), "Boeing's ousted CEO departs with $62 million, even without severance pay", NBC News: www.nbcnews.com/business/business-news/boeing-s-ousted-ceo-departs-62-million-even-without-severance-n1114061

4   Andrew Clark (15 October 2009), "Goldman Sachs breaks record with $16.7bn bonus pot", *The Guardian*: www.theguardian.com/business/2009/oct/15/goldman-sachs-record-bonus-pot

5   Suyin Haynes (28 May 2020), "'The saddest, bitterest thing of all'. From the Great Depression to today, a long history of food

destruction in the face of hunger", *Time*: https://time.com/5843136/covid-19-food-destruction/#:~:text=Government%20intervention%20in%20the%20early,would%20lead%20to%20higher%20prices

6   John Steinbeck (1939), *The Grapes of Wrath*, Penguin Classics.

15 WHEN IS ENOUGH?

1   Suzanne Collins (2009), *The Hunger Games*, Scholastic.
2   Mike Judge (dir.) (2006), *Idiocracy*, screenplay by Mike Judge and Etan Cohen; 20th Century Fox.
3   Lana Wachowski and Lilly Wachowski (dir.) (1999), *The Matrix*, screenplay by Lana Wachowski and Lilly Wachowski; Warner Brothers and Roadshow Entertainment.
4   Greg Moorlock (24 July 2018), "A look inside the murky world of the illegal organ trade", *Independent*: www.independent.co.uk/voices/organ-trade-dealing-donation-illegal-black-market-donors-transplants-a8461216.html
5   *Dr Who*, Series 10 Episode 5, "Oxygen", by Steven Moffat, Chris Chibnall, Mark Gatiss, Toby Whitehouse, Richard Curtis, Simon Nye, director Charles Palmer, BBC, 13 May 2017.
6   Owen Bowcott (4 April 2011), "Number of solicitors triples in 30 years", *The Guardian*: www.theguardian.com/law/2011/apr/04/number-of-solicitors-uk
7   Mark Hilliard (8 January 2018), "Shopkeeper sued by burglar who injured himself during break-in", *The Irish Times*: www.irishtimes.com/news/offbeat/shopkeeper-sued-by-burglar-who-injured-himself-during-break-in-1.3348803
8   BBC (23 September 2009), *State of the Planet*, "Global warning", a statement made by David Attenborough on Easter Island: www.bbc.co.uk/programmes/p004hsk7

16 ALTERNATIVE SOCIETY

1   BBC News (6 May 2016), "'Boaty McBoatface' polar ship named after Attenborough": www.bbc.co.uk/news/uk-36225652
2   Scott Adams (2020), *The Dilbert Principle*, Boxtree; Scott Adams (2002), *The Best of Dilbert* Volume 1, Boxtree.

3   Wikipedia, "Universal basic income": https://en.wikipedia.org/wiki/Universal_basic_income

17 BACK TO REALITY

1   John Steinbeck (1939), *The Grapes of Wrath*, Penguin Classics.
2   Suyin Haynes (28 May 2020), "'The saddest, bitterest thing of all'. From the Great Depression to today, a long history of food destruction in the face of hunger", *Time:* https://time.com/5843136/covid-19-food-destruction/#:~:text=Government%20intervention%20in%20the%20early,would%20lead%20to%20higher%20prices

18 LAST LAUGH, CLOSING THOUGHTS AND FINAL WORDS

1   Scott Adams (2020), *The Dilbert Principle*, Boxtree.

Milton Keynes UK
Ingram Content Group UK Ltd.
UKHW022104040724
445034UK00017B/298